MW01493856

Fundamentals

OF MUSIC THEORY FOR THE WINDBAND STUDENT

A *NEW* Music Theory Workbook For Band

Welcome Back!

*You are about to begin the third and final book in the **Fundamentals of Music Theory Series**. Book Three is designed for the older learner (high school students) but can easily be used by advanced middle school students who have completed the first two books in the series.*

Book Three begins with a review of material from Books One and Two. This feature allows students new to your band program to begin their study of theory while you continue yours. All students should read and complete the Review Units as they contain several new approaches that were not covered in the first two books. Students are also reminded to:

- *Read all lesson material carefully.*
- *Ask questions if you do not understand.*
- *Complete all exercises in pencil.*
- *Keep all your theory workbooks for future reference.*

Once you have finished this book, you will have gained the skills necessary for a lifetime of music making and learning. Best wishes!

Eric Harris

Eric Harris, Author

By Eric Harris

WARNING!
Reproduction of this material in whole or in part, by any means, without the express written consent of the publisher is a violation of copyright law. DO NOT COPY!

North Land
MUSIC PUBLISHERS
P.O. Box 2101 Huntersville, NC 28070

COPYRIGHT © 2005
by Eric Harris.
All Rights Reserved. Printed in the USA.
For orders or questions please call:
1-704-875-6240

ISBN 0-9676157-3-9

TABLE OF CONTENTS

© 2005. Eric Harris. All Rights Reserved.

TABLE OF CONTENTS

© 2005. Eric Harris. All Rights Reserved.

ABOUT THE AUTHOR

 Eric Harris worked as a band director in Charlotte, North Carolina for twelve years. During this time, his middle and high school bands earned numerous superior ratings in concert and marching events across the state. Mr. Harris holds the Bachelor of Music Education Degree from Winthrop University in Rock Hill, South Carolina where he studied conducting with Dr. William F. Malambri. He also holds the Master of Music Education Degree from the University of Southern Mississippi (in Hattiesburg) where he studied conducting with Dr. Thomas V. Fraschillo and Dr. Gary W. Adam. Mr. Harris is an elected member of the American School Band Director's Association and has enjoyed teaching, conducting, and judging invitations in North Carolina, South Carolina, Virginia, and Mississippi.

SPECIAL THANKS

Many friends, mentors, colleagues, and students have offered support and encouragement for me and for this work. Through their kind words, personal endorsements, and editorial work, they have helped to make the publication of these books a wonderful reality. Many thanks to you all.

Susan Stroud
President, *NorthLand Music Publishers*; Huntersville, NC

Ruth Petersen
Director of Bands, *Bradley Middle School*; Huntersville, NC

Edward T. Benson
Instrumental Music Coordinator (Ret.), *Charlotte-Mecklenburg Schools*; Charlotte, NC

June McKinnon
Assistant Principal of Instruction (Ret.), *J.M. Alexander Middle School*; Huntersville, NC

Dr. Steve Canipe
Principal (Ret.), *J.M. Alexander Middle School*; Huntersville, NC

Robert H. Black
Director of Bands (Ret.), *East Gaston High School & Mount Holly Junior High School*; Mount Holly, NC

Dr. Thomas V. Fraschillo
Director of Bands, *The University of Southern Mississippi*; Hattiesburg, MS

Dr. Gary W. Adam
Associate Director of Bands, *The University of Southern Mississippi*; Hattiesburg, MS

Dr. Joseph L. Brumbeloe
Professor of Music Theory, *The University of Southern Mississippi*; Hattiesburg, MS

Dr. Christopher J. Goertzen
Professor of Music History, *The University of Southern Mississippi*; Hattiesburg, MS

David Montgomery
Assistant Director of Bands, *Western Michigan University*; Kalamazoo, MI

Annette Montgomery
Strings Teacher; Kalamazoo, MI

Mohamad and Susan Schuman
Directors of Bands, *Stone High School*; Wiggins, MS

Michael Luley
Director of Bands, *Falls Church High School*; Falls Church, VA

Scott Clowes
Director of Bands, *East Mecklenburg High School*; Charlotte, NC

Lesli Clowes
Director of Bands, *Crestdale Middle School*; Matthews, NC

Richard Holmes
Director of Bands, *Grandview Middle School*; Hickory, NC

Marsha Smithwick
Director of Bands (Ret.), *Bertie High School*; Bertie, NC

Lynn and Phyllis Harris
My Parents; Mount Holly, NC

FOR COLIN AND LAURA: TWO OF THE BEST

During my twelve years of teaching I was privileged to work with hundreds of wonderful young people. All of them – in some way – contributed to this book. Two, however, were an essential part of our editorial team and offered many suggestions which found their way into the final copy. Colin Thomson and Laura Ellsaesser brought warmth, wisdom, talent, intellect, and good humor to rehearsal each day. This book is affectionately dedicated to them.

"How often do we come in contact with men and women in whose presence
we may dwell only for a short time, yet we can never look on their countenance
or be in any way associated with them without being made better, or lifted up."
• Booker T. Washington

© 2005. Eric Harris. All Rights Reserved.

LESSON 1: STAFF AND CLEF REVIEW

1. Music is written on a set of five lines and four spaces called a **staff**. The lines and spaces of the staff are numbered from the bottom to the top.

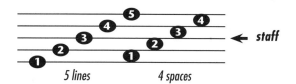

2. **Notes** are written symbols used to represent musical sounds. Notes can be written on the lines of the staff and in the spaces between the lines of the staff.

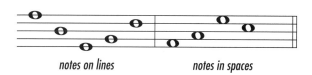

3. Lower notes are written at the bottom of the staff. Higher notes are written at the top of the staff. How high or low a note sounds is called its **pitch**.

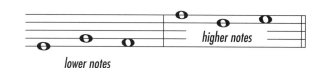

4. All musical sounds have four characteristics:
   - **pitch** – how high or low it sounds.
   - **duration** – how long it lasts.
   - **intensity** – how loud or soft it sounds.
   - **timbre** – (pronounced tam'bur) – the identifying quality of the sound. (Is it a clarinet or a trumpet?)

5. **Bar lines** are used to divide the staff into measures. A **measure** is the space between two bar lines. A **double bar line** is used to mark the end of a piece of music. A **thin double bar line** is sometimes used to mark the end of a movement or section of a piece.

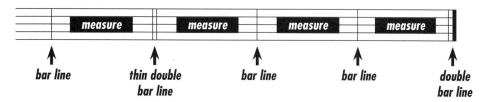

6. The lines and spaces of the staff are named using the first seven letters of the alphabet. Once the pattern reaches G, it begins again on A. This creates a repeating **musical alphabet pattern**. The distance from one note to the next note, up or down, with the same letter name is called an **octave** (A to A, B to B, etc.).

7. **Clefs** are used to assign letter names to the lines and spaces of the staff. The **treble clef** is an old form of the letter G. The treble clef (also called the G Clef) circles around line number two on the staff and calls it "G." The other lines and spaces of the staff can be named by going forward and backward in the musical alphabet pattern.

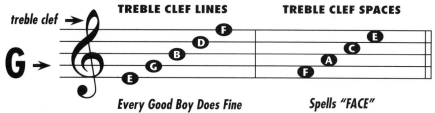

The slogan, "Every Good Boy Does Fine," is used to help students remember the names of the treble clef lines. The spaces of the treble clef spell the word "FACE."

© 2005. Eric Harris. All Rights Reserved.

8. The **bass clef** is an old form of the letter F. The bass clef (also called the F Clef) has a big dot that sits on line four and two smaller dots (one above and one below) that identify line four and call it "F." The other lines and spaces of the staff can be named by going forward and backward in the musical alphabet pattern.

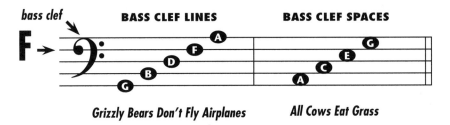

Grizzly Bears Don't Fly Airplanes   *All Cows Eat Grass*

The slogan, "Grizzly Bears Don't Fly Airplanes," is used to help students remember the names of the bass clef lines. The slogan, "All Cows Eat Grass," is used to help students remember the names of the bass clef spaces.

9. **Ledger lines** are used to extend the staff in either direction. The musical alphabet pattern continues when using ledger lines. It is important to remember that the musical alphabet pattern goes forward when moving up and above the staff. The musical alphabet pattern goes backward when moving down and below the staff.

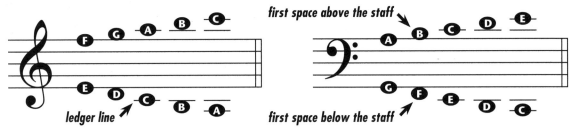

10. If we join a treble staff and a bass staff with a left bar line and a brace, we create a **grand staff** (or **great staff**).

11. **Middle C** is written on the first ledger line below the treble staff or on the first ledger line above the bass staff.

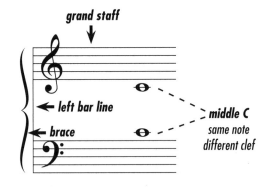

12. Reading music on the grand staff is just like reading music on a single staff. All line and space names remain the same.

13. The grand staff is used primarily for piano, organ, and some choral music. Many church hymnals contain music which is written on a grand staff.

14. It is important to remember that notes written below middle C (on ledger lines) are actually bass clef notes. Notes written above middle C (on ledger lines) are actually treble clef notes. Some students prefer to think of middle C as a "gateway" pitch; anything above it is treble clef while anything below it is bass clef.

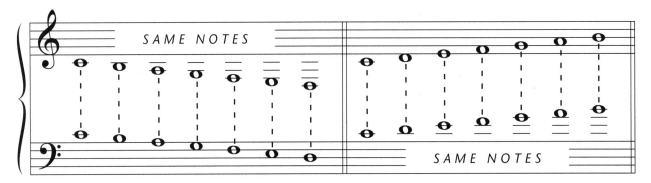

© 2005. Eric Harris. All Rights Reserved.

Manuscript Review 1

Handwritten music is called **manuscript**. The most important rule when writing music by hand is to be neat. Study, trace, and draw on your own, the manuscript techniques shown below.

Treble Clef

Draw a straight line that extends above and below the staff. Next draw a right curve that begins at the top of the straight line and curves down to staff line four. Then draw a left curve that begins at staff line four and connects at staff line one. Finally, draw a curl around line two.

Trace the clef drawing steps below.   *Draw five treble clefs on your own.*

   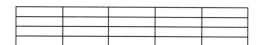

Bass Clef

Begin by drawing a big dot on line four of the staff. Next draw a backwards "C" that begins on the big dot, curves up to the top line of the staff, and then extends down to the second line of the staff. Finally, draw two smaller dots – one in the space above line four, one in the space below line four.

Trace the clef drawing steps below.   *Draw five bass clefs on your own.*

Notes

When writing notes on the staff, be sure the note head is centered on the line or fills the entire space. Note heads are oval, not round.

Trace the notes on the line below.   *Trace the notes in the space below.*

Draw six notes on the line on your own.   *Draw six notes in the space on your own.*

Ledger Lines

Ledger lines should be spaced the same distance apart as the lines of the staff. It is also important to remember that notes written on ledger lines should not be "capped." In other words, an extra line written above (or below) the note is unnecessary.

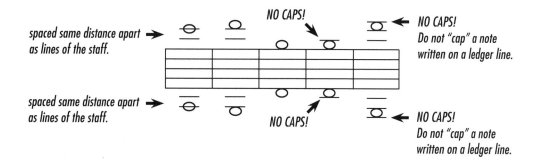

© 2005. Eric Harris. All Rights Reserved.

Exercise 1.1 - Line and Space Number Identification

Directions: Identify the line (L) or space (S) number on which the notes are placed.

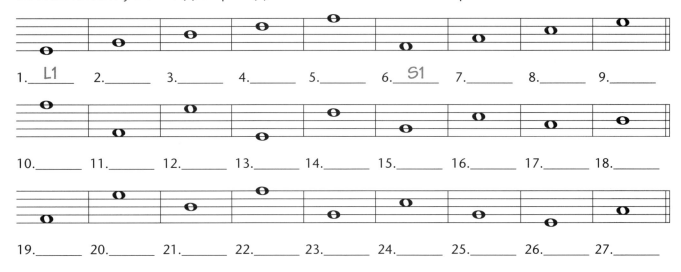

1. _L1_ 2. _____ 3. _____ 4. _____ 5. _____ 6. _S1_ 7. _____ 8. _____ 9. _____

10. _____ 11. _____ 12. _____ 13. _____ 14. _____ 15. _____ 16. _____ 17. _____ 18. _____

19. _____ 20. _____ 21. _____ 22. _____ 23. _____ 24. _____ 25. _____ 26. _____ 27. _____

Exercise 1.2 - Pitch Relationships

Directions: Determine whether the second note in each measure is higher than (H), lower than (L), or the same as (S) the first note in each measure.

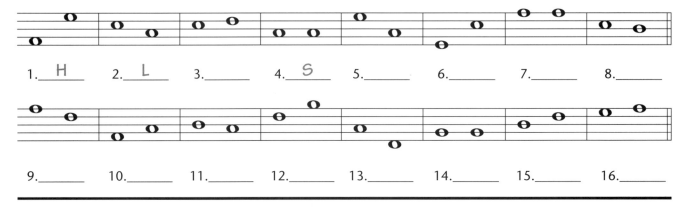

1. _H_ 2. _L_ 3. _____ 4. _S_ 5. _____ 6. _____ 7. _____ 8. _____

9. _____ 10. _____ 11. _____ 12. _____ 13. _____ 14. _____ 15. _____ 16. _____

Exercise 1.3 - Musical Alphabet Patterns

Directions: Complete the musical alphabet patterns below.

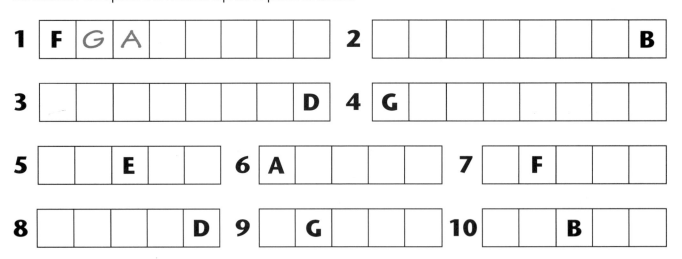

1 | F | G | A | | | | |
2 | | | | | | | B |
3 | | | | | | | D |
4 | G | | | | | | |
5 | | | E | | | |
6 | A | | | | | |
7 | | F | | | | |
8 | | | | D | |
9 | | G | | | |
10 | | | B | | |

© 2005. Eric Harris. All Rights Reserved.

Exercise 1.4 - Treble Clef Note Identification

Directions: Name each note given below.

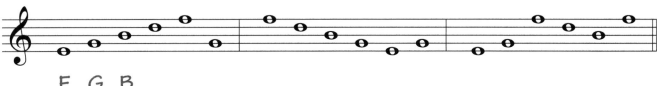

E G B

1.   2.   3.

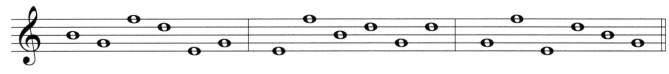

4.   5.   6.

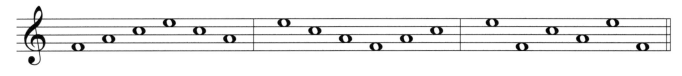

7.   8.   9.

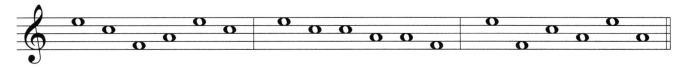

10.   11.   12.

13.   14.   15.

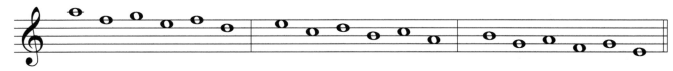

16.   17.   18.

19.   20.   21.

© 2005. Eric Harris. All Rights Reserved.

Exercise 1.5 - Treble Clef Note Identification

Directions: Name each note given below.

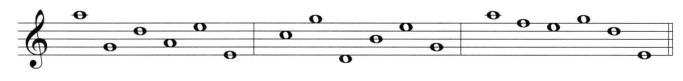

1. _____   2. _____   3. _____

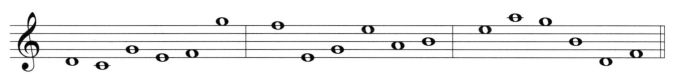

4. _____   5. _____   6. _____

7. _____   8. _____   9. _____

10. _____   11. _____   12. _____

13. _____   14. _____   15. _____

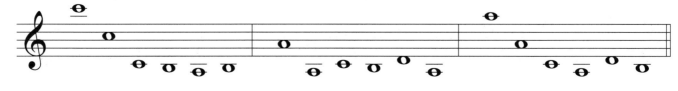

16. _____   17. _____   18. _____

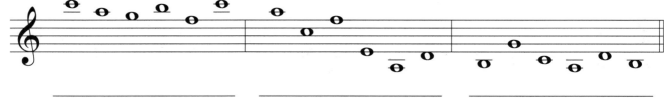

19. _____   20. _____   21. _____

© 2005. Eric Harris. All Rights Reserved.

Exercise 1.6 - Bass Clef Note Identification

Directions: Name each note given below.

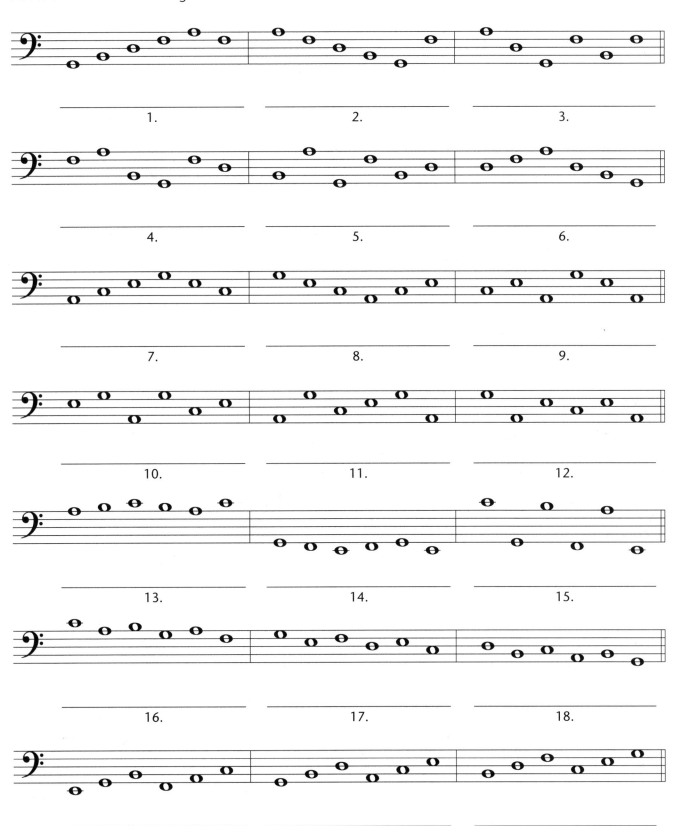

© 2005. Eric Harris. All Rights Reserved.

Exercise 1.7 - Bass Clef Note Identification

Directions: Name each note given below.

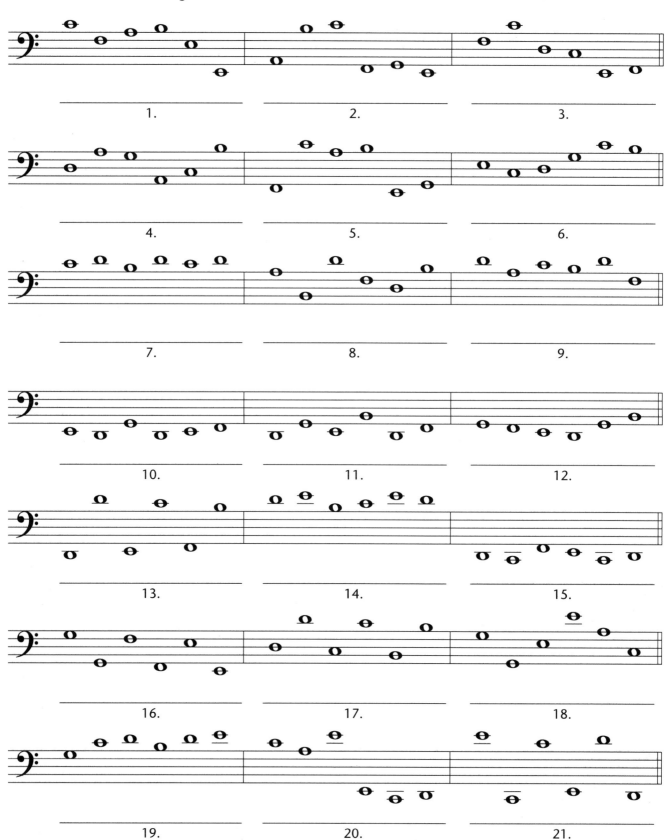

© 2005. Eric Harris. All Rights Reserved.

Exercise 1.8 - Treble and Bass Clef Extreme Ledger Lines

Directions: Name each note given below. Count letter names carefully when naming notes written on ledger lines.

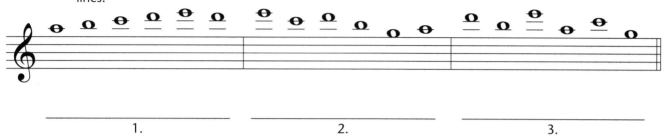

1.   2.   3.

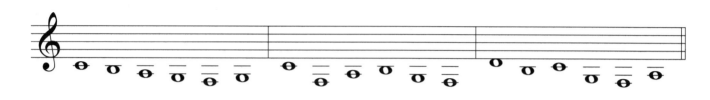

4.   5.   6.

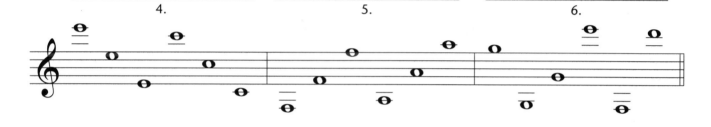

7.   8.   9.

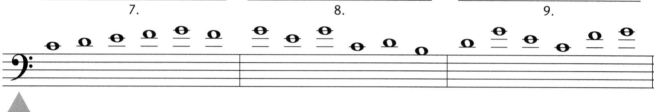

Check Clef

10.   11.   12.

13.   14.   15.

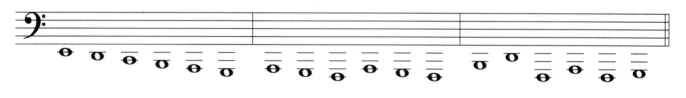

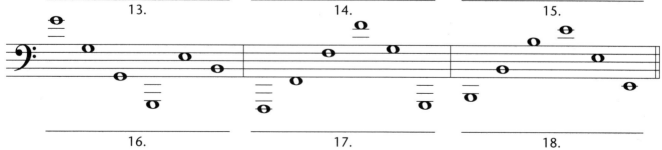

16.   17.   18.

© 2005. Eric Harris. All Rights Reserved.

Exercise 1.9 - Writing Notes On The Staff

Staff 1 • Directions: Draw a treble clef and write the requested notes **on the staff** (on lines and in spaces).

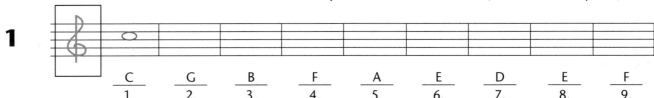

C	G	B	F	A	E	D	E	F
1.	2.	3.	4.	5.	6.	7.	8.	9.

Staff 2 • Directions: Draw a treble clef and write the requested notes **above the staff**. Use ledger lines when necessary.

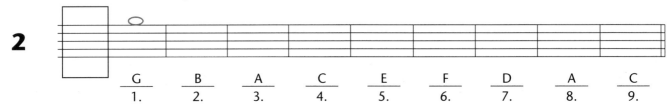

G	B	A	C	E	F	D	A	C
1.	2.	3.	4.	5.	6.	7.	8.	9.

Staff 3 • Directions: Draw a treble clef and write the requested notes **below the staff**. Use ledger lines when necessary.

C	F	A	D	G	B	C	A	G
1.	2.	3.	4.	5.	6.	7.	8.	9.

Staff 4 • Directions: Draw a <u>bass</u> <u>clef</u> and write the requested notes **on the staff** (on lines and in spaces).

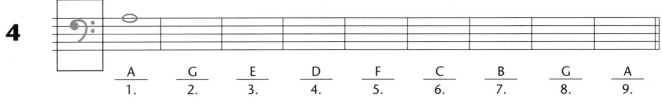

A	G	E	D	F	C	B	G	A
1.	2.	3.	4.	5.	6.	7.	8.	9.

Staff 5 • Directions: Draw a <u>bass</u> <u>clef</u> and write the requested notes **above the staff**. Use ledger lines when necessary.

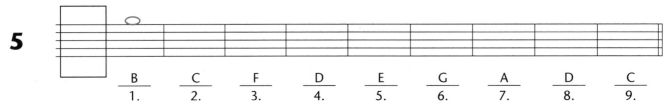

B	C	F	D	E	G	A	D	C
1.	2.	3.	4.	5.	6.	7.	8.	9.

Staff 6 • Directions: Draw a <u>bass</u> <u>clef</u> and write the requested notes **below the staff**. Use ledger lines when necessary.

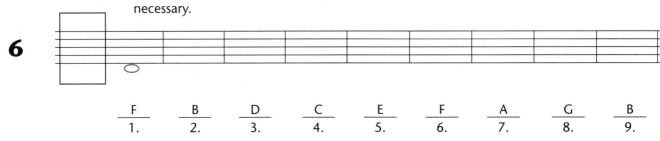

F	B	D	C	E	F	A	G	B
1.	2.	3.	4.	5.	6.	7.	8.	9.

© 2005. Eric Harris. All Rights Reserved.

Exercise 1.10 - Writing Notes On The Grand Staff

Directions: Write each note in four places on the grand staff. Use ledger lines if necessary.

1) G	2) E	3) F	4) C	5) A	6) D	7) B

Exercise 1.11 - Rewriting Treble To Bass, And Bass To Treble

Directions: Rewrite the given treble clef notes to bass clef.

1.	2.	3.	4.	5.	6.	7.	8.	9.	10.

Directions: Rewrite the given bass clef notes to treble clef.

11.	12.	13.	14.	15.	16.	17.	18.	19.	20.

Exercise 1.12 - Creating Grand Staves

Directions: Create grand staves by adding a left bar line, a brace, a treble clef, and a bass clef to each.

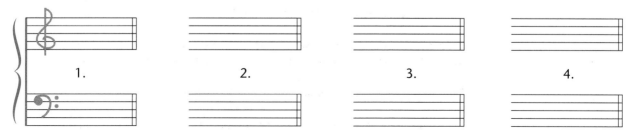

1.	2.	3.	4.

© 2005. Eric Harris. All Rights Reserved.

Unit Review Questions

Directions: Answer the questions below.

1. _____ Music is written on a set of five lines and four spaces called a ?

2. _____ The lines and spaces of the staff are ? from the bottom to the top.

3. _____ Written symbols used to represent musical sounds are called ?

4. _____ Notes can be written on the lines of the staff and in the ? between the lines of the staff.

5. _____ Lower notes are written at the ? of the staff.

6. _____ Higher notes are written at the ? of the staff.

7. _____ How high or low a note sounds is called its ?

8. _____ How long a note sounds is called its ?

9. _____ How loud or soft a note sounds is called its ?

10. _____ The identifying quality of a sound is called its ?

11. _____ These are used to divide the staff into measures.

12. _____ The space between two bar lines is called a ?

13. _____ A ? bar line is used to mark the end of a piece of music.

14. _____ A ? double bar line is sometimes used to mark the end of a movement or section of a piece.

15. _____ The lines and spaces of the staff are named using the first ? letters of the alphabet.

16. _____ List the seven letters of the musical alphabet pattern in order.

17. _____ Once the pattern reaches G, it begins again on ?

18. _____ These symbols are used to assign letter names to the lines and spaces of the staff.

19. _____ This clef is an old form of the letter G. (Name it and draw it.)

20. _____ This clef is an old form of the letter F. (Name it and draw it.)

21. _____ This clef identifies line number two on the staff and calls it "G."

22. _____ This clef identifies line number four on the staff and calls it "F."

23. _____ If we know the location of any single pitch on the staff (such as F and G), we can go forward or backward in the ? to name the other lines and spaces.

24. _____ The lines of the treble clef are ? (Write all five answers in the blank.)

25. _____ The spaces of the treble clef are ? (Write all four answers in the blank.)

© 2005. Eric Harris. All Rights Reserved.

26. _____ The lines of the bass clef are _?_ (Write all five answers in the blank.)

27. _____ The spaces of the bass clef are _?_ (Write all four answers in the blank.)

28. _____ These tiny lines are used to extend the staff in either direction.

29. _____ The musical alphabet pattern continues when using ledger lines. (True/False)

30. _____ When moving up the staff, the musical alphabet pattern goes _?_

31. _____ When moving down the staff, the musical alphabet pattern goes _?_

32. _____ If we join a treble staff and a bass staff with a left bar line and a brace, we create a _?_ staff.

33. _____ This note is written on the first ledger line below the treble staff or on the first ledger line above the bass staff.

34. _____ Notes written below middle C are actually _?_ clef notes.

35. _____ Notes written above middle C are actually _?_ clef notes.

36. _____ Handwritten music is called _?_

37. _____ The most important rule to follow when writing music by hand is to be _?_

38. _____ Note heads are _?_, not round.

39. _____ Notes written on the staff should be centered on the line or should fill the entire _?_

40. _____ When writing ledger lines above and below the staff, they should be spaced the same _?_ apart as the lines of the staff.

41. _____ It is important to remember that notes written above or below the staff on ledger lines should not be _?_. In other words, an extra line written above or below the note is unnecessary.

Items 42 - 49: Name the notes from lowest to highest in each measure of the grand staff example below.

	42.	43.	44.	45.	46.	47.	48.	49.
A								
E								
C								
A								

© 2005. Eric Harris. All Rights Reserved.

LESSON 2: NOTE & REST VALUE REVIEW

1. **Notes** (also called note values) are written symbols used to represent musical sounds. Different types of notes tell us how long the sounds will last. Different note values are created by combining **note heads**, **stems**, and **flags**.

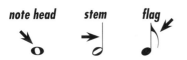

2. **Rests** (also called rest values) are written symbols used to represent silence in music. Every note value has a companion rest of equal value.

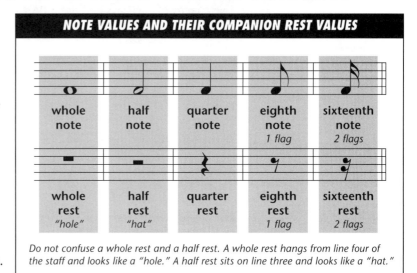

NOTE VALUES AND THEIR COMPANION REST VALUES

whole note	half note	quarter note	eighth note *1 flag*	sixteenth note *2 flags*
whole rest *"hole"*	half rest *"hat"*	quarter rest	eighth rest *1 flag*	sixteenth rest *2 flags*

Do not confuse a whole rest and a half rest. A whole rest hangs from line four of the staff and looks like a "hole." A half rest sits on line three and looks like a "hat."

3. Instead of writing multiple eighth or sixteenth notes using flags, musicians often connect these notes with heavy lines called **beams**. Eighth notes have one flag and are connected by one beam. Sixteenth notes have two flags and are connected by two beams. Eighth and sixteenth notes can also be connected in combinations using beams. Study each example below.

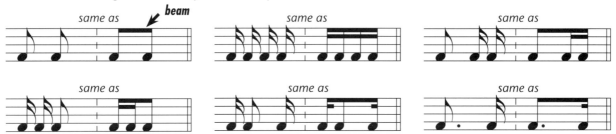

4. Note and rest values work like fractions. Each note value divides into two smaller note values.

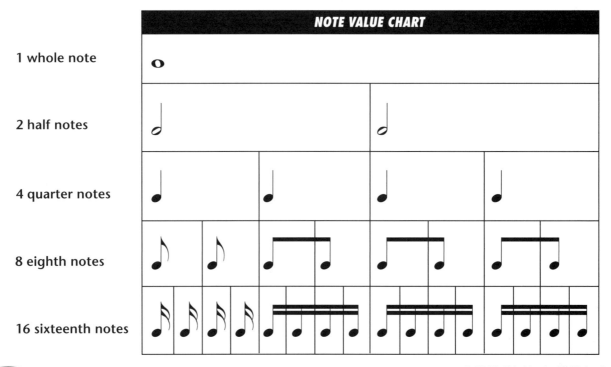

NOTE VALUE CHART

| 1 whole note |
| 2 half notes |
| 4 quarter notes |
| 8 eighth notes |
| 16 sixteenth notes |

© 2005. Eric Harris. All Rights Reserved.

5. Here is the chart of rest values. It works just like the chart of note values on the previous page.

REST VALUE CHART							

1 whole rest	▬							
2 half rests	▬				▬			
4 quarter rests	𝄽		𝄽		𝄽		𝄽	
8 eighth rests	𝄾	𝄾	𝄾	𝄾	𝄾	𝄾	𝄾	𝄾
16 sixteenth rests	𝄿 𝄿	𝄿 𝄿	𝄿 𝄿	𝄿 𝄿	𝄿 𝄿	𝄿 𝄿	𝄿 𝄿	𝄿 𝄿

6. A **dot** after a note head increases the value of that note by one half of its original value. It can also be noticed that a dotted note equals *three* of the next smaller note value on the note value chart.

7. A **tie** is a curved line that connects two or more notes of the *same* pitch and adds their values. A tie functions like a musical "plus" (+) sign. Tied notes are played as one single, sustained sound.

8. Rests can also have dots. The dot is always written in the third space. Dotted rests work just like dotted notes.

      dotted whole   dotted half   dotted quarter   dotted eighth   dotted sixteenth

9. Stems on notes may go up or down. Musicians follow a three-part rule when placing stems on notes.

THE STEM RULE

- If the note head is BELOW the third line of the staff, the stem will go UP and is attached to the RIGHT side of the note head.

- If the note head is ABOVE the third line of the staff, the stem will go DOWN and is attached to the LEFT side of the note head.

- If the note head is ON the third line of the staff, the stem may go UP or DOWN; the final decision is made by the individual writer.

© 2005. Eric Harris. All Rights Reserved.

Manuscript Review 2

Study, trace, and draw on your own, the note and rest values shown below.

Whole Notes – oval, not round.

trace   draw two   draw two   draw two

Half Notes – like whole notes with stems.

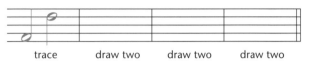

trace   draw two   draw two   draw two

Quarter Notes – note heads are filled-in.

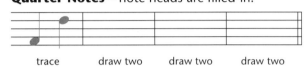

trace   draw two   draw two   draw two

Eighth Notes – one flag attached to the right.

trace   draw two   draw two   draw two

Sixteenth Notes – two flags.

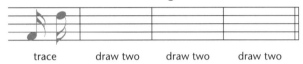

trace   draw two   draw two   draw two

Whole Rests – hang from line 4, like a "hole."

trace   draw one   draw one   draw one

Half Rests – sit on line three, like a "hat."

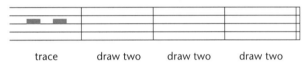

trace   draw two   draw two   draw two

Quarter Rests – draw a "Z" then attach a "C."

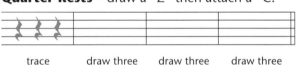

trace   draw three   draw three   draw three

Eighth Rests – like a "7" with a dot in space 3.

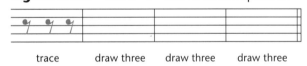

trace   draw three   draw three   draw three

Sixteenth Rests – two flags; start in space 3.

trace   draw three   draw three   draw three

Stem Practice • Draw a stem on each note head below. Remember the stem rule from page 19!

Flag Practice • Add one flag to each stem below. This will create eighth notes. Remember, flags attach to the right side of the stem. Flags always fly to the right!

Flag Practice • Add two flags to each stem below. This will create sixteenth notes. Flags fly to the right.

20

© 2005. Eric Harris. All Rights Reserved.

Exercise 2.1 - Note and Rest Value Identification

Directions: Name each note or rest value shown below.

1.	2.	3.	4.	5.

6.	7.	8.	9.	10.

Exercise 2.2 - Note and Rest Value Charts

Directions: Draw a note and a rest value chart (like the ones in the lesson). Be sure the note values line-up correctly. Use beams on eighth and sixteenth notes.

NOTE VALUE CHART

REST VALUE CHART

Exercise 2.3 - Beaming Exercise

Directions: Match each flagged measure with its beamed equivalent.

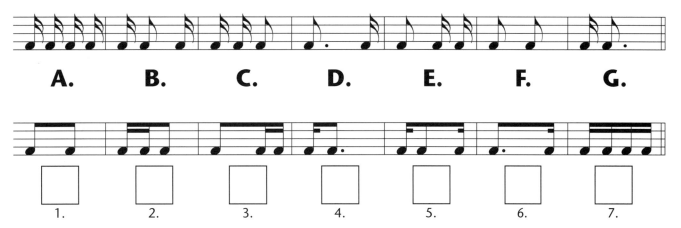

| A. | B. | C. | D. | E. | F. | G. |

1.	2.	3.	4.	5.	6.	7.

© 2005. Eric Harris. All Rights Reserved.

Exercise 2.4 - Note Value Equations

Directions: Write *one* note in the blank that is equal in duration to the combined notes in the equation.

1. ♩ + ♩ + ♩ = _____
2. ♪ + ♪ = _____
3. ♩ + ♪ = _____
4. 𝅗𝅥 + ♪ + ♬ + ♬ + ♩ = _____
5. 𝅗𝅥 + 𝅗𝅥 + 𝅗𝅥 = _____
6. ♩ + ♩ + ♩ = _____
7. 𝅗𝅥 + ♩ + ♩ = _____
8. ♪ + ♪ + ♩ + ♪ + ♪ = _____
9. ♪ + ♩ + ♪ = _____
10. 𝅗𝅥. + ♩ = _____
11. ♬ + ♩. + ♬ = _____
12. ♪ + 𝅗𝅥 + ♪ = _____
13. ♪ + ♩. = _____
14. ♩. + ♩. = _____
15. ♬ + ♬ + ♪ + ♪ = _____
16. 𝅗𝅥 + ♩ = _____
17. 𝅝 + 𝅗𝅥 = _____

18. ♬ + ♬ = _____
19. ♩ + ♩ = _____
20. ♪ + ♪ + ♪ + ♪ = _____
21. ♪ + ♪ + ♪ + ♪ = _____
22. ♪ + ♪ + ♪ = _____
23. ♪ + 𝅗𝅥 + ♪ + ♬ = _____
24. ♪. + ♩ + ♬ = _____
25. ♬ + ♪ = _____
26. ♪ + ♩ = _____
27. ♪ + ♪ + ♬ = _____
28. ♪. + ♬ = _____
29. 𝅝 – 𝅗𝅥 = _____
30. ♪ – ♬ = _____
31. ♩ – ♪ = _____
32. 𝅗𝅥. – ♩ = _____
33. ♪ + ♪ + ♬ + ♬ + ♪ = _____
34. ♪ + ♪ + ♬ = _____

Exercise 2.5 - Working With Ties

Directions: Write *one* note in the blank that is equal in duration to the tied notes.

1. 𝅗𝅥 ⌣ ♩ = _____
2. ♩ ⌣ ♩ ⌣ 𝅗𝅥 = _____
3. ♪ ⌣ ♪ = _____
4. ♩ ⌣ ♩ ⌣ ♪ = _____

5. 𝅗𝅥 ⌣ 𝅗𝅥 = _____
6. 𝅗𝅥. ⌣ ♩ = _____
7. ♪ ⌣ ♪ ⌣ ♪ = _____
8. 𝅗𝅥. ⌣ ♪ = _____

© 2005. Eric Harris. All Rights Reserved.

Exercise 2.6 - Working With Note Groups

Directions: Write *one* note in the blank that is equal in duration to the note groups shown below.

1. ♫♫ = _____   6. ♫. = _____

2. ♩♫ = _____   7. ♪ ♩ ♪ = _____

3. ♫♪ = _____   8. ♩. ♫ = _____

4. ♫♩ = _____   9. ♩. ♪ = _____

5. ♩. ♫ = _____   10. ♪ ♩. = _____

Exercise 2.7 - Word Problems

Directions: Complete the following statements.

1. One whole note equals _____ half notes.
2. One whole note equals _____ quarter notes.
3. One whole note equals _____ eighth notes.
4. One whole note equals _____ sixteenth notes.
5. One half note equals _____ quarter notes.
6. One half note equals _____ eighth notes.
7. One half note equals _____ sixteenth notes.
8. One quarter note equals _____ eighth notes.
9. One quarter note equals _____ sixteenth notes.
10. One eighth note equals _____ sixteenth notes.
11. One dotted-half note equals _____ quarter notes.
12. One dotted-half note equals _____ eighth notes.
13. One dotted-half note equals _____ sixteenth notes.

14. One dotted-quarter note equals _____ eighth notes.
15. One dotted-quarter note equals ___ sixteenth notes.
16. One dotted-eighth note equals _____ sixteenth notes.
17. One dotted-whole note equals ___ half notes.
18. Six sixteenth notes equal _____ eighth notes.
19. Eight sixteenth notes equal _____ quarter notes.
20. Four eighth notes equal _____ quarter notes.
21. Six eighth notes equal _____ sixteenth notes.
22. Three half notes equal _____ sixteenth notes.
23. Three quarter notes equal _____ eighth notes.
24. One half note equals _____ eighth notes.
25. Six quarter notes equal _____ half notes.
26. Nine eighth notes equal ___ dotted-quarter notes.

© 2005. Eric Harris. All Rights Reserved.

Unit Review Questions

Directions: Answer the questions below.

1. _____ Written symbols used to represent musical sound are called ?

2. _____ Written symbols used to represent silence in music are called ?

3. _____ Each note value has a companion rest of ? value.

4. _____ Draw an eighth rest and a single eighth note.

5. _____ Draw a whole rest and a whole note.

6. _____ Draw a half rest and a half note.

7. _____ Draw a quarter rest and a quarter note.

8. _____ Draw a sixteenth rest and a sixteenth note.

9. _____ Eighth notes and eighth rests have ? flag(s).

10. _____ Sixteenth notes and sixteenth rests have ? flag(s).

11. _____ If the note head is above the third line, the stem will go ?

12. _____ If the note head is below the third line, the stem will go ?

13. _____ If the note head is on the third line, the stem may go ? or ? (Write both answers.)

14. _____ Flags are always attached to the ? side of the stem.

15. _____ If the stem goes down, it is attached to the ? side of the note head.

16. _____ If the stem goes up, it is attached to the ? side of the note head.

17. _____ The ? rest hangs from line four and looks like a "hole."

18. _____ The ? rest sits on line three and looks like a "hat."

19. _____ The quarter rest is drawn by attaching a ? to a ? (Write both answers.)

20. _____ The eighth rest looks like a ? with a dot placed in space three.

21. _____ Instead of writing eighth notes and sixteenth notes with flags, musicians will often connect these notes with heavy lines called ?

22. _____ This curved line connects two notes of the same pitch and adds their values.

23. _____ A dotted note equals ? of the next value down on the note value chart.

24. _____ A dot increases the value of a note by ? of its original value.

25. _____ When dotted rests are used, the dot is always placed in space ? of the staff.

26. _____ Dotted rests function just like dotted notes (True/False).

© 2005. Eric Harris. All Rights Reserved.

LESSON 3: PIANO KEYBOARD REVIEW

1. The piano keyboard is an important tool for all musicians. While you may never wish to learn to play the piano, it is important that you understand how the keys are named and how they relate to one another.

2. The piano keyboard has black keys and white keys. The black keys are grouped into sets of two and three. Just to the left of each group of two black keys is the white key "C." Just to the left of each group of three black keys is the white key "F." If we follow the musical alphabet pattern, we can easily name the remaining white keys.

NAMING WHITE KEYS ON THE PIANO

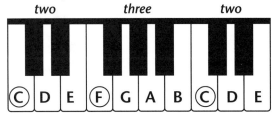

To the right is higher. ➡

⬅ *To the left is lower.*

3. As we move to the right on the piano keyboard, the sound (pitch) of each key becomes higher. As we move to the left on the piano keyboard, the sound (pitch) of each key becomes lower. Remember: to the right is higher or up; to the left is lower or down.

4. The distance from one key to the next closest key (with no key in between) is called a **half step**. Half steps most often appear between white keys and black keys. Notice however, that there is no black key between E and F or between B and C. A white key to a white key can also be a half step, if there is no black key in between.

HALF STEPS ON THE PIANO KEYBOARD

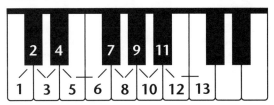

1 to 2 is a half step. 7 to 8 is a half step.
2 to 3 is a half step. 8 to 9 is a half step.
3 to 4 is a half step. 9 to 10 is a half step.
4 to 5 is a half step. 10 to 11 is a half step.
5 to 6 is a half step. 11 to 12 is a half step.
6 to 7 is a half step. 12 to 13 is a half step.

5. To make half steps easier to understand, the keys on the piano keyboard to the right have been numbered. The distance from one number to the next number (in order) is a half step. Notice the "zig-zag" pattern.

6. Special symbols called **accidentals** are used to raise or lower the sound of notes. A **sharp** (♯) raises the sound of a note a half step. (Example: C to C-sharp is a half step up.) Sharps are typically played on the black keys to the right of each white key on the piano. Because there is no black key between E and F or between B and C, to sharp E we must play F. To sharp B we must play C. Put simply, to sharp any note, play the next closest key to the right.

SHARPS ON THE PIANO KEYBOARD

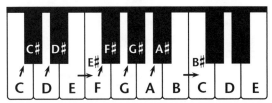

To the right is higher. Sharps raise to the right. ➡

7. A **flat** (♭) lowers the sound of a note a half step. (Example: D to D-flat is a half step down.) Flats are typically played on the black keys to the left of each white key on the piano. Because there is no black key between E and F or between B and C, to flat F we must play E. To flat C we must play B. Put simply, to flat any note, play the next closest key to the left.

FLATS ON THE PIANO KEYBOARD

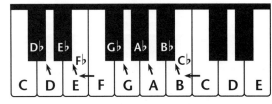

⬅ *To the left is lower. Flats lower to the left.*

8. A **natural** (♮) is used to cancel a sharp or flat. Notes without sharps or flats are called **natural notes**. Natural notes are always played on the white keys of the piano. It is not necessary to place a natural before each note – notes without sharps or flats are assumed to be natural. If we apply a natural to a sharped note, (C♯ to C♮) we actually lower the pitch (back down to natural or normal). If we apply a natural to a flatted note, (D♭ to D♮) we actually raise the pitch (back up to natural or normal).

© 2005. Eric Harris. All Rights Reserved.

9. The black keys on the piano keyboard each have two names. One set of names (with sharps) is used when raising the sound of natural notes. The other set of names (with flats) is used when lowering the sound of natural notes. Four of the white keys also have two names. E can be called F-flat. B can be called C-flat. F can be called E-sharp. C can be called B-sharp.

KEYBOARD WITH ALL KEY NAMES AND ENHARMONICS

Memorize this diagram!

10. When two notes have the same sound (because they are played by the same piano key) but have two different names, they are said to be **enharmonic**. For example, C♯ and D♭ are enharmonic.

11. Enharmonic notes will use the same fingerings on a wind instrument. If you encounter a note for which you do not know the fingering (like D♯), you probably know the fingering for its enharmonic equal (E♭).

12. Since all of the black keys and four of the white keys each have two names, the question, "What is a half step above A?" can obviously have two answers (A♯ or B♭). Two types of half steps exist in music. A **chromatic half step** (CHS) occurs when two notes a half step apart share the same letter name (like A and A♯ for example). A **diatonic half step** (DHS) occurs when two notes a half step apart have different (but consecutive) letter names (like A and B♭). Find the examples below on the keyboard above.

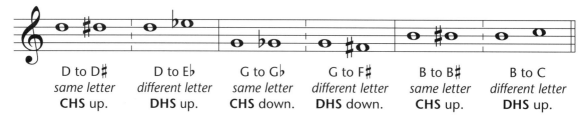

D to D♯	D to E♭	G to G♭	G to F♯	B to B♯	B to C
same letter	*different letter*	*same letter*	*different letter*	*same letter*	*different letter*
CHS up.	**DHS** up.	**CHS** down.	**DHS** down.	**CHS** up.	**DHS** up.

13. Two half steps combine to create one **whole step**. A whole step will always involve a skipped key on the piano. Whole steps must also use consecutive letter names. E♭ to E♯ will sound like a whole step, but the spelling is wrong – whole steps must use consecutive letter names. The correct spelling would be E♭ to F.

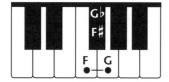
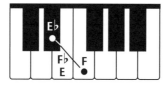

The whole step F to G skips the black key F♯/G♭.

The whole step E♭ to F skips the white key E/F♭.

The whole step A♭ to B♭ skips the white key A.

14. When written on the staff, accidentals are placed before the note they are to affect on the same line or space as the note they are to affect. While we say "C-sharp" and "E-flat" (and we write our answers to theory questions this way too), on the staff we write "sharp-C" and "flat-E" and place the accidental before the letter name (note).

© 2005. Eric Harris. All Rights Reserved.

15. When playing accidentals in written music, musicians follow the **rule of accidentals**. It has two parts:

- Accidentals are good for one measure only. They cancel at the bar line.

F   F   F♯ F♯   F   G   A♭ B♭   B   A   G   F   F♯ A   C   F♯

- An accidental may be carried into the next measure if the note is tied across the bar line. When ties are used, the accidental dies at the end of the tie.

D   E   F   G♯ G♯   F   E   G   F   G   A   B♭   B♭ A   B   A

Manuscript Review 3

Study, trace, and draw on your own, the accidentals shown below. Remember to place all accidentals before the note they are to affect on the same line or space as the note they are to affect.

Sharps

Sharps look like the pound sign on your telephone. Sharps are drawn like a small tic-tac-toe board. Be sure the "little box" in the center of the sharp fills the entire space or sits squarely on the line.

Trace the sharps below.

Write a sharp before each note below, then name the note.

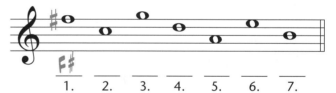

F♯
1.   2.   3.   4.   5.   6.   7.

Flats

Flats look like an oddly shaped "b." They are drawn by attaching a stem to half a heart shape. Be sure the open space in the middle of the flat fills the entire space or sits squarely on the line.

Trace the flats below.

Write a flat before each note below, then name the note.

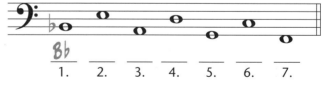

B♭
1.   2.   3.   4.   5.   6.   7.

Naturals

Naturals are drawn by attaching an "L" shape to a "7" shape. Remember that notes without naturals are assumed to be natural. We are just practicing writing the naturals on the staff. Be sure the little box in the center of the natural fills the entire space or sits squarely on the line.

Trace the naturals below.

Write a natural before each note below, then name the note.

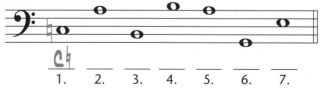

C♮
1.   2.   3.   4.   5.   6.   7.

© 2005. Eric Harris. All Rights Reserved.

Exercise 3.1 - Naming The White Keys

Directions: Label all C's and F's.

1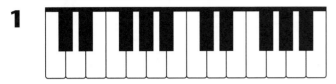

Directions: Label all D's and G's.

2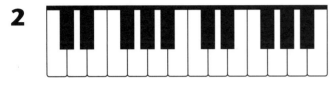

Directions: Label all E's and A's.

3

Directions: Label all B's.

4

Directions: Label all the white keys.

5

Directions: Label all the white keys. (Be careful.)

6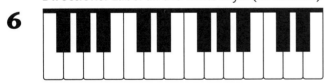

Directions: Name the numbered keys below.

7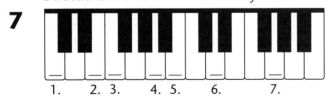

Directions: Name the numbered keys below.

8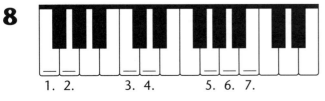

Directions: Name the numbered keys below.

9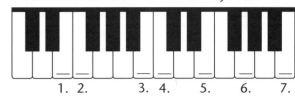

Directions: Name the numbered keys below.

10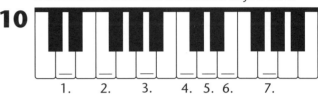

Directions: Name the numbered keys below.

11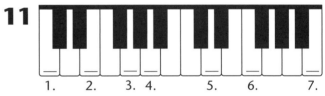

Directions: Name the numbered keys below.

12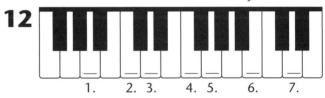

Directions: Name the numbered keys below.

13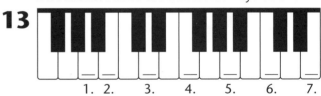

Directions: Name the numbered keys below.

14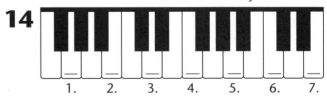

Directions: Name the numbered keys below.

15

© 2005. Eric Harris. All Rights Reserved.

Exercise 3.2 - Naming The Black Keys

1 **Directions:** Label all of the white keys on the keyboard below.

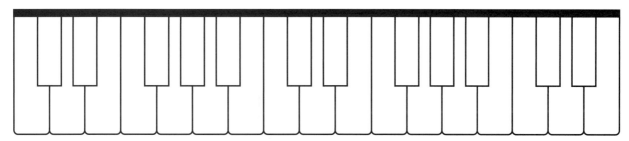

2 **Directions:** Label all of the black keys using SHARP NAMES.

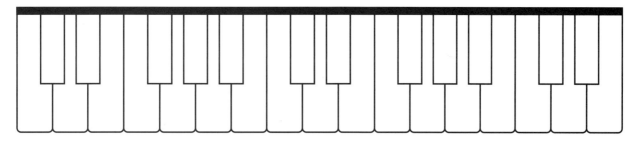

3 **Directions:** Label all of the black keys using FLAT NAMES.

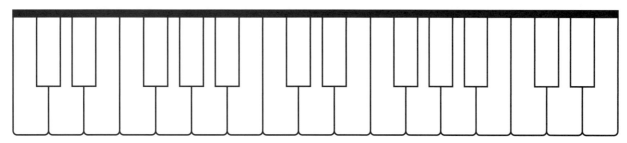

4 **Directions:** Label all E's, F's, B's, and C's with BOTH NAMES.

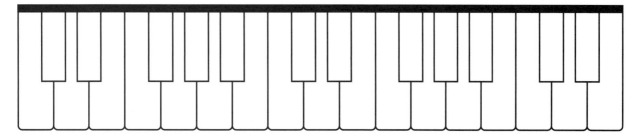

5 **Directions:** Label all keys (white and black). Include BOTH NAMES WHERE APPROPRIATE.

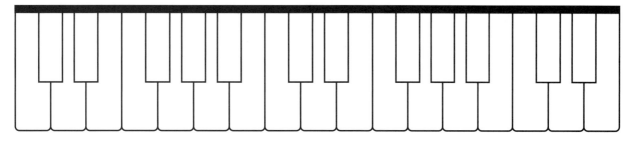

© 2005. Eric Harris. All Rights Reserved.

Exercise 3.3 - Name The Keys Speed Drill

Directions: Name the numbered keys on the piano keyboard below. You should be able to complete this exercise in less than one minute.

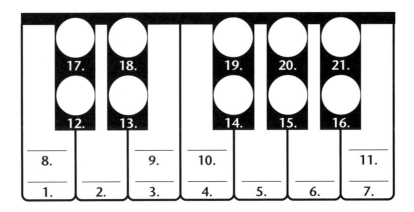

Exercise 3.4 - Relating Notes On The Staff To The Piano Keyboard

Directions: Name each note below; then draw a line to the piano key with the same letter name.

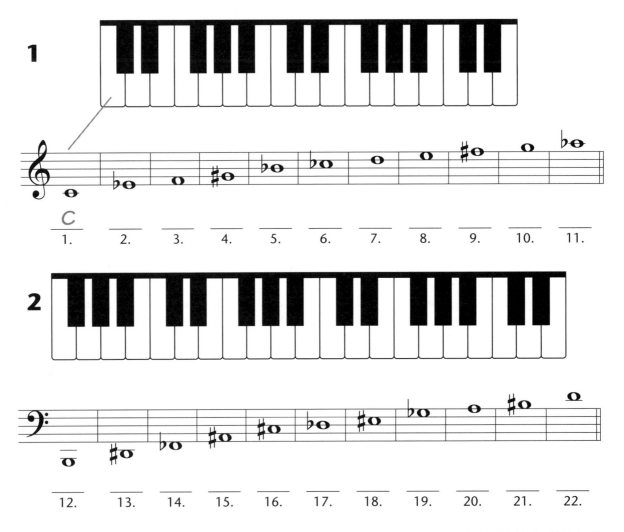

© 2005. Eric Harris. All Rights Reserved.

Exercise 3.5 - Relating Enharmonics On The Staff To The Piano Keyboard

Directions: Name the notes in each enharmonic pair below. Be careful, the clefs change. Then draw a line from each enharmonic pair to the matching key on the piano that will play both notes.

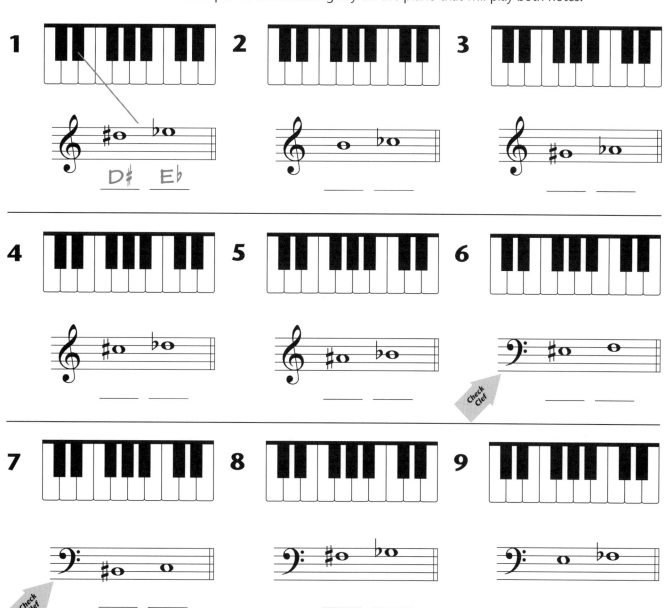

Exercise 3.6 - Name The Enharmonic

Directions: Give the enharmonic spelling for each note below.

1. Db	2. B	3. Gb	4. A#	5. Fb	6. G#	7. C	8. D#	9. B#
10. Bb	11. E#	12. Ab	13. C#	14. Eb	15. F#	16. E	17. Cb	18. F

© 2005. Eric Harris. All Rights Reserved.

Exercise 3.7 - Higher, Lower, or Enharmonic?

Directions: Name the notes in each measure below, then determine whether the **second** note in each measure is higher than, lower than, or enharmonic with the first note in each measure.

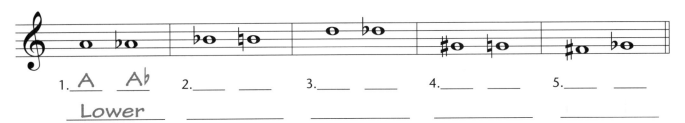

1. A Ab
Lower
2.____   3.____   4.____   5.____
____   ____   ____   ____

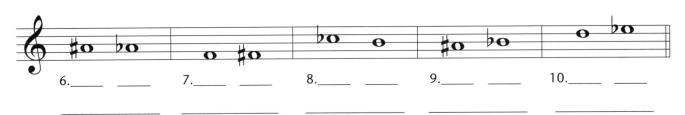

6.____   7.____   8.____   9.____   10.____
____   ____   ____   ____   ____

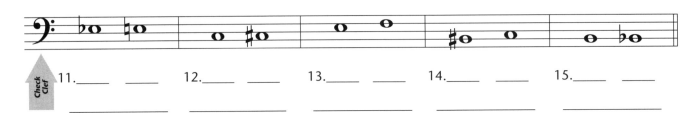

Check Clef
11.____   12.____   13.____   14.____   15.____
____   ____   ____   ____   ____

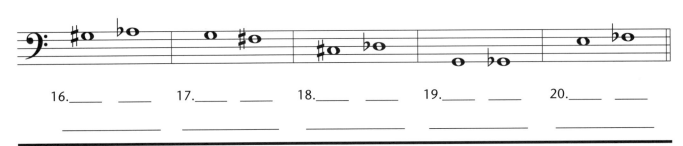

16.____   17.____   18.____   19.____   20.____
____   ____   ____   ____   ____

Exercise 3.8 - Half Step Identification

Directions: If the keys marked in each item are a half step apart, check "yes;" if they are not, check "no."

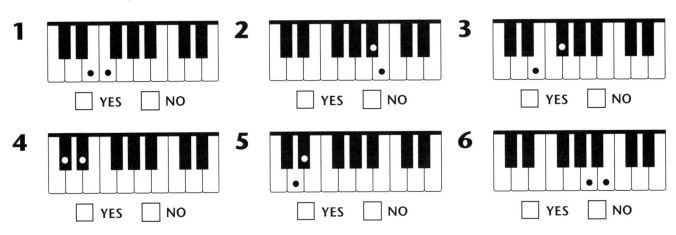

1 ☐ YES ☐ NO   2 ☐ YES ☐ NO   3 ☐ YES ☐ NO

4 ☐ YES ☐ NO   5 ☐ YES ☐ NO   6 ☐ YES ☐ NO

© 2005. Eric Harris. All Rights Reserved.

Exercise 3.9 - Half Step Check

Directions: Using the keyboard below, answer the following questions.

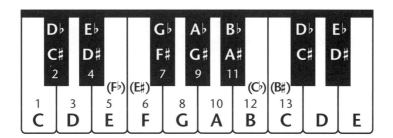

1. What key number is one half step above 1? ____

2. What key number is one half step above 4? ____

3. What key number is one half step above 5? ____

4. What key number is one half step above 9? ____

5. What key number is one half step above 3? ____

6. What key number is one half step below 13? ____

7. What key number is one half step below 7? ____

8. What key number is one half step below 6? ____

9. What key number is one half step below 5? ____

10. What key number is one half step below 10? ____

SPECIAL QUESTIONS

1. On the piano keyboard, which direction is higher, right or left? _____

2. On the piano keyboard, which direction is lower, right or left? _____

Exercise 3.10 - Half Step Check

Directions: Using your knowledge of the piano keyboard, determine whether each item below is true (T) or false (F).

1. ___T___ C to C♯ is a half step up.

2. _____ D to D♭ is a half step down.

3. _____ E♭ to F♭ is a half step up.

4. _____ B♭ to C is a half step up.

5. _____ G to F♯ is a half step down.

6. _____ A♯ to A is a half step down.

7. _____ C to B♭ is a half step down.

8. _____ D♭ to E♭ is a half step up.

9. _____ G to A♯ is a half step up.

10. _____ F♭ to G is a half step up.

11. _____ A to B is a half step up.

12. _____ A♭ to G is a half step down.

13. _____ E to E♭ is a half step down.

14. _____ B to B♯ is a half step up.

15. _____ D♭ to D♯ is a half step up.

16. _____ B♭ to A♭ is a half step down.

17. _____ F♯ to E♯ is a half step down.

18. _____ C♯ to D is a half step up.

19. _____ G♭ to F is a half step down.

20. _____ C♯ to B♯ is a half step down.

© 2005. Eric Harris. All Rights Reserved.

Exercise 3.11 - Spelling Chromatic Half Steps

Directions: Build a chromatic half step (CHS) above or below the given pitch as requested.

> **!** Remember, chromatic half steps use the same letter name. C to C-sharp is a chromatic half step up. A to A-flat is a chromatic half step down.

C♯					
CHS above C	CHS above D	CHS above F	CHS above G	CHS above A	CHS above B
1.	2.	3.	4.	5.	6.
CHS above E	CHS below C♯	CHS below D♯	CHS below E♯	CHS below F♯	CHS below G♯
7.	8.	9.	10.	11.	12.
CHS below A♯	CHS below B♯	CHS above C♭	CHS above D♭	CHS above E♭	CHS above F♭
13.	14.	15.	16.	17.	18.
CHS above G♭	CHS above A♭	CHS above B♭			
19.	20.	21.			

Exercise 3.12 - Spelling Diatonic Half Steps

Directions: Build a diatonic half step (DHS) above or below the given pitch as requested.

> **!** Remember, diatonic half steps use different letter names. C to D-flat is a diatonic half step up. E-flat to D is a diatonic half step down.

D♭					
DHS above C	DHS above D	DHS above E	DHS above F	DHS above G	DHS above A
1.	2.	3.	4.	5.	6.
DHS above B	DHS below D♭	DHS below E♭	DHS below F	DHS below G♭	DHS below A♭
7.	8.	9.	10.	11.	12.
DHS below B♭	DHS below C	DHS above C♯	DHS above D♯	DHS above E♯	DHS above F♯
13.	14.	15.	16.	17.	18.
DHS above G♯	DHS above A♯	DHS above B♯			
19.	20.	21.			

© 2005. Eric Harris. All Rights Reserved.

Exercise 3.13 - Whole Step Identification

Directions: If the keys marked in each item are a whole step apart, check "yes;" if they are not, check "no."

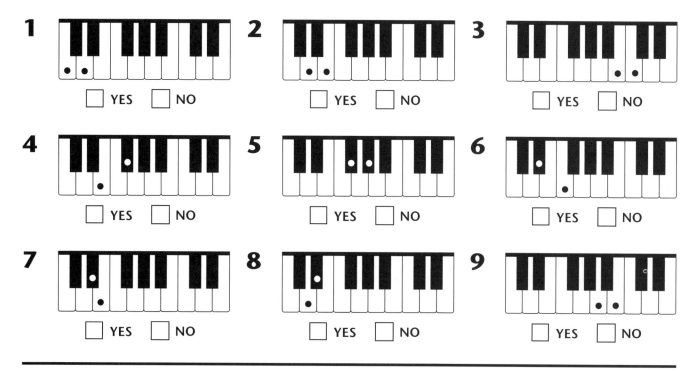

1 ☐ YES ☐ NO

2 ☐ YES ☐ NO

3 ☐ YES ☐ NO

4 ☐ YES ☐ NO

5 ☐ YES ☐ NO

6 ☐ YES ☐ NO

7 ☐ YES ☐ NO

8 ☐ YES ☐ NO

9 ☐ YES ☐ NO

Exercise 3.14 - Whole Step Check

Directions: Using the keyboard below, answer the following questions.

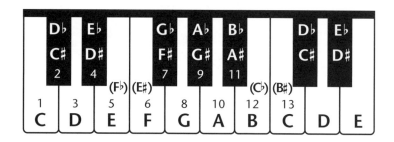

1. What key number is one whole step above 1? _____

2. What key number is one whole step above 2? _____

3. What key number is one whole step above 4? _____

4. What key number is one whole step above 5? _____

5. What key number is one whole step above 9? _____

6. What key number is one whole step above 3? _____

7. What key number is one whole step below 10? ___

8. What key number is one whole step below 13? ___

9. What key number is one whole step below 11? ___

10. What key number is one whole step below 6? _____

11. What key number is one whole step below 7? _____

12. What key number is one whole step below 3? _____

© 2005. Eric Harris. All Rights Reserved.

Exercise 3.15 - Name The Skipped Key

Directions: Answer the questions below.

1. The whole step C to D skips the black key __C♯/ D♭__.

2. The whole step E♭ to F skips the white key _____/_____.

3. The whole step A♭ to B♭ skips the white key _____.

4. The whole step B to C♯ skips the white key _____/_____.

5. The whole step F♯ to G♯ skips the white key _____.

6. The whole step D♭ to E♭ skips the white key _____.

7. The whole step E to F♯ skips the white key _____/_____.

8. The whole step A to B skips the black key _____/_____.

9. The whole step G♭ to A♭ skips the white key _____.

10. The whole step D to E skips the black key _____/_____.

11. The whole step G♯ to A♯ skips the white key _____.

12. The whole step B♭ to C skips the white key _____/_____.

Exercise 3.16 - Spelling Whole Steps

Directions: Build a whole step (WS) above or below the given pitch as requested.

 Remember, whole steps always use the next letter name. E to G-flat would sound the same as E to F-sharp, but E to G-flat skips the letter name F. E to F-sharp is the correct spelling.

WS above C 1.	WS above D 2.	WS above E 3.	WS above F 4.	WS above G 5.	WS above A 6.
WS above B 7.	WS below C 8.	WS below D 9.	WS below E 10.	WS below F 11.	WS below G 12.
WS below A 13.	WS below B 14.	WS above C♯ 15.	WS above D♯ 16.	WS above F♯ 17.	WS above G♯ 18.
WS above A♯ 19.	WS below D♭ 20.	WS below E♭ 21.	WS below G♭ 22.	WS below A♭ 23.	WS below B♭ 24.
WS below C♯ 25.	WS below D♯ 26.	WS below E♯ 27.	WS below F♯ 28.	WS below G♯ 29.	WS below A♯ 30.
WS below B♯ 31.	WS above D♭ 32.	WS above E♭ 33.	WS above F♭ 34.	WS above G♭ 35.	WS above A♭ 36.
WS above B♭ 37.	WS above C♭ 38.				

© 2005. Eric Harris. All Rights Reserved.

Exercise 3.17 - On The Staff

Directions: Determine whether the notes in each measure form a chromatic half step (CHS), diatonic half step (DHS), whole step (WS) or are enharmonic (E).

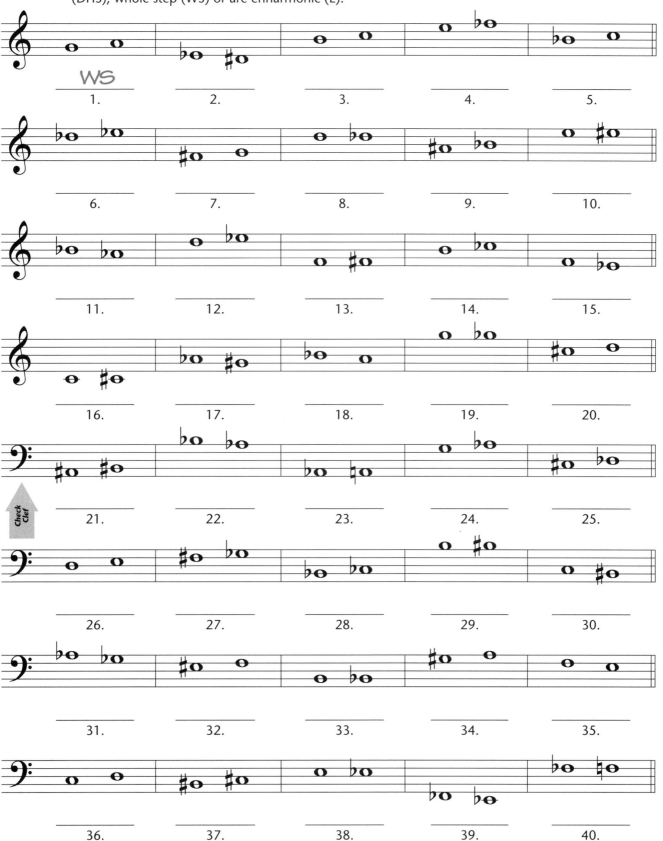

© 2005. Eric Harris. All Rights Reserved.

LESSON 4: DOUBLE SHARPS & DOUBLE FLATS

1. Three basic accidentals are used in music: sharps (♯), which raise the sound of notes a half step; flats (♭), which lower the sound of notes a half step; and naturals (♮), which cancel sharps or flats.

2. Two important but less frequently used accidentals can also be found in music. The **double sharp** (✕), which raises the sound of a note a whole step (or raises a sharped note another chromatic half step); and the **double flat** (♭♭), which lowers the sound of a note a whole step (or lowers a flatted note another chromatic half step).

DOUBLE SHARPS ON THE PIANO

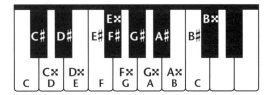

Right is higher. Sharps raise to the right. ➡

- C to C-sharp is a half step up.
- C to C-double sharp is a whole step up.
- C-double sharp can be used to raise C-sharp another chromatic half step.

DOUBLE FLATS ON THE PIANO

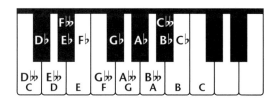

⬅ *Left is lower. Flats lower to the left.*

- D to D-flat is a half step down.
- D to D-double flat is a whole step down.
- D-double flat can be used to lower D-flat another chromatic half step.

3. Notice that the use of double sharps and double flats gives each white key on the piano three enharmonic names!

4. Double accidentals make it easy to spell previously difficult whole steps and half steps. For example:

   Problem: Spell a whole step above E♯ – which is actually F. A whole step above F is G.
              We can't say E♯ to G because this skips a letter name (F).
              So we call G by its enharmonic name: F✕.

   Problem: Spell a chromatic half step below B♭. The white key A is a half step below B♭ but
              we must use the same letter name when spelling chromatic half steps. So we call A by
              its enharmonic name: B♭♭.

   Problem: Spell a whole step below F♭ – which is actually E. A whole step below E is D.
              We can't say F♭ to D because this skips a letter name (E).
              So we call D by its enharmonic name: E♭♭.

5. Double sharps are written on the staff in the form of a small "x." Double flats are written on the staff in the form of two flats placed closely, side by side.

Trace each double sharp below. Then write one of your own beside each.

Trace each double flat below. Then write one of your own beside each.

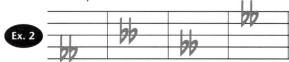

Ex. 1

Ex. 2

© 2005. Eric Harris. All Rights Reserved.

Exercise 3.18 - Complex Pitch Sets On The Keyboard

Directions: Each item below contains a set of three ascending or three descending pitches. Write the letter name of each pitch in the set on the corresponding piano keyboard below each item.

G, G-sharp, G-double sharp.

1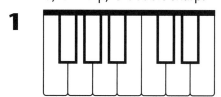

D, D-flat, D-double flat.

5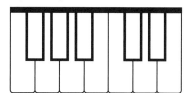

A, A-sharp, A-double sharp.

9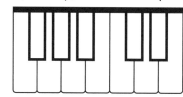

D, D-sharp, D-double sharp.

2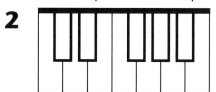

A, A-flat, A-double flat.

6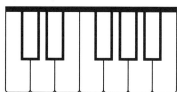

C, C-sharp, C-double sharp.

10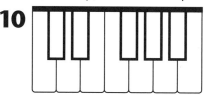

F, F-sharp, F-double sharp.

3

F, F-flat, F-double flat.

7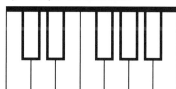

G, G-flat, G-double flat.

11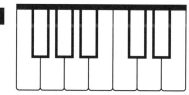

E, E-sharp, E-double sharp.

4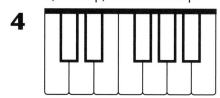

C, C-flat, C-double flat.

8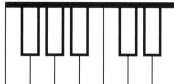

B, B-flat, B-double flat.

12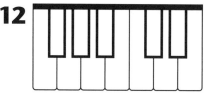

Exercise 3.19 - Using Double Accidentals

Directions: Provide the correct pitch name for each problem below; "↑" means above, "↓" means below.

1. _____ CHS ↓ Db
2. _____ CHS ↑ B♯
3. _____ CHS ↓ Ab
4. _____ CHS ↑ F♯
5. _____ WS ↓ Cb
6. _____ WS ↓ Fb
7. _____ WS ↑ E♯

8. _____ WS ↑ B♯
9. _____ CHS ↓ Gb
10. _____ CHS ↑ C♯
11. _____ CHS ↓ Eb
12. _____ CHS ↑ A♯
13. _____ CHS ↓ Bb
14. _____ CHS ↑ D♯

15. The enharmonic spellings for C are _____ and _____.
16. The enharmonic spellings for G are _____ and _____.
17. The enharmonic spellings for F are _____ and _____.
18. The enharmonic spellings for A are _____ and _____.
19. The enharmonic spellings for E are _____ and _____.
20. The enharmonic spellings for D are _____ and _____.
21. The enharmonic spellings for B are _____ and _____.

© 2005. Eric Harris. All Rights Reserved.

Exercise 3.20 - Writing Notes On The Staff

Directions: Write the requested notes on the staves below. Use whole notes. Remember, accidentals are placed before the note they are to affect on the same line or space as the note they are to affect.

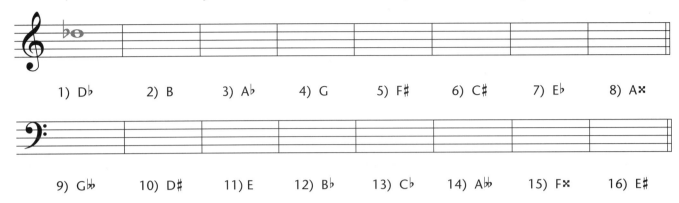

1) Db   2) B   3) Ab   4) G   5) F#   6) C#   7) Eb   8) A𝄪

9) Gbb   10) D#   11) E   12) Bb   13) Cb   14) Abb   15) F𝄪   16) E#

Exercise 3.21 - Finding Pitches On The Piano

Directions: Mark the pitch with a dot on the corresponding piano key.

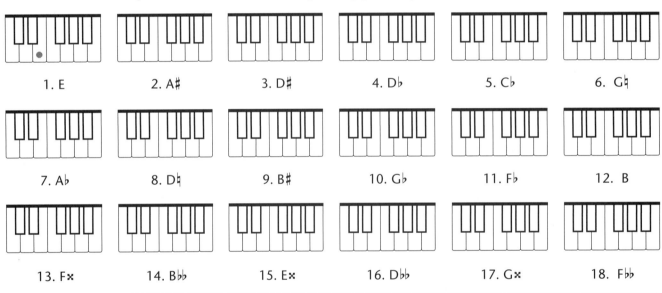

1. E   2. A#   3. D#   4. Db   5. Cb   6. G♮

7. Ab   8. D♮   9. B#   10. Gb   11. Fb   12. B

13. F𝄪   14. Bbb   15. E𝄪   16. Dbb   17. G𝄪   18. Fbb

Exercise 3.22 - Naming Notes On The Staff

Directions: Using your knowledge of the rule of accidentals, name the notes in each musical example below.

1. 2. 3. 4. 5. 6. 7. 8. 9. 10. 11. 12. 13. 14. 15. 16. 17.18.19.20.

1. 2. 3. 4. 5. 6. 7. 8. 9. 10. 11. 12. 13. 14.

© 2005. Eric Harris. All Rights Reserved.

Unit Review Questions

Directions: Answer the questions below.

1. _____ The piano keyboard has white keys and ? keys.

2. _____ The black keys are grouped into sets of ? and three.

3. _____ Just to the left of each group of three black keys is the white key ?

4. _____ Just to the left of each group of two black keys is the white key ?

5. _____ If we know the location of C and F on the piano keyboard, we can follow the ? pattern to name the remaining white keys.

6. _____ As we move to the right on the piano keyboard, the pitch of each key becomes ?

7. _____ As we move to the left on the piano keyboard, the pitch of each key becomes ?

8. _____ On the piano, higher is to the ?, lower is to the ? (Write both answers in the blank.)

9. _____ The distance from one key to the next closest key on the piano (with no key in between) is called a ?

10. _____ Most half steps occur between white keys and ? keys.

11. _____ There is no black key between ? and ? or between ? and ? (Write all four answers in the blank.)

12. _____ A white key to a white key can also be a half step if there is no ? key in between.

13. _____ When using a numbered piano keyboard, the distance from one number up or down to the next number in order is a ?

14. _____ Special symbols used to raise or lower the sound of a note are called ?

15. _____ This accidental lowers the sound of a note a half step. (Name it and draw it.)

16. _____ This accidental raises the sound of a note a half step. (Name it and draw it.)

17. _____ A ? is used to cancel a sharp or flat. (Name it and draw it.)

18. _____ Applying a natural will actually ? a flatted note.

19. _____ Applying a natural will actually ? a sharped note.

20. _____ All of the black keys on the piano each have ? names.

21. _____ One set of black key names uses ? (for raising the sound of notes).

22. _____ One set of black key names uses ? (for lowering the sound of notes).

23. _____ E can also be called ?

© 2005. Eric Harris. All Rights Reserved.

24. _____ B can also be called ?

25. _____ F can also be called ?

26. _____ C can also be called ?

27. _____ When two notes have the same sound (because they are played by the same piano key) but have two different letter names, they are said to be ?

28. _____ Enharmonic notes will use the same ? on a wind instrument.

29. _____ A ? exists when two notes a half step apart share the same letter name (C and C-sharp for example).

30. _____ A ? exists when two notes a half step apart have different (but consecutive) letter names (C and D-flat for example).

31. _____ Two half steps combine to create a ?

32. _____ A whole step will always involve a ? key on the piano.

33. _____ Whole steps must always use ? letter names.

34. _____ When written on the staff, accidentals are placed ? the note they are to affect on the same line or space as the note they are to affect.

35. _____ Accidentals are good for ? measure only.

36. _____ Accidentals ? at the bar line.

37. _____ An accidental may be carried into the next measure if the note is ? across the bar line.

38. _____ When a note with an accidental is tied across the bar line, the accidental ? at the end of the tie.

39. _____ A ? raises the sound of a note a whole step.

40. _____ A ? lowers the sound of a note a whole step.

41. _____ A ? also raises a sharped note another chromatic half step.

42. _____ A ? also lowers a flatted note another chromatic half step.

43. _____ The use of a double sharp or double flat gives each white key on the piano ? enharmonic names.

44. _____ Draw a double sharp.

45. _____ Draw a double flat.

46. _____ Double accidentals make it easy to spell previously difficult whole steps and half steps. (True/False)

© 2005. Eric Harris. All Rights Reserved.

LESSON 5: TIME SIGNATURE REVIEW

1. **Time signatures** are large fractions placed at the beginning of a piece of music.

↖ **time signature**

2. Time signatures with a top number of two, three, or four are called **simple time** signatures. The following are all simple time signatures.

$$\frac{2}{2} \quad \frac{3}{2} \quad \frac{4}{2} \qquad \frac{2}{4} \quad \frac{3}{4} \quad \frac{4}{4} \qquad \frac{2}{8} \quad \frac{3}{8} \quad \frac{4}{8}$$

most common

Two-four, three-four, and four-four time are the most frequently encountered time signatures and will be the focus of this lesson.

3. In simple time, each number of the time signature gives us an important piece of information.

4 The *top number* tells us the number of beats that will be found in each measure.

4 The *bottom number* is a "code" that tells us the note value that will get one beat. (The number four means "quarter note.")*

The **beat** is the pulse of the music kept by tapping the foot. *One foot-tap equals one beat.*

4. The note value indicated by the bottom number of the time signature is called the **beat value**. In simple time, each beat divides into two smaller note values called the **division value**. In all time signatures with four as the bottom number, the beat value will be a quarter note, and the division value will be an eighth note (two of them).

* The number two means "half note;" eight means "eighth note."

TWO-FOUR TIME	THREE-FOUR TIME	FOUR-FOUR TIME
2 Two beats in each measure. **4** The quarter note gets one beat (one foot-tap).	**3** Three beats in each measure. **4** The quarter note gets one beat (one foot-tap).	**4** Four beats in each measure. **4** The quarter note gets one beat (one foot-tap).

Each measure of two-four time will contain two quarter notes or some combination of notes (and/or rests) that equals two quarter notes.

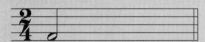

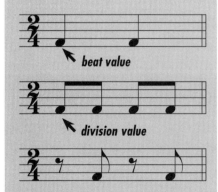

← **beat value**

← **division value**

Note: A whole rest fills an entire measure with silence in all time signatures (even in two-four time).

Each measure of three-four time will contain three quarter notes or some combination of notes (and/or rests) that equals three quarter notes.

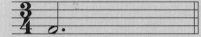

← **beat value**

← **division value**

Note: A whole rest fills an entire measure with silence in all time signatures (even in three-four time).

Each measure of four-four time will contain four quarter notes or some combination of notes (and/or rests) that equals four quarter notes.

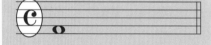

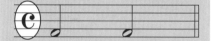

← **beat value**

← **division value**

*Four-four time is also called **Common Time** and can be indicated by a large C written in place of the time signature.*

© 2005. Eric Harris. All Rights Reserved.

5. In all time signatures with four as the bottom number, notes (and their matching rests) will get the following beats:

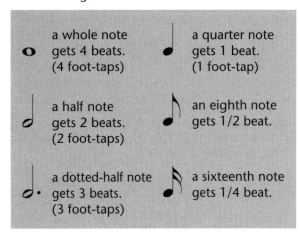

a whole note gets 4 beats. (4 foot-taps)

a quarter note gets 1 beat. (1 foot-tap)

a half note gets 2 beats. (2 foot-taps)

an eighth note gets 1/2 beat.

a dotted-half note gets 3 beats. (3 foot-taps)

a sixteenth note gets 1/4 beat.

We must remember that the time signature sets the maximum number of beats for each measure. A whole note (since it gets four beats) will never appear in a measure of three-four time and a dotted-half note (since it gets three beats) will never appear in a measure of two-four time.

6. Some musicians refer to the time signature as the **meter signature**. These two terms are interchangeable and have the same meaning.

7. We have already learned to identify simple time signatures (where the top number is two, three, or four). However, we can further describe these time signatures by classifying them as duple, triple, or quadruple.

Time signatures with a top number of two are said to be in **simple-duple meter**.

2 **2** **2**
2 **4** **8**
(♩) (♩) (♪)

Time signatures with a top number of three are said to be in **simple-triple meter**.

3 **3** **3**
2 **4** **8**

Time signatures with a top number of four are said to be in **simple-quadruple meter**.

4 **4** **4**
2 **4** **8**

Exercise 4.1 - Review Questions

Directions: Answer the questions below.

1. _____ Large fractions placed at the beginning of a piece of music are called ?

2. _____ Time signatures with a top number of two, three, or four are called ? signatures.

3. _____ The most frequently encountered time signatures are ? (Write all three answers in the blank.)

4. _____ In a simple time signature, this number tells us how many beats will be in each measure.

5. _____ In a simple time signature, this number is a "code" that tells us what note value will get one beat.

6. _____ The ? is the pulse of the music kept by tapping the foot.

7. _____ One ? equals one beat.

8. _____ If the bottom number of the time signature is four, what note value will get one beat?

9. _____ How many beats are in each measure of two-four time?

10. _____ In two-four time, what note value gets one beat?

11. _____ What single note value will fill an entire measure with sound in two-four time?

12. _____ How many beats are in each measure of three-four time?

© 2005. Eric Harris. All Rights Reserved.

13. _____ In three-four time, what note value gets one beat?

14. _____ What single note value will fill an entire measure with sound in three-four time?

15. _____ How many beats are in each measure of four-four time?

16. _____ In four-four time, what note value gets one beat?

17. _____ What single note value will fill an entire measure with sound in four-four time?

18. _____ What kind of rest will fill an entire measure with silence in <u>all</u> time signatures?

19. _____ Another name for four-four time (indicated with a large "C") is ? time.

20. _____ How many quarter notes can fit into a measure of two-four time?

21. _____ How many quarter notes can fit into a measure of three-four time?

22. _____ How many quarter notes can fit into a measure of four-four time?

23. _____ How many eighth notes can fit into a measure of two-four time?

24. _____ How many eighth notes can fit into a measure of three-four time?

25. _____ How many eighth notes can fit into a measure of four-four time?

26. _____ How many sixteenth notes can fit into a measure of two-four time?

27. _____ How many sixteenth notes can fit into a measure of three-four time?

28. _____ How many sixteenth notes can fit into a measure of four-four time?

29. _____ Can a dotted-half note fit into a measure of two-four time? (Yes/No)

30. _____ Can a whole note fit into a measure of three-four time? (Yes/No)

31. _____ How many beats does a whole note get?

32. _____ How many beats does a half note get?

33. _____ How many beats does a dotted-half note get?

34. _____ How many beats does a quarter note get?

35. _____ How many beats does an eighth note get? (Only one – not a pair.)

36. _____ How many beats does a sixteenth note get?

Classify the time signatures in items 37 through 45 as simple-duple (SD), simple-triple (ST), or simple-quadruple (SQ).

$\frac{4}{8}$ $\frac{2}{2}$ $\frac{3}{2}$ $\frac{3}{8}$ $\frac{4}{4}$ $\frac{2}{4}$ $\frac{3}{4}$ $\frac{4}{2}$ $\frac{2}{8}$

37. ____ 38. ____ 39. ____ 40. ____ 41. ____ 42. ____ 43. ____ 44. ____ 45. ____

© 2005. Eric Harris. All Rights Reserved.

LESSON 6: COUNTING REVIEW

1. Musicians number each beat in each measure. This process is called **counting**. Counting helps musicians learn, recognize, and accurately perform rhythms. *All rhythms should be counted aloud with a steady foot-tap.* Each beat gets one foot-tap.

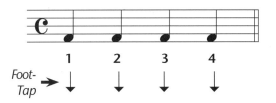

2. **Wedges** (>) are used to indicate sustained beats that exist within longer note values.

3. Each measure begins with "1."

4. Rests are not counted aloud. Simply continue to tap the foot.

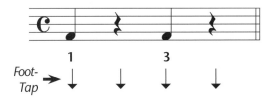

5. Eighth notes travel in pairs. The first eighth note in each pair is given a **beat number** (1, 2, 3, or 4). The second eighth note in each pair is called the "**and**" of the beat and is indicated with a "+." When counting eighth notes with a foot-tap, the foot will *tap the floor on the beat* and will *come up on the "and" of the beat.* This is why the "and" of the beat is sometimes called the "upbeat" or "offbeat."

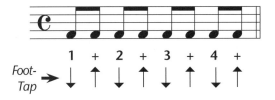

6. An eighth note followed by an eighth rest is counted, played, and will sound like a short (staccato) quarter note.

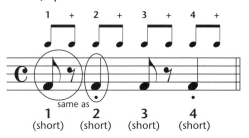

7. An eighth rest followed by an eighth note is counted and played by tapping the foot on the beat (the rest) and speaking or playing as the foot comes up on "and." Look for the pairs!

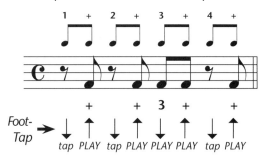

8. **Classic beams** are the result of old printing practices. Do not let odd beaming combinations confuse you. Just look for the pairs. You may wish to draw lines to make seeing the pairs (and thus counting the pairs) easier.

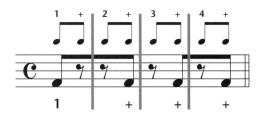

9. Eighth notes are sometimes beamed in groups of four. Do not let this confuse you. The counting remains the same. Look for the pairs!

Look at these eighth notes beamed in a group of six in three-four time. Look for the pairs!

© 2005. Eric Harris. All Rights Reserved.

10. Notes that are tied together are counted as one single, sustained note value.

11. If we tie the second eighth note in a pair to the first eighth note in the next pair, we create a quarter note value that begins on the "and" of the beat. This effect is called **syncopation**.

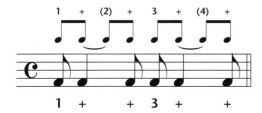

Note: Students may write any counting in parentheses to help with complex rhythms. This counting, however, is only part of the thinking process and is never spoken.

12. One dotted-quarter note contains three eighth notes (two for the quarter note and one for the dot). It is important to realize that the dot is actually the first eighth note in the next pair. This is why we count "One-the-dot-is-two," or "Two-the-dot-is-three," or "Three-the-dot-is-four." The abbreviation "TDI" is used to mean "the-dot-is" when writing the counting under a measure of rhythm.

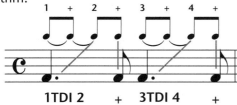

13. If we write three notes of the same value in the same time/space normally occupied by two (like three eighth notes in the space of two) we create a **triplet**. Triplets are counted using the "One-la-le" method. The first note in the triplet is given a beat number. The second note in the triplet is called the "la" of the beat. The third note is called the "le" of the beat.

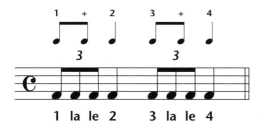

14. Sixteenth notes travel in sets of four. The first sixteenth note in a set is given a beat number. The second sixteenth is called the "e" of the beat. The third sixteenth is called the "and" of the beat. The fourth sixteenth is called the "a" of the beat. Notice that the "and" in a set of four sixteenth notes matches the "and" in a pair of eighth notes. This is because two sixteenth notes equal one eighth note.

15. Two more rhythms can be created by tying the first two or the last two sixteenths together to create an eighth note.

16. Another two rhythms can be created by tying the first three or the last three sixteenths together to create a dotted-eighth note.

© 2005. Eric Harris. All Rights Reserved.

17. If we tie the middle two sixteenth notes together, we get the rhythm used in the folk tune *Turkey In The Straw.*

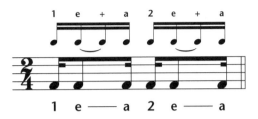

18. Other rhythms can be created by replacing one of the four sixteenth notes in a group with a sixteenth rest. Many of these sound similar to rhythms we have already learned to count.

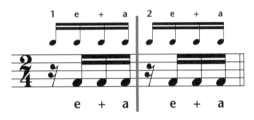

SOUND-ALIKES

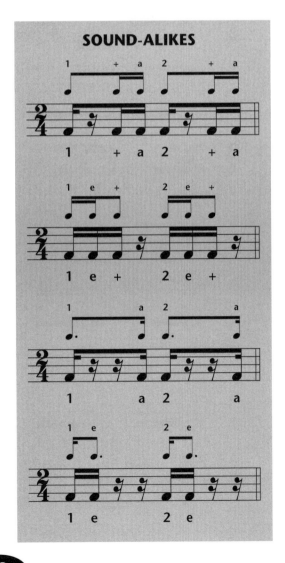

SOUND-ALIKES (cont.)

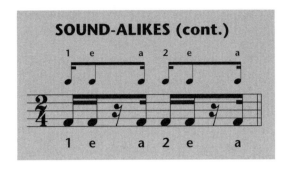

19. Two final rhythms involve the dotted-quarter note.

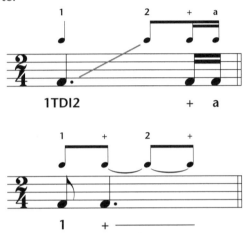

20. Most of the music we play uses combinations of the rhythms we have just learned. The key to successful rhythm reading is the ability to separate and recognize the patterns in each measure. Once this is accomplished, you can reassemble the entire measure of rhythm and perform it. This process sounds complicated but it becomes very easy with practice. Lines are used to separate the patterns in each measure below.

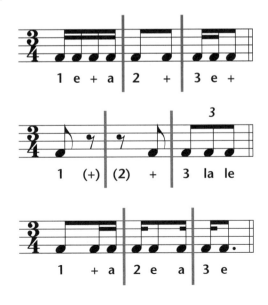

© 2005. Eric Harris. All Rights Reserved.

21. Notes that come before the first full measure of music are called **pick-up notes** or the **anacrusis**. Pick-up notes can occur in any time signature and can be any fraction of a full measure. The missing beats of a pick-up measure can be found in the last measure of the piece.

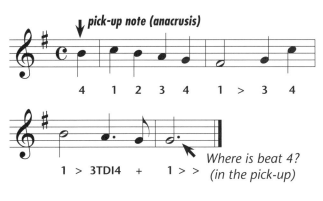

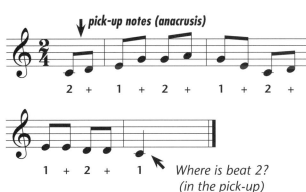

22. The chart below summarizes the rhythms covered in this unit. The Sound-Alikes are each placed beside an associated Basic Rhythm for reference.

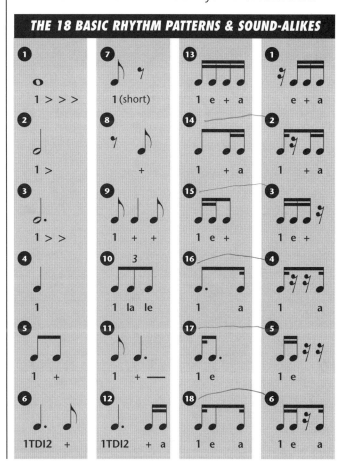

Exercise 4.2 - Rhythm Counting Exercise

Directions: Write the counting under each measure below.

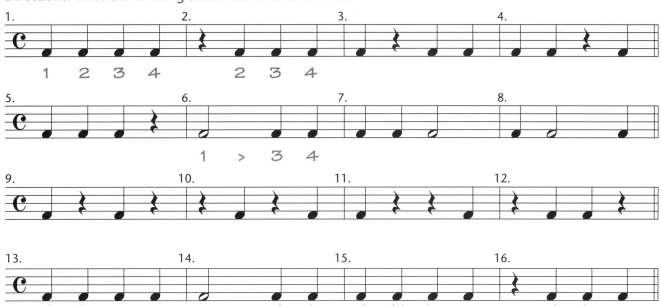

© 2005. Eric Harris. All Rights Reserved.

Exercise 4.3 - Rhythm Counting Exercise

Directions: Write the counting under each measure of rhythm below. Play the rhythms on your tuning note.

> **!** Two-four time and three-four time are counted just like four-four time; the only difference is the total number of beats in each measure.

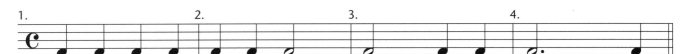

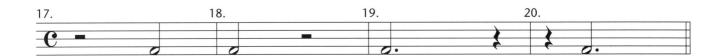

Check time sig.

© 2005. Eric Harris. All Rights Reserved.

Exercise 4.4 - Rhythm Counting Exercise

Directions: Write the counting under each measure of rhythm below. Play the rhythms on your tuning note.

1   2   3   4

(1) + (2) + 3(+) 4(+)

Exercise 4.5 - Find The Beat

Directions: Identify the beat or part of the beat (the "and" of the beat) to which the arrow is pointing.

Write your answers here.

and of 1   beat 3

1. _____   2. _____   3. _____   4. _____   5. _____   6. _____

7. _____   8. _____   9. _____   10. _____   11. _____   12. _____

© 2005. Eric Harris. All Rights Reserved.

Exercise 4.6 - Rhythm Counting Exercise

Directions: Write the counting under each measure of rhythm below. Play the rhythms on your tuning note.

1.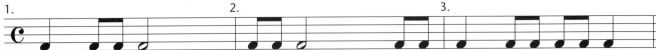

4.

7.

10.

13.

1TDI 2 + 3 4

16.

19.

1 +(2) + 3 4

22.

25.

1 la le 2 3 la le 4

28.

© 2005. Eric Harris. All Rights Reserved.

Exercise 4.7 - Rhythm Counting Exercise

Directions: Write the counting under each measure of rhythm below. Play the rhythms on your tuning note.

1 e + a 2

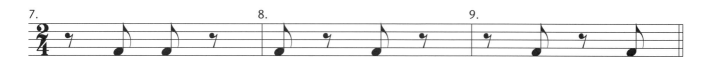

1 + a 2 +

1 e + 2 +

1 a 2 +

© 2005. Eric Harris. All Rights Reserved.

Exercise 4.8 - Rhythm Counting Exercise

Directions: Write the counting under each measure of rhythm below. Play the rhythms on your tuning note.

1 e a 2 +

© 2005. Eric Harris. All Rights Reserved.

Exercise 4.9 - Rhythm Counting Exercise

Directions: Write the counting under each measure of rhythm below. Play the rhythms on your tuning note.

© 2005. Eric Harris. All Rights Reserved.

Exercise 4.10 - Rhythm Counting Exercise

Directions: Write the counting under each measure of rhythm below. Play the rhythms on your tuning note.

Exercise 4.11 - Name The Time Signature

Directions: Provide the time signature for each measure below (two-four, three-four, or four-four).

 With the exception of eighth notes (which are often beamed in sets of four or six), a beam is used to group note values within a single beat. All of the beamed figures in the Eighteen Basic Rhythm Patterns and the Sound-Alike Rhythms equal one quarter note (one beat).

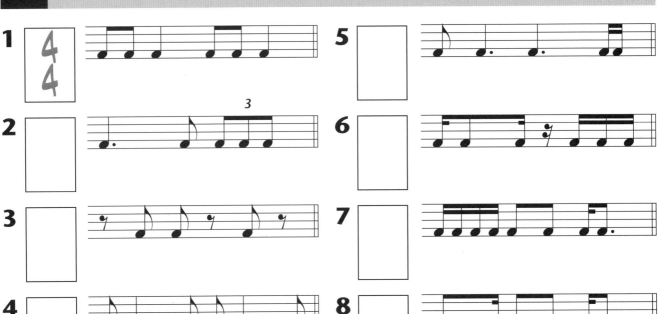

© 2005. Eric Harris. All Rights Reserved.

Unit Review Questions

Directions: Identify the beat or part of the beat to which the arrow is pointing.

Write your answers here.

1.	2.	3.	4.	5.	6.

e of 1

7.	8.	9.	10.	11.	12.

13.	14.	15.	16.	17.	18.

Directions: Answer the questions below.

1. _____ Counting helps musicians learn, recognize, and accurately perform ?

2. _____ All rhythms should be counted aloud with a steady ?

3. _____ This symbol is used to indicate sustained beats that exist within longer note values. (Name it and draw it.)

4. _____ When counting, each measure begins with ?

© 2005. Eric Harris. All Rights Reserved.

5. _____ Rests [are/are not] counted aloud. (Choose the correct answer.)

6. _____ Eighth notes travel in ?

7. _____ The first eighth note in a pair is given a beat ?

8. _____ The second eighth note in a pair is called the ? of the beat.

9. _____ When counting eighth notes with a foot-tap, the foot taps the floor on the ?

10. _____ When counting eighth notes with a foot-tap, the foot comes up on the ? of the beat.

11. _____ The "and" of the beat can also be called the ? or the offbeat.

12. _____ An eighth note followed by an eighth rest is counted, played, and will sound like a ? (staccato) quarter note.

13. _____ An eighth rest followed by an eighth note is counted and played by tapping the foot on the beat and playing as the foot comes up on ?

14. _____ These special beams are the result of old printing practices.

15. _____ When counting eighth notes, you may wish to draw lines to help you see the ?

16. _____ Eighth notes are sometimes beamed in groups of four and/or six. (True/False)

17. _____ When eighth notes are beamed in groups of four or six, the counting remains the same. (True/False)

18. _____ Notes that are ? together are counted as one single, sustained note value.

19. _____ If we tie the second eighth note in a pair to the first eighth note in the next pair, we create a quarter note value that begins on the ? of the beat. This effect is called syncopation.

20. _____ When counting dotted-quarter notes, it is important to remember that the dot is the ? eighth note in the next pair.

21. _____ This abbreviation is used to mean "the-dot-is."

22. _____ If we write three eighth notes in the same time/space normally occupied by two eighth notes we create a ?

23. _____ Sixteenth notes travel in sets of ?

24. _____ The first sixteenth note in a set is given a beat ?

25. _____ The second sixteenth note in a set is called the ? of the beat.

26. _____ The third sixteenth note in a set is called the ? of the beat.

27. _____ The fourth sixteenth note in a set is called the ? of the beat.

28. _____ If we tie the first two sixteenth notes in a set together, we create this rhythm. (Draw it.)

© 2005. Eric Harris. All Rights Reserved.

29. _____ If we tie the last two sixteenth notes in a set together, we create this rhythm. (Draw it.)

30. _____ If we tie the first three sixteenth notes in a set together, we create this rhythm. (Draw it.)

31. _____ If we tie the last three sixteenth notes in a set together, we create this rhythm. (Draw it.)

32. _____ If we tie the middle two sixteenth notes in a set together, we create this rhythm. (Draw it.)

33. _____ The key to successful rhythm reading is the ability to separate and recognize the ? in each measure.

34. _____ Notes that come before the first full measure of music are called ? notes or the anacrusis.

35. _____ When counting rhythms in two-four, three-four, and four-four time, the only difference is the total number of ? in each measure.

36. _____ Time signatures with a top number of two, three, or four are called ? time signatures.

37. _____ The ? number of the time signature is a "code" that tells us what note value will get one beat.

38. _____ The ? number of the time signature tells us the number of beats that will be in each measure.

39. _____ The ? is the pulse of the music kept by tapping the foot.

40. _____ One foot-tap equals one ?

41. _____ In ? time, there will be two quarter notes in each measure or some combination of notes (and/or rests) that equals two quarter notes.

42. _____ In ? time, there will be four quarter notes in each measure or some combination of notes (and/or rests) that equals four quarter notes.

43. _____ In ? time, there will be three quarter notes in each measure or some combination of notes (and/or rests) that equals three quarter notes.

44. _____ A ? rest will fill an entire measure with silence in all time signatures.

45. _____ Another term which is used interchangeably with time signature is ? signature.

46. _____ If we are in simple time and there are two beats in each measure, the meter is said to be ? (simple-duple, simple-triple, or simple-quadruple).

47. _____ If we are in simple time and there are three beats in each measure, the meter is said to be ? (simple-duple, simple-triple, or simple-quadruple).

48. _____ If we are in simple time and there are four beats in each measure, the meter is said to be ? (simple-duple, simple-triple, or simple-quadruple).

© 2005. Eric Harris. All Rights Reserved.

LESSON 7: MAJOR SCALE REVIEW

1. Major scales can be created by combining whole steps and half steps in the pattern shown below. This is called the **major scale pattern**.

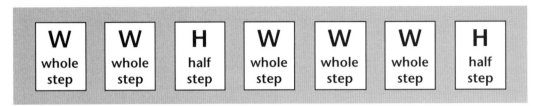

2. This pattern of whole steps and half steps can easily be seen in the C major scale shown below.

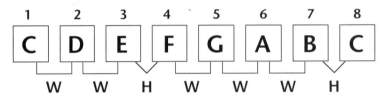

3. If we look carefully at the C major scale above, we can see characteristics found in all major scales.

   • Major scales contain eight notes. The first note and the last note are the same and are located an octave apart. The first note of the scale gives the scale its name.

   • Major scales are built entirely of whole steps with the exception of half steps which occur between the third and fourth notes of the scale and again between the seventh and eighth notes of the scale.

   • Major scales are built using the basic musical alphabet patterns. This means each letter will be used only once (except for the octave) and will always be found in alphabetical order.

4. If we maintain the major scale pattern of whole and half steps, we can build a major scale starting on any note. All major scales (with the exception of C major) require one or more sharps or flats to maintain the whole step/half step pattern. Major scales will contain sharps only or flats only, *never a combination*.

The D major scale requires two sharps (F♯ and C♯) to maintain the pattern.

	1	2	3	4	5	6	7	8
	D	E	F♯	G	A	B	C♯	D
		W	W	H	W	W	W	H

The B♭ major scale requires two flats (B♭ and E♭) to maintain the pattern.

	1	2	3	4	5	6	7	8
	B♭	C	D	E♭	F	G	A	B♭
		W	W	H	W	W	W	H

*Note: When writing major scales, always begin by first writing out the basic alphabet pattern and then, **working left to right**, check the size of each step (whole or half) adding sharps or flats as needed to maintain the major scale pattern. Always **work left to right** to avoid errors.*

5. Scales can be written ascending (going up – like those you've seen thus far) and descending (going down). To write a descending scale, simply write the scale backward. Look at the B♭ major scale shown above. Here it is descending (going down – or backward): B♭, A, G, F, E♭, D, C, B♭.

© 2005. Eric Harris. All Rights Reserved.

6. The sharps or flats used in a major scale can be compiled into a list (called the **key signature**) and placed at the beginning of a piece of music. The key signature not only tells musicians which notes to sharp or flat, it also indicates the scale that was used to write the piece.

B♭ Major Scale – requires two* flats: B♭ and E♭.

A Major Scale – requires three sharps: F♯, C♯, and G♯.

D♭ Major Scale – requires five flats, B♭, E♭, A♭, D♭, and G♭.

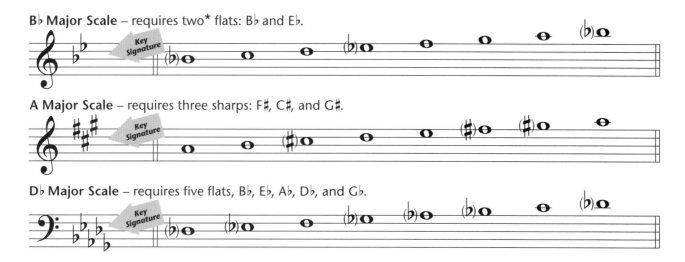

7. Sharps and flats placed in the key signature are always written on specific lines and spaces and always follow a specific order. *It is important to note that the accidentals will not appear in the scale in the same order they appear in the key signature.*

Note: This is another style of brace. It functions just like the one you learned to draw in Unit 1.

The **order of sharps** is F, C, G, D, A, E, B.

The sharps will always appear in this order:
One sharp – F♯.
Two sharps – F♯ and C♯.
Three sharps – F♯, C♯, and G♯.
Four sharps – F♯, C♯, G♯, and D♯.
Five sharps – F♯, C♯, G♯, D♯, and A♯.
Six sharps – F♯, C♯, G♯, D♯, A♯, and E♯.
Seven sharps – F♯, C♯, G♯, D♯, A♯, E♯, and B♯.

The **order of flats** is B, E, A, D, G, C, F.

The flats will always appear in this order:
One flat – B♭.
Two flats – B♭ and E♭.
Three flats – B♭, E♭, and A♭.
Four flats – B♭, E♭, A♭, and D♭.
Five flats – B♭, E♭, A♭, D♭, and G♭.
Six flats – B♭, E♭, A♭, D♭, G♭, and C♭.
Seven flats – B♭, E♭, A♭, D♭, G♭, C♭, and F♭.

8. Notice that the order of flats is simply the order of sharps in reverse.

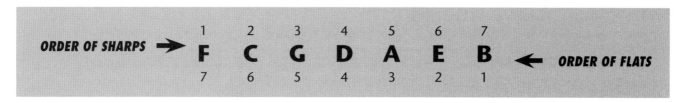

*Please note that while appearing twice in the scale, B♭ is only written in the key signature once, and only counts as one of the two flats. Accidentals in the key signature affect every note with that letter name, regardless of the line, space, or ledger line on which they are written. One B♭ in the key signature means that all B's are flat, no matter where or how many times they appear.

© 2005. Eric Harris. All Rights Reserved.

9. Musicians memorize fifteen major scales and their matching key signatures. Seven scales require sharps to maintain the major scale pattern. Seven scales require flats to maintain the major scale pattern. One scale (C major) requires no sharps or flats to maintain the major scale pattern.

MAJOR SCALES AND KEY SIGNATURES WHICH USE SHARPS

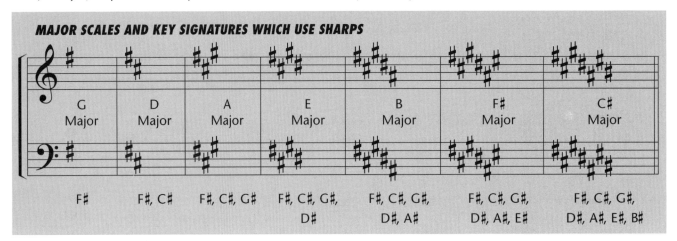

The G major scale requires one sharp – F♯ – to maintain the major scale pattern of whole and half steps.

The D major scale requires two sharps – F♯ and C♯ – to maintain the major scale pattern.

The A major scale requires three sharps – F♯, C♯, and G♯ – to maintain the major scale pattern.

The E major scale requires four sharps – F♯, C♯, G♯, and D♯ – to maintain the major scale pattern.

The B major scale requires five sharps – F♯, C♯, G♯, D♯, and A♯ – to maintain the major scale pattern.

The F# major scale requires six sharps – F♯, C♯, G♯, D♯, A♯, and E♯ – to maintain the major scale pattern.

The C# major scale requires seven sharps – F♯, C♯, G♯, D♯, A♯, E♯, and B♯ – to maintain the pattern.

MAJOR SCALES AND KEY SIGNATURES WHICH USE FLATS

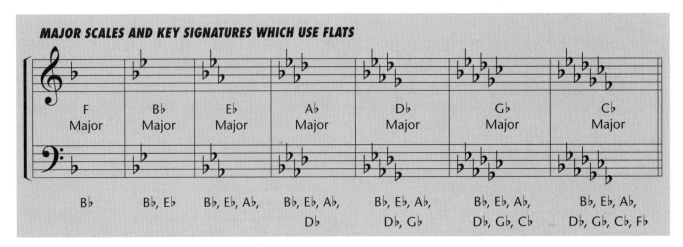

The F major scale requires one flat – B♭ – to maintain the major scale pattern of whole and half steps.

The B♭ major scale requires two flats – B♭ and E♭ – to maintain the major scale pattern.

The E♭ major scale requires three flats – B♭, E♭, and A♭ – to maintain the major scale pattern.

The A♭ major scale requires four flats – B♭, E♭, A♭, and D♭ – to maintain the major scale pattern.

The D♭ major scale requires five flats – B♭, E♭, A♭, D♭, and G♭ – to maintain the major scale pattern.

The G♭ major scale requires six flats – B♭, E♭, A♭, D♭, G♭, and C♭ – to maintain the major scale pattern.

The C♭ major scale requires seven flats – B♭, E♭, A♭, D♭, G♭, C♭, and F♭ – to maintain the pattern.

10. Students can use their knowledge of key signatures to write major scales quickly and with little chance for error. To write a major scale, simply begin with the basic alphabet pattern, and then add the accidentals from the key signature. For example, to write an E♭ major scale, write the E to E basic alphabet pattern (E, F, G, A, B, C, D, E) and then add the accidentals from the E♭ major key signature (B♭, E♭, and A♭). The answer would be: E♭, F, G, A♭, B♭, C, D, E♭. *Remember, accidentals do not appear in the scale in the same order they appear in the key signature.*

© 2005. Eric Harris. All Rights Reserved.

11. Musicians use many tools to help them memorize the fifteen major key signatures. The most popular is the **Circle of Fifths**, which shows all of the signatures on a clock-like device. The circle begins with C major at the top. Moving clockwise to the right, are the sharp keys. Moving counterclockwise to the left, are the flat keys. The sharp and flat keys cross at the bottom of the circle and show the three enharmonic keys.

12. The **Chart of Fifths** is the same information presented in a vertical chart. The right side of the chart shows the sharp keys; the left side of the chart shows the flat keys. The enharmonic keys are connected with dotted lines at the bottom of the chart.

13. Both charts move up or down in order by fifths (hence the name "of fifths"). This means each new key is five letter names *higher* than the one before on the sharp side; each new key is five letter names *lower* than the one before on the flat side.

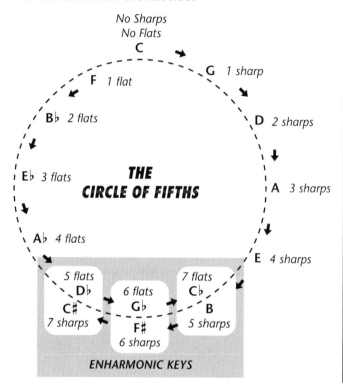

THE CHART OF FIFTHS

C Major - *No Sharps, No Flats*

FLAT KEY SIGNATURES		SHARP KEY SIGNATURES	
F major	1 flat	G major	1 sharp
B♭ major	2 flats	D major	2 sharps
E♭ major	3 flats	A major	3 sharps
A♭ major	4 flats	E major	4 sharps
D♭ major	5 flats	B major	5 sharps
G♭ major	6 flats	F♯ major	6 sharps
C♭ major	7 flats	C♯ major	7 sharps
ENHARMONIC KEYS			

14. The bottom of each chart shows the **enharmonic keys**. Each pair of scales is spelled differently but will sound the same and will use the same keys on the piano and the same fingerings on a wind instrument.

15. There are several important observations that students should make when working with key signatures:

• Only two of the sharp keys (F♯ and C♯) have the term "sharp" in the key name.

• All of the flat keys have the term "flat" in the key name (with the exception of F major).

• In flat keys, the next to the last flat will always reveal the name of the key (except for F major).

• In sharp keys, one half step above the last sharp will reveal the name of the key.

• When writing sharp key signatures on the treble staff, the third sharp will always be placed on the first space above the staff.

• When writing flat key signatures on the bass staff, the last flat will always be placed on the first space below the staff.

• C major has no sharps or flats; C♯ major has all sharps; C♭ major has all flats. C is "all or nothing."

© 2005. Eric Harris. All Rights Reserved.

Exercise 5.1 - Writing Major Scales

Directions: Using the major scale pattern, write the following scales. Mark the matching keys on the piano.

1. F G A Bb C D E F

2. Bb ___ ___ ___ ___ ___ ___ ___

3. Eb ___ ___ ___ ___ ___ ___ ___

4. Ab ___ ___ ___ ___ ___ ___ ___

5. Db ___ ___ ___ ___ ___ ___ ___

6. Gb ___ ___ ___ ___ ___ ___ ___

7. Cb ___ ___ ___ ___ ___ ___ ___

8. G ___ ___ ___ ___ ___ ___ ___

9. D ___ ___ ___ ___ ___ ___ ___

10. A ___ ___ ___ ___ ___ ___ ___

11. E ___ ___ ___ ___ ___ ___ ___

12. B ___ ___ ___ ___ ___ ___ ___

13. F# ___ ___ ___ ___ ___ ___ ___

14. C# ___ ___ ___ ___ ___ ___ ___

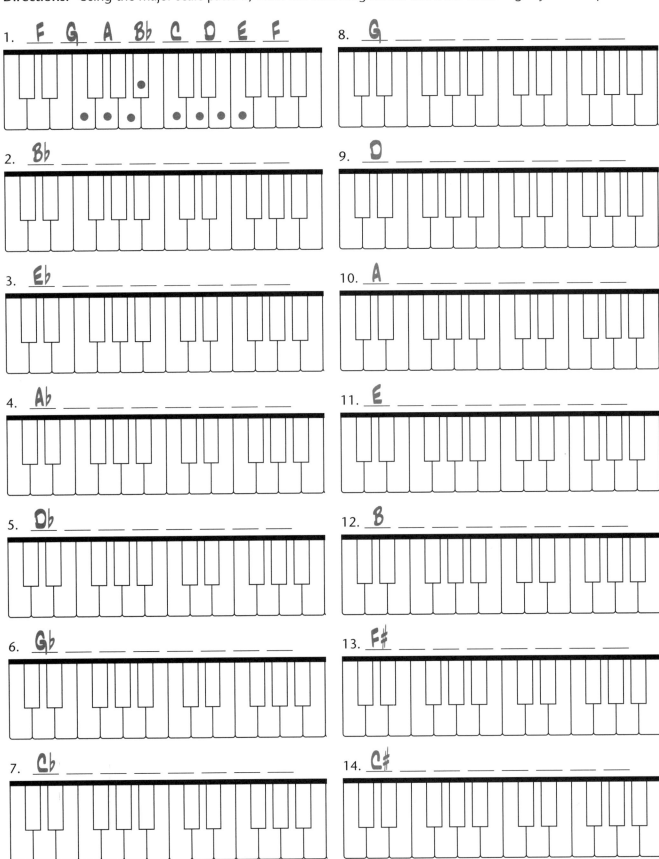

© 2005. Eric Harris. All Rights Reserved.

Exercise 5.2 - Identifying Major Scales

Directions: Answer "yes" or "no" to each question below.

1. Is the scale below the D major scale? _____

2. Is the scale below the E♭ major scale? _____

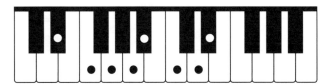

3. Is the scale below the A major scale? _____

4. Is the scale below the B♭ major scale? _____

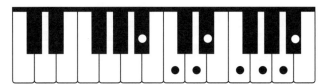

5. Is the scale below the F♯ major scale? _____

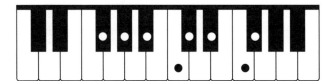

6. Is the scale below the C♭ major scale? _____

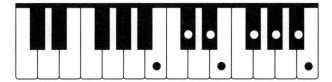

7. Is the scale below the C♯ major scale? _____

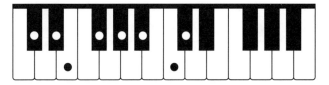

8. Is the scale below the A♭ major scale? _____

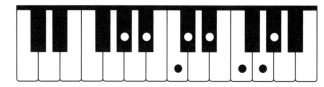

9. Is the scale below the E major scale? _____

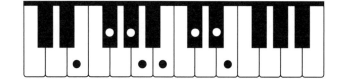

10. Is the scale below the D♭ major scale? _____

11. Is the scale below the B major scale? _____

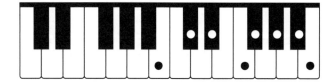

12. Is the scale below the F major scale? _____

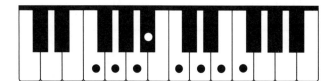

13. Is the scale below the G major scale? _____

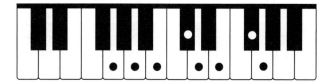

14. Is the scale below the G♭ major scale? _____

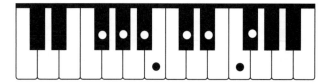

© 2005. Eric Harris. All Rights Reserved.

Exercise 5.3 - Major Key Signature Review

Directions: Provide the missing information for the chart below.

Major Key	Key Signature	Key Signature	Major Key	Mix	Mix
1. E major	4 sharps	26. No sharps No flats	C major	51. 2 sharps	D major
2. E♭ major		27. 1 sharp		52. D♭ major	5 flats
3. D♭ major		28. 1 flat		53. 4 flats	
4. B♭ major		29. 2 sharps		54. A major	
5. A♭ major		30. 2 flats		55. 1 flat	
6. G♭ major		31. 3 sharps		56. F♯ major	
7. C♭ major		32. 3 flats		57. 4 sharps	
8. D major		33. 4 sharps		58. E♭ major	
9. E major		34. 4 flats		59. 7 flats	
10. G major		35. 5 sharps		60. C♯ major	
11. F♯ major		36. 5 flats		61. 2 flats	
12. A major		37. 6 sharps		62. B major	
13. C♯ major		38. 6 flats		63. 1 sharp	
14. B major		39. 7 sharps		64. G♭ major	
15. F major		40. 7 flats		65. 1 flat	
16. G major		41. 1 flat		66. C♯ major	
17. E♭ major		42. 3 flats		67. 2 sharps	
18. F♯ major		43. 2 flats		68. E♭ major	
19. D major		44. 5 flats		69. 5 sharps	
20. B♭ major		45. 6 sharps		70. G major	
21. E major		46. 2 sharps		71. 4 flats	
22. A♭ major		47. 1 sharp		72. E major	
23. B major		48. 4 sharps		73. 3 sharps	
24. G♭ major		49. 7 flats		74. B♭ major	
25. A major		50. 7 sharps		75. 6 sharps	

© 2005. Eric Harris. All Rights Reserved.

Exercise 5.4 - Major Key Signature Review

Directions: Provide the number, type, and a list of the accidentals found in each major key signature below.

1. C major no sharps no flats _____
2. G major 1 sharp F# _____
3. D major _____ _____
4. A major _____ _____
5. E major _____ _____
6. B major _____ _____
7. F# major _____ _____
8. C# major _____ _____
9. C major _____ _____
10. F major _____ _____
11. Bb major _____ _____
12. Eb major _____ _____
13. Ab major _____ _____
14. Db major _____ _____
15. Gb major _____ _____
16. Cb major _____ _____
17. A major _____ _____
18. Ab major _____ _____
19. E major _____ _____
20. Eb major _____ _____
21. D major _____ _____
22. Db major _____ _____
23. B major _____ _____
24. Bb major _____ _____
25. G major _____ _____
26. Gb major _____ _____
27. F major _____ _____
28. F# major _____ _____
29. C major _____ _____

30. E major _____ _____
31. F major _____ _____
32. C# major _____ _____
33. Gb major _____ _____
34. D major _____ _____
35. B major _____ _____
36. Ab major _____ _____
37. C major _____ _____
38. Eb major _____ _____
39. A major _____ _____
40. Db major _____ _____
41. G major _____ _____
42. Cb major _____ _____
43. F# major _____ _____
44. Bb major _____ _____
45. G major _____ _____
46. F major _____ _____
47. D major _____ _____
48. Bb major _____ _____
49. A major _____ _____
50. Eb major _____ _____
51. Ab major _____ _____
52. E major _____ _____
53. Db major _____ _____
54. B major _____ _____
55. F# major _____ _____
56. Gb major _____ _____
57. C# major _____ _____
58. Cb major _____ _____

© 2005. Eric Harris. All Rights Reserved.

Exercise 5.5 - Writing Major Key Signatures – Trace Exercise

Directions: Trace the key signatures shown below. *Notice that the third sharp is written on the first space above the staff in treble clef. The last flat is written on the first space below the staff in bass clef.*

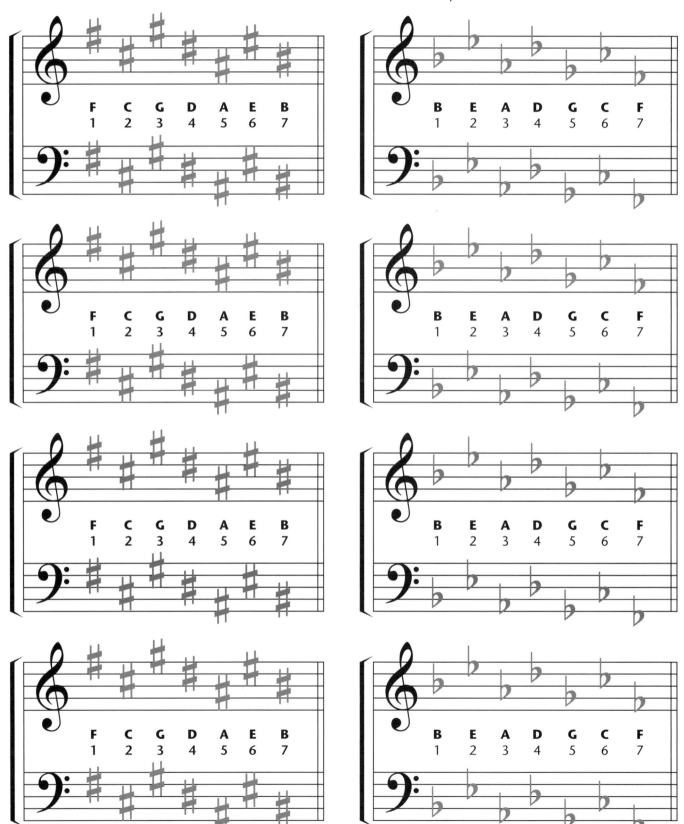

© 2005. Eric Harris. All Rights Reserved.

Exercise 5.6 - Writing Major Key Signatures (Sharp Keys Only)

Directions: Write the requested major key signature. Be sure to follow the exact placement and order shown on pages 61 and 62.

1. G major   2. D major   3. A major   4. E major

5. B major   6. F♯ major   7. C♯ major   8. B major

9. F♯ major   10. A major   11. E major   12. C♯ major

13. G major   14. B major   15. D major   16. F♯ major

Clef Change

17. G major   18. D major   19. A major   20. E major

21. B major   22. F♯ major   23. C♯ major   24. A major

25. C♯ major   26. E major   27. G major   28. B major

29. D major   30. F♯ major   31. A major   32. C♯ major

© 2005. Eric Harris. All Rights Reserved.

Exercise 5.7 - Writing Major Key Signatures (Flats Keys Only)

Directions: Write the requested major key signature. Be sure to follow the exact placement and order shown on pages 61 and 62.

1. F major   2. B♭ major   3. E♭ major   4. A♭ major

5. D♭ major   6. G♭ major   7. C♭ major   8. B♭ major

9. D♭ major   10. F major   11. A♭ major   12. C♭ major

13. E♭ major   14. G♭ major   15. B♭ major   16. D♭ major

Clef Change

17. F major   18. B♭ major   19. E♭ major   20. A♭ major

21. D♭ major   22. G♭ major   23. C♭ major   24. A♭ major

25. C♭ major   26. E♭ major   27. G♭ major   28. B♭ major

29. D♭ major   30. F major   31. A♭ major   32. C♭ major

© 2005. Eric Harris. All Rights Reserved.

Exercise 5.8 - Writing Major Key Signatures (Sharp and Flat Keys)

Directions: Write the requested major key signature. Be sure to follow the exact placement and order shown on pages 61 and 62.

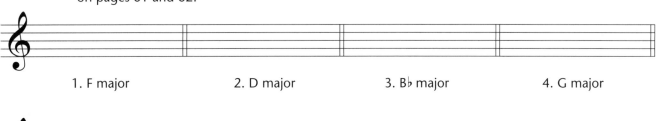

1. F major   2. D major   3. B♭ major   4. G major

5. A major   6. D♭ major   7. E major   8. A♭ major

9. E♭ major   10. B major   11. G♭ major   12. C♯ major

13. F♯ major   14. C♭ major   15. E major   16. B♭ major

17. C♯ major   18. C♭ major   19. F♯ major   20. G♭ major

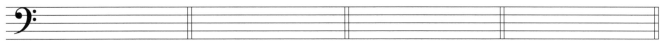

21. B major   22. D♭ major   23. E♭ major   24. D major

25. A♭ major   26. F major   27. G major   28. E major

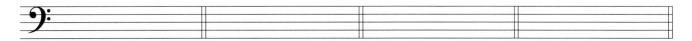

29. B♭ major   30. A major   31. D major   32. F major

© 2005. Eric Harris. All Rights Reserved.

Exercise 5.9 - Writing Major Key Signatures (Sharp and Flat Keys)

Directions: Write the requested major key signature. Be sure to follow the exact placement and order shown on pages 61 and 62.

| 1. F♯ major | 2. C♭ major | 3. G major | 4. D♭ major |

| 5. A♭ major | 6. A major | 7. B♭ major | 8. G major |

| 9. F major | 10. D major | 11. E♭ major | 12. E major |

| 13. B major | 14. F major | 15. C♯ major | 16. G♭ major |

Clef Change

| 17. G♭ major | 18. G major | 19. A♭ major | 20. A major |

| 21. B♭ major | 22. B major | 23. C♭ major | 24. C♯ major |

| 25. D♭ major | 26. D major | 27. E♭ major | 28. E major |

| 29. F major | 30. F♯ major | 31. C♯ major | 32. C♭ major |

© 2005. Eric Harris. All Rights Reserved.

Exercise 5.10 - Identifying Major Key Signatures

Directions: Name each major key given below.

1. _____ major   2. _____ major   3. _____ major   4. _____ major

5. _____ major   6. _____ major   7. _____ major   8. _____ major

9. _____ major   10. _____ major   11. _____ major   12. _____ major

13. _____ major   14. _____ major   15. _____ major   16. _____ major

17. _____ major   18. _____ major   19. _____ major   20. _____ major

21. _____ major   22. _____ major   23. _____ major   24. _____ major

25. _____ major   26. _____ major   27. _____ major   28. _____ major

29. _____ major   30. _____ major   31. _____ major   32. _____ major

© 2005. Eric Harris. All Rights Reserved.

Exercise 5.11 - Identifying Major Key Signatures

Directions: Name each major key given below.

1. _____ major   2. _____ major   3. _____ major   4. _____ major

5. _____ major   6. _____ major   7. _____ major   8. _____ major

9. _____ major   10. _____ major   11. _____ major   12. _____ major

13. _____ major   14. _____ major   15. _____ major   16. _____ major

17. _____ major   18. _____ major   19. _____ major   20. _____ major

21. _____ major   22. _____ major   23. _____ major   24. _____ major

25. _____ major   26. _____ major   27. _____ major   28. _____ major

29. _____ major   30. _____ major   31. _____ major   32. _____ major

© 2005. Eric Harris. All Rights Reserved.

Exercise 5.12 - Sharp Key Review

Directions: Write the requested major key signature in treble and bass clef.

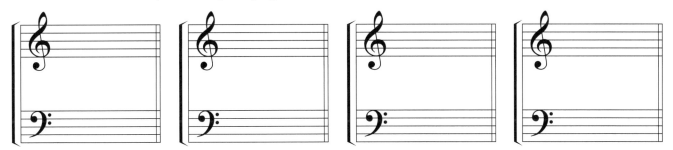

1. G major   2. D major   3. A major   4. E major

5. B major   6. F# major   7. C# major

Directions: Using your knowledge of key signatures, write the requested major scales below. The first note is given.

1	C							
2	G							
3	D							
4	A							
5	E							
6	B							
7	F#							
8	C#							

© 2005. Eric Harris. All Rights Reserved.

Exercise 5.13 - Flat Key Review

Directions: Write the requested major key signature in treble and bass clef.

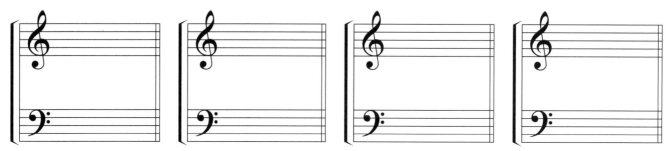

1. F major   2. B♭ major   3. E♭ major   4. A♭ major

5. D♭ major   6. G♭ major   7. C♭ major

Directions: Using your knowledge of key signatures, write the requested major scales below. The first note is given.

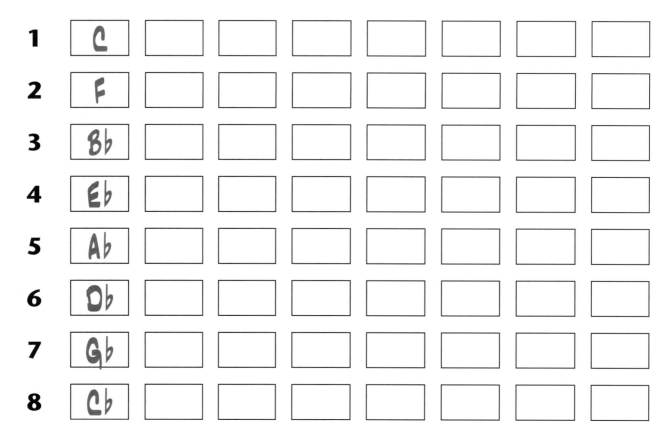

1   C

2   F

3   B♭

4   E♭

5   A♭

6   D♭

7   G♭

8   C♭

© 2005. Eric Harris. All Rights Reserved.

Exercise 5.14 - Writing Major Scales

Directions: Write the requested major scale, ascending only, in whole notes. Do not write a key signature.

1. **A major**

9. **B♭ major**

2. **D♭ major**

10. **C major**

3. **G major**

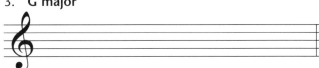

11. **A♭ major**

4. **F major**

12. **D major**

5. **C major**

13. **C♯ major**

6. **E major**

14. **E♭ major**

7. **C♭ major**

15. **F♯ major**

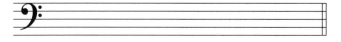

8. **B major**

16. **G♭ major**

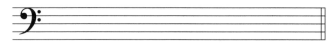

© 2005. Eric Harris. All Rights Reserved.

Exercise 5.15 - Writing Major Scales

Directions: Write the requested major scale, ascending only, in whole notes. Do not write a key signature.

1. **C major**

9. **B major**

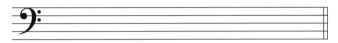

2. **D major**

10. **Cb major**

3. **Bb major**

11. **G major**

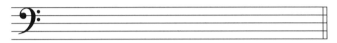

4. **Eb major**

12. **F major**

5. **Gb major**

13. **C# major**

6. **Ab major**

14. **E major**

7. **C# major**

15. **Db major**

8. **F# major**

16. **A major**

© 2005. Eric Harris. All Rights Reserved.

Exercise 5.16 - Writing Major Scales – Descending

Directions: Write the requested major scale, **descending** only, in whole notes. Do not write a key signature.

1. **C major**

9. **D major**

2. **E major**

10. **F major**

3. **G major**

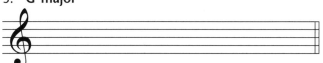

11. **A major**

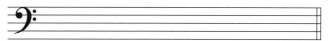

4. **B♭ major**

12. **C♯ major**

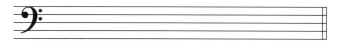

5. **D♭ major**

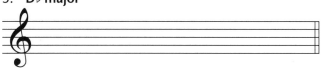

13. **E♭ major**

6. **F♯ major**

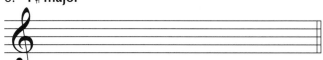

14. **G♭ major**

7. **A♭ major**

15. **B major**

8. **C♭ major**

16. **G major**

© 2005. Eric Harris. All Rights Reserved.

LESSON 8: DEGREE NAME REVIEW

1. Each note in a major scale can be referred to by **letter name**, **degree number***, **solfège syllable**, or by **proper degree name**. Look at the C major scale example below.

LETTER NAMES

C	D	E	F	G	A	B	C

DEGREE NUMBERS*

1	2	3	4	5	6	7	8

SOLFÈGE SYLLABLES

Do	Re	Mi	Fa	Sol	La	Ti	Do

PROPER DEGREE NAMES

Tonic	Supertonic	Mediant	Subdominant	Dominant	Submediant	Leading Tone	Tonic

2. Degree numbers, solfège syllables, and proper degree names remain the same for all major scales. Look at the A♭ major example shown below.

LETTER NAMES

A♭	B♭	C	D♭	E♭	F	G	A♭

DEGREE NUMBERS

1	2	3	4	5	6	7	8

SOLFÈGE SYLLABLES

Do	Re	Mi	Fa	Sol	La	Ti	Do

PROPER DEGREE NAMES

Tonic	Supertonic	Mediant	Subdominant	Dominant	Submediant	Leading Tone	Tonic

3. Degree numbers, solfège syllables, and proper degree names remain the same for all major scales.
   In a major scale:

   scale degree 1 is always Tonic or Do;
   scale degree 2 is always Supertonic or Re;
   scale degree 3 is always Mediant or Mi;
   scale degree 4 is always Subdominant or Fa;

   scale degree 5 is always Dominant or Sol;
   scale degree 6 is always Submediant or La;
   scale degree 7 is always Leading Tone or Ti;
   scale degree 8 is always Tonic or Do.

4. In some theory books, students will see a special symbol called a carat (^) placed over a scale degree number. For example, the fourth note of a scale would be referred to as "scale degree four" or $\hat{4}$.

   *Each note of a scale is called a "scale degree" and is given a number. The first note of a scale is called "scale degree one." The second note of a scale is called "scale degree two." The third note of a scale is called "scale degree three," and so on.

© 2005. Eric Harris. All Rights Reserved.

Exercise 5.17 - Thinking In Keys

Directions: You are given the name of a major key. You are also given the proper degree name, the solfège syllable, or the scale degree number. Provide the matching pitch name.

	Key	Degree	Pitch Name		Key	Degree	Pitch Name
1.	D major	Supertonic	E	26.	F major	Submediant	
2.	F major	Fa		27.	G major	Sol	
3.	B major	Mediant		28.	E major	Dominant	
4.	E major	Re		29.	C major	7	
5	G major	5		30.	B major	Subdominant	
6.	C major	Subdominant		31.	D♭ major	Mi	
7.	A major	Ti		32.	F major	Dominant	
8.	F♯ major	Dominant		33.	E♭ major	Re	
9.	B♭ major	La		34.	G♭ major	Mediant	
10.	G♭ major	Submediant		35.	A major	La	
11.	F♯ major	3		36.	A♭ major	Leading Tone	
12.	C♯ major	Tonic		37.	E major	Do	
13.	G♭ major	Sol		38.	F♯ major	Submediant	
14.	D♭ major	Leading Tone		39.	F major	Ti	
15.	C major	2		40.	B major	Tonic	
16.	E major	Mediant		41.	B♭ major	4	
17.	G major	Do		42.	C♯ major	Leading Tone	
18.	B♭ major	Subdominant		43.	C major	6	
19.	D major	6		44.	C♭ major	Dominant	
20.	F major	Supertonic		45.	D major	Sol	
21.	A♭ major	Fa		46.	C♭ major	Re	
22.	C♯ major	Mediant		47.	E♭ major	Leading Tone	
23.	E♭ major	Dominant		48.	A♭ major	6	
24.	F major	Leading Tone		49.	C♭ major	Fa	
25.	A major	2		50.	D♭ major	Supertonic	

© 2005. Eric Harris. All Rights Reserved.

Exercise 5.18 - Thinking In Keys

Directions: You are given the name of a major key. You are also given the proper degree name, the solfège syllable, or the scale degree number. Provide the matching pitch name.

	Key	Degree	Pitch Name		Key	Degree	Pitch Name
1.	E major	Tonic		26.	G major	Re	
2.	G major	Dominant		27.	A♭ major	Sol	
3.	B♭ major	Mi		28.	B major	Ti	
4.	D major	2		29.	C major	3	
5	F♯ major	6		30.	D♭ major	7	
6.	A♭ major	1		31.	E major	5	
7.	C major	Re		32.	F♯ major	Supertonic	
8.	E♭ major	La		33.	G♭ major	Tonic	
9.	G♭ major	Mi		34.	A major	Leading Tone	
10.	B major	Leading Tone		35.	B♭ major	8	
11.	D♭ major	Subdominant		36.	C♯ major	4	
12.	F major	Mediant		37.	D major	5	
13.	A major	2		38.	E♭ major	Fa	
14.	B♭ major	3		39.	F major	Do	
15.	C♯ major	7		40.	G major	La	
16.	D♭ major	Sol		41.	A♭ major	Supertonic	
17.	E major	Fa		42.	B major	Dominant	
18.	F♯ major	Ti		43.	C♭ major	Mediant	
19.	G♭ major	Do		44.	D♭ major	5	
20.	A♭ major	2		45.	E major	7	
21.	B major	6		46.	F♯ major	2	
22.	C♭ major	4		47.	G♭ major	4	
23.	D major	Submediant		48.	A major	Re	
24.	E♭ major	Tonic		49.	B♭ major	Ti	
25.	F major	Subdominant		50.	C major	Fa	

© 2005. Eric Harris. All Rights Reserved.

Exercise 5.19 - Thinking In Keys

Directions: Answer the questions below.

1. _____ In this major scale, F is the subdominant.

2. _____ In this major scale, G is the mediant.

3. _____ In this major scale, C♯ is the supertonic.

4. _____ In this major scale, F is the submediant.

5. _____ In this major scale, F is the mediant.

6. _____ In this major scale, E is the submediant.

7. _____ In this major scale, C is the supertonic.

8. _____ In this major scale, B♭ is the leading tone.

9. _____ In this major scale, G is the subdominant.

10. _____ In this major scale, A is the tonic.

11. _____ In this major scale, G♯ is the dominant.

12. _____ In this major scale, B is the subdominant.

13. _____ In this major scale, D♯ is the leading tone.

14. _____ In this major scale, C is the dominant.

15. _____ In this major scale, F is the leading tone.

16. _____ In this major scale, E is Ti.

17. _____ In this major scale, B♭ is Re.

18. _____ In this major scale, G is Sol.

19. _____ In this major scale, A♭ is Fa.

20. _____ In this major scale, D is Do.

21. _____ In this major scale, C♯ is Mi.

22. _____ In this major scale, F♯ is La.

23. _____ In this major scale, G is scale degree seven.

24. _____ In this major scale, A is scale degree two.

25. _____ In this major scale, B is scale degree five.

26. _____ In this major scale, E♭ is scale degree six.

27. _____ In this major scale, C is scale degree three.

28. _____ In this major scale, D is scale degree four.

© 2005. Eric Harris. All Rights Reserved.

Unit Review Questions

Directions: Answer the questions below.

1. _____ All major scales have half steps between _?_ and _?_ and also between _?_ and _?_ (Give scale degree numbers. Write all four answers in the blank.)

2. _____ All major scales begin and end with the _?_ letter name.

3. _____ The sharps or flats found in a major key signature are the sharps or flats used in a major scale to maintain the whole step-half step pattern. (True/False)

4. _____ Sharps or flats (do/do not) appear in the scale in the same order they appear in the key signature.

5. _____ There will never be a combination of sharps and flats in a major key signature or major scale. (True/False)

6. _____ The scale/key of D-flat major is enharmonic with the scale/key of _?_ major.

7. _____ The scale/key of F-sharp major is enharmonic with the scale/key of _?_ major.

8. _____ The scale/key of B-major is enharmonic with the scale/key of _?_ major.

9. _____ Enharmonic scales will sound alike. (True/False)

10. _____ Enharmonic scales will use the same keys on the piano. (True/False)

11. _____ Enharmonic scales will use the same fingerings on a wind instrument. (True/False)

12. _____ The G major scale requires _?_ sharp to maintain the major scale pattern.

13. _____ The F major scale requires _?_ flat to maintain the major scale pattern.

14. _____ The D major scale requires _?_ sharps to maintain the major scale pattern.

15. _____ The B-flat major scale requires _?_ flats to maintain the major scale pattern.

16. _____ The A major scale requires _?_ sharps to maintain the major scale pattern.

17. _____ The E-flat major scale requires _?_ flats to maintain the major scale pattern.

18. _____ The E major scale requires _?_ sharps to maintain the major scale pattern.

19. _____ The A-flat major scale requires _?_ flats to maintain the major scale pattern.

20. _____ The B major scale requires _?_ sharps to maintain the major scale pattern.

21. _____ The D-flat major scale requires _?_ flats to maintain the major scale pattern.

22. _____ The C-sharp major scale requires _?_ sharps to maintain the major scale pattern.

23. _____ The C-flat major scale requires _?_ flats to maintain the major scale pattern.

24. _____ The C major scale requires _?_ sharps or flats to maintain the major scale pattern.

25. _____ The order of sharps is _?_ (Write all seven answers in the blank, in order.)

26. _____ The order of flats is _?_ (Write all seven answers in the blank, in order.)

© 2005. Eric Harris. All Rights Reserved.

27. _____ If there are three sharps in the key signature, they will be ? (Write all three answers in the blank.)

28. _____ If there are six flats in the key signature, they will be ? (Write all six answers in the blank.)

29. _____ If there are five sharps in the key signature, they will be ? (Write all five answers in the blank.)

30. _____ If there are four flats in the key signature, they will be ? (Write all four answers in the blank.)

31. _____ The solfège syllable for the first note of a major scale is ?

32. _____ The solfège syllable for the second note of a major scale is ?

33. _____ The solfège syllable for the third note of a major scale is ?

34. _____ The solfège syllable for the fourth note of a major scale is ?

35. _____ The solfège syllable for the fifth note of a major scale is ?

36. _____ The solfège syllable for the sixth note of a major scale is ?

37. _____ The solfège syllable for the seventh note of a major scale is ?

38. _____ The proper degree name for the first note of a major scale is ?

39. _____ The proper degree name for the second note of a major scale is ?

40. _____ The proper degree name for the third note of a major scale is ?

41. _____ The proper degree name for the fourth note of a major scale is ?

42. _____ The proper degree name for the fifth note of a major scale is ?

43. _____ The proper degree name for the sixth note of a major scale is ?

44. _____ The proper degree name for the seventh note of a major scale is ?

45. _____ When writing sharp key signatures on the treble staff, the ? sharp will always be placed on the first space above the staff.

46. _____ When writing flat key signatures on the bass staff, the ? flat will always be placed on the first space below the staff.

47. _____ The order of flats is simply the order of sharps in ?

48. _____ Musicians memorize ? major scales and their matching key signatures.

49. _____ Name the two sharp keys that have the term "sharp" in the key name.

50. _____ Name the only flat key that does not have the term "flat" in the key name.

51. _____ This symbol is used to mean "scale degree" in some music theory books. (Name it and draw it.)

52. _____ Because scales which begin with C have all sharps, all flats, or no sharps or flats at all, C is said to be ?

© 2005. Eric Harris. All Rights Reserved.

LESSON 9: THE CHURCH MODES

1. **Modes** are ancient scale patterns that were used in the chant music of the Roman Catholic church during the Middle Ages (about 500 to 1400 A.D.).

2. Modes are still used today in classical, jazz, rock, pop, and movie music.

3. Modes are sometimes called the "Church Modes" or the "Ecclesiastical Modes." (The word "ecclesiastical" means "church.")

4. There are seven modes. Each mode has a specific pattern of whole and half steps. These patterns can best be seen (and heard) by playing the modes using only the white keys of the piano.

   The **Ionian Mode** is the same as our major scale played from scale degree one to scale degree one.
   (1 to 1) C - D - E - F - G - A - B - C.   (step pattern: W-W-H-W-W-W-H)

   The **Dorian Mode** is the same as our major scale played from scale degree two to scale degree two.
   (2 to 2) D - E - F - G - A - B - C - D.   (step pattern: W-H-W-W-W-H-W)

   The **Phrygian Mode** is the same as our major scale played from scale degree three to scale degree three.
   (3 to 3) E - F - G - A - B - C - D - E.   (step pattern: H-W-W-W-H-W-W)

   The **Lydian Mode** is the same as our major scale played from scale degree four to scale degree four.
   (4 to 4) F - G - A - B - C - D - E - F.   (step pattern: W-W-W-H-W-W-H)

   The **Mixolydian Mode** is the same as our major scale played from scale degree five to scale degree five.
   (5 to 5) G - A - B - C - D - E - F - G.   (step pattern: W-W-H-W-W-H-W)

   The **Aeolian Mode** is the same as our major scale played from scale degree six to scale degree six.
   (6 to 6) A - B - C - D - E - F - G - A.   (step pattern: W-H-W-W-H-W-W)

   The **Locrian Mode** is the same as our major scale played from scale degree seven to scale degree seven.
   (7 to 7) B - C - D - E - F - G - A - B.   (step pattern: H-W-W-H-W-W-W)
   Note: The Locrian mode was never used in chant. It existed only as a theoretical possibility.

THE SEVEN CHURCH MODES						
Ionian	Dorian	Phrygian	Lydian	Mixolydian	Aeolian	Locrian
1 to 1	2 to 2	3 to 3	4 to 4	5 to 5	6 to 6	7 to 7

5. A mode can be written starting on any pitch as long as the pattern of whole steps and half steps required for that mode is maintained. Instead of memorizing seven different step patterns, musicians often relate modes to major scales. Study the examples shown below.

Problem: Write a G Dorian Mode.
- Know that the Dorian Mode is based on the second scale degree of a major scale.
- Ask the question, "G is the second note of what major scale?" (The answer is F major.)
- Write the G to G alphabet pattern:
  G A B C D E F G
- Insert the F major key signature (B♭):
  G A B♭ C D E F G

Problem: Write an A♭ Lydian Mode.
- Know that the Lydian Mode is based on the fourth scale degree of a major scale.
- Ask the question, "A♭ is the fourth note of what major scale?" (The answer is E♭ major.)
- Write the A to A alphabet pattern:
  A B C D E F G A
- Insert the E♭ major key signature (B♭, E♭, A♭):
  A♭ B♭ C D E♭ F G A♭

© 2005. Eric Harris. All Rights Reserved.

Unit Review Questions

Directions: Write the following modes.

1. ___ ___ ___ ___ ___ ___ ___
   C Lydian

2. ___ ___ ___ ___ ___ ___ ___
   E♭ Phrygian

3. ___ ___ ___ ___ ___ ___ ___
   D Locrian

4. ___ ___ ___ ___ ___ ___ ___
   B Aeolian

5. ___ ___ ___ ___ ___ ___ ___
   F Mixolydian

6. ___ ___ ___ ___ ___ ___ ___
   F♯ Dorian

7. ___ ___ ___ ___ ___ ___ ___
   G♭ Ionian

8. ___ ___ ___ ___ ___ ___ ___
   A♯ Phrygian

9. ___ ___ ___ ___ ___ ___ ___
   E Lydian

10. ___ ___ ___ ___ ___ ___ ___
    B♭ Dorian

11. ___ ___ ___ ___ ___ ___ ___
    F Aeolian

12. ___ ___ ___ ___ ___ ___ ___
    C♯ Mixolydian

Directions: Write the following modes on the staff–ascending only. Be careful, the clefs change. Be sure to place accidentals before the notes they are to affect on the exact same line or space as the notes they are to affect.

1. **A Lydian**

2. **G Phrygian**

3. **E Locrian**

4. **D Aeolian**

5. **F♯ Mixolydian**

6. **E♭ Dorian**

7. **C♯ Ionian**

8. **B♭ Lydian**

© 2005. Eric Harris. All Rights Reserved.

Directions: Answer the following questions.

1. _____ Modes are ancient _?_ patterns that were used hundreds of years ago.

2. _____ Modes were used in the _?_ music of the Roman Catholic church.

3. _____ Modes and Chant were used during the _?_, which lasted from about 500 to 1400 A.D.

4. _____ Modes are sometimes called _?_ or _?_ modes. (Write both answers in the blank, one over the other.)

5. _____ There are _?_ modes (give the number).

6. _____ Each mode has a specific _?_ of whole and half steps.

7. _____ These patterns are most easily seen if we play the modes using only the _?_ keys of the piano.

8. _____ The _?_ mode is the same as our major scale played from 1 to 1.

9. _____ The _?_ mode is the same as our major scale played from 2 to 2.

10. _____ The _?_ mode is the same as our major scale played from 3 to 3.

11. _____ The _?_ mode is the same as our major scale played from 4 to 4.

12. _____ The _?_ mode is the same as our major scale played from 5 to 5.

13. _____ The _?_ mode is the same as our major scale played from 6 to 6.

14. _____ The _?_ mode is the same as our major scale played from 7 to 7.

15. _____ This mode was never used in chant, it existed only as a theoretical possibility.

16. _____ A mode can be written starting on any pitch as long as the _?_ of whole steps and half steps required for that mode is maintained.

17. _____ Instead of memorizing seven different step patterns, musicians often relate modes to _?_ scales.

Directions: Identify the mode. (This is easy; just take the accidentals and create a key signature!)

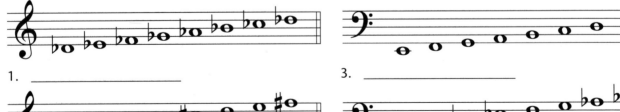

1. _____ 3. _____

2. _____ 4. _____

© 2005. Eric Harris. All Rights Reserved.

LESSON 10: COMPOUND TIME

1. Time signatures with a top number of six, nine, or twelve are called **compound time signatures**. The following are all compound time signatures.

$$\frac{6}{2} \quad \frac{9}{2} \quad \frac{12}{2} \qquad \frac{6}{4} \quad \frac{9}{4} \quad \frac{12}{4} \qquad \boxed{\frac{6}{8} \quad \frac{9}{8} \quad \frac{12}{8}}$$
most common

Six-eight, nine-eight, and twelve-eight time are the most frequently encountered compound time signatures and will be the focus of this lesson.

2. In compound time, the time signature must be mathematically processed to give us the information we need.

$$\frac{6}{8}$$

The top number must be divided by three to get the total number of beats in each measure. ($6 \div 3 = 2$)

The note value indicated by the bottom number must be multiplied by three to determine the note value that will get one beat. (The number eight means "eighth note.")

♪ x 3 = ♩.

3. In compound time, the note value indicated by the bottom number must be multiplied by three to determine the beat value. Therefore, each beat *divides* into three smaller note values (like triplets) called the division value. In all time signatures with eight as the bottom number, the beat value will be a dotted-quarter note, and the division value will be an eighth note (three of them).

SIX-EIGHT TIME	**NINE-EIGHT TIME**	**TWELVE-EIGHT TIME**
$\frac{6}{8}$ $6 \div 3 = 2$. Two beats in each measure. ♪ x 3 = ♩. Dotted-quarter note gets one beat.	$\frac{9}{8}$ $9 \div 3 = 3$. Three beats in each measure. ♪ x 3 = ♩. Dotted-quarter note gets one beat.	$\frac{12}{8}$ $12 \div 3 = 4$. Four beats in each measure. ♪ x 3 = ♩. Dotted-quarter note gets one beat.

Each measure of six-eight time will contain *two* dotted-quarter notes or some combination of notes (and/or rests) that equals two dotted-quarter notes.

Each measure of nine-eight time will contain *three* dotted-quarter notes or some combination of notes (and/or rests) that equals three dotted-quarter notes.

Each measure of twelve-eight time will contain *four* dotted-quarter notes or some combination of notes (and/or rests) that equals four dotted-quarter notes.

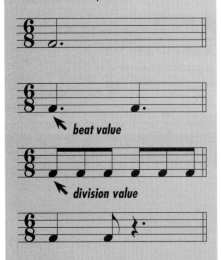

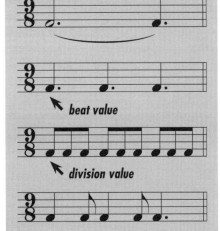

Note: A whole rest fills an entire measure with silence (even in six-eight time) regardless of the time signature.

Note: No single note value can fill an entire measure with sound in 9/8 time. Two or more notes must be tied. A whole rest fills an entire measure with silence.

Note: A whole rest fills an entire measure with silence (even in twelve-eight time) regardless of the time signature.

© 2005. Eric Harris. All Rights Reserved.

4. In all compound time signatures with eight as the bottom number, notes (and their matching rests) will get the following beats. (Notice that larger note values are dotted in compound meter.)

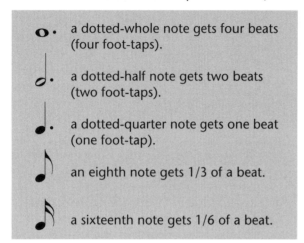

- a dotted-whole note gets four beats (four foot-taps).
- a dotted-half note gets two beats (two foot-taps).
- a dotted-quarter note gets one beat (one foot-tap).
- an eighth note gets 1/3 of a beat.
- a sixteenth note gets 1/6 of a beat.

Remember, the time signature sets the maximum number of beats for each measure. A dotted-whole note will never appear in a measure of six-eight time (since it gets four beats and there are only two beats in a measure of six-eight time).

5. Just as we can classify simple time signatures as duple, triple, or quadruple, so too can compound time signatures be classified.

Time signatures with a top number of six are said to be in **compound-duple meter**. (6 ÷ 3 = 2).

$$\frac{6}{2} \quad \frac{6}{4} \quad \frac{6}{8}$$

Time signatures with a top number of nine are said to be in **compound-triple meter**. (9 ÷ 3 = 3).

$$\frac{9}{2} \quad \frac{9}{4} \quad \frac{9}{8}$$

Time signatures with a top number of twelve are said to be in **compound-quadruple meter**. (12 ÷ 3 = 4).

$$\frac{12}{2} \quad \frac{12}{4} \quad \frac{12}{8}$$

6. In six-eight, nine-eight, and twelve-eight time, eighth notes travel in sets of three (like triplets).

Exercise 7.1 - Review Questions

Directions: Answer the questions below.

1. _____ Time signatures with a top number of six, nine, or twelve are called _?_ time signatures.

2. _____ The most frequently encountered compound time signatures are _?_ (Write all three answers in the blank.)

3. _____ In a compound time signature, the top number must be divided by _?_ to determine the total number of beats in each measure.

4. _____ In a compound time signature, the note value indicated by the bottom number must be multiplied by _?_ to determine what note value will get one beat.

5. _____ In compound time, if the bottom number of the time signature is eight, what note value will get one beat? (Name it and draw it.)

6. _____ How many beats are in each measure of six-eight time?

7. _____ In six-eight time, what note value will get one beat? (Name it and draw it.)

8. _____ How many beats are in each measure of nine-eight time?

9. _____ In nine-eight time, what note value will get one beat? (Name it and draw it.)

10. _____ How many beats are in each measure of twelve-eight time?

© 2005. Eric Harris. All Rights Reserved.

11. _____ In twelve-eight time, what note value will get one beat? (Name it and draw it.)

12. _____ What single note value will fill an entire measure with sound in six-eight time? (Name it and draw it.)

13. _____ What single note value will fill an entire measure with sound in twelve-eight time? (Name it and draw it.)

14. _____ Can a single note value fill an entire measure with sound in nine-eight time?

15. _____ To fill an entire measure with sustained sound in nine-eight time, we must ? two or more note values together.

16. _____ How many dotted-quarter notes can fit into a measure of six-eight time?

17. _____ How many dotted-quarter notes can fit into a measure of nine-eight time?

18. _____ How many dotted-quarter notes can fit into a measure of twelve-eight time?

19. _____ How many eighth notes can fit into a measure of six-eight time?

20. _____ How many eighth notes can fit into a measure of nine-eight time?

21. _____ How many eighth notes can fit into a measure of twelve-eight time?

22. _____ Can a dotted-whole note fit into a measure of six-eight time?

23. _____ Can a dotted-whole note fit into a measure of nine-eight time?

24. _____ In twelve-eight time, how many beats does a dotted-whole note get?

25. _____ In twelve-eight time, how many beats does a dotted-half note get?

26. _____ In twelve-eight time, how many beats does a dotted-quarter note get?

27. _____ In twelve-eight time, how many beats does an eighth note get?

28. _____ In twelve-eight time, how many beats does a sixteenth note get?

29. _____ In six-eight time, how many beats does a dotted-quarter note get?

30. _____ In six-eight time, how many beats does a dotted-half note get?

31. _____ In six-eight time, how many beats does an eighth note get?

32. _____ In nine-eight time, how many beats does a dotted-quarter note get?

Classify the time signatures in items 33 through 41 as compound-duple (CD), compound-triple (CT), or compound-quadruple (CQ).

$\frac{6}{8}$	$\frac{12}{8}$	$\frac{9}{8}$	$\frac{9}{2}$	$\frac{12}{4}$	$\frac{9}{4}$	$\frac{6}{2}$	$\frac{6}{4}$	$\frac{12}{2}$
___	___	___	___	___	___	___	___	___
33.	34.	35.	36.	37.	38.	39.	40.	41.

© 2005. Eric Harris. All Rights Reserved.

LESSON 11: COUNTING IN COMPOUND TIME

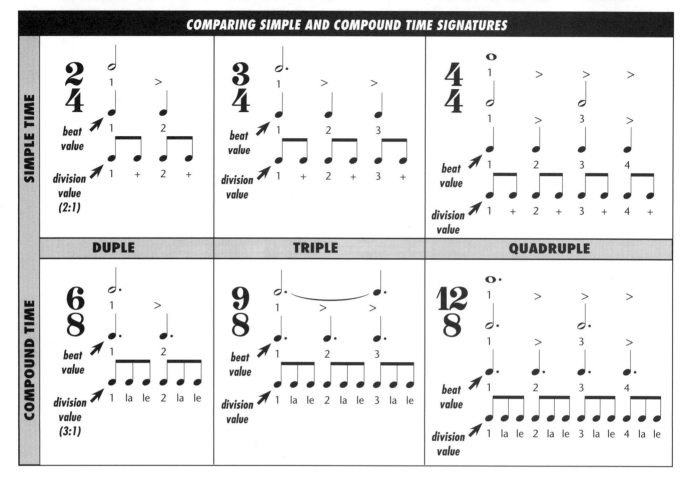

COMPARING SIMPLE AND COMPOUND TIME SIGNATURES

1. Time signatures with a top number of two, three, or four are called **simple time** signatures.

2. Time signatures with a top number of six, nine, or twelve are called **compound time** signatures.

3. In simple time, the beat value divides at a 2:1 ratio (two eighth notes for each quarter note).

4. In compound time, the beat value divides at a 3:1 ratio (three eighth notes for each dotted quarter note – like a triplet).

5. The duplet ( ) does not exist naturally in compound time. It is borrowed from simple time. A small "2" is placed over the duplet to remind us that the figure is a **borrowed division**. A duplet is counted just like an eighth note pair (1 +).

6. The triplet ( ) does not exist naturally in simple time. It is borrowed from compound time. A small "3" is placed over the triplet to remind us that this figure is also a borrowed division.

7. Notice the similarities between two-four time and six-eight time. Six-eight time is counted just like two-four time with a triplet on each beat.

8. Notice the similarities between three-four time and nine-eight time. Nine-eight time is counted just like three-four time with a triplet on each beat.

9. Notice the similarities between four-four time and twelve-eight time. Twelve-eight time is counted just like four-four time with a triplet on each beat.

10. In six-eight time, the dotted-half note ( ) fills an entire measure with sound.

11. In nine-eight time, no single note value can fill an entire measure with sound. A tie must be used to connect two or more note values for this purpose.

12. In twelve-eight time, the dotted-whole note ( ) fills an entire measure with sound.

13. A whole rest is used to fill an entire measure with silence in all time signatures – both simple and compound.

© 2005. Eric Harris. All Rights Reserved.

14. Study the six-eight time counting samples below. ***Rhythms written in nine-eight and twelve-eight time look and are counted the same as those found in six-eight time. The only difference is the total number of beats in each measure.***

1 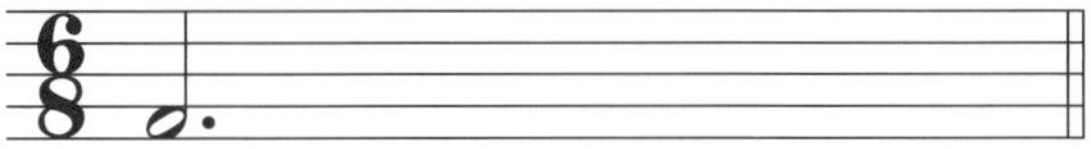

1 >

2 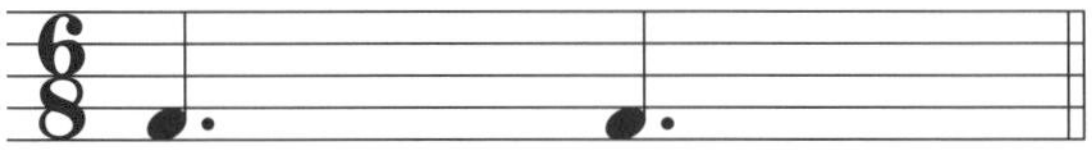

1 2

3 

1 la le 2 la le

4 

1 le 2 la le

5 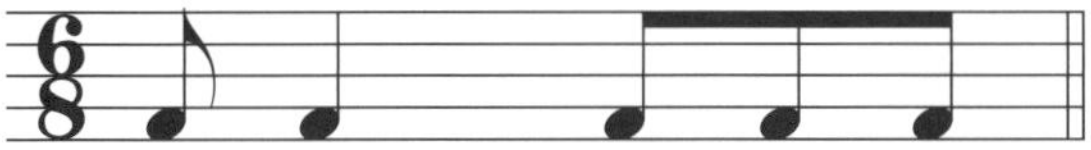

1 la 2 la le

6 

1 (la) le 2

Do not confuse with a duplet – has no "2."

7 

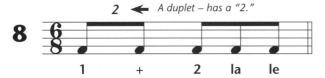

1 la le (2) la le

2 ← A duplet – has a "2."

8 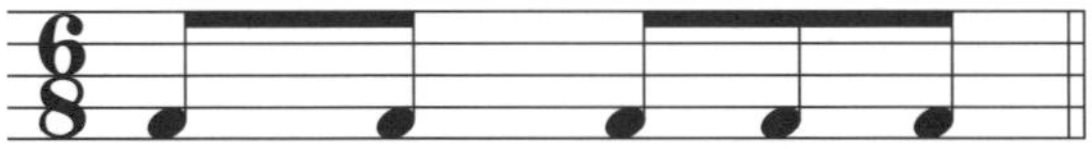

1 + 2 la le

9 

(1) la le 2 la (le)

15. Sixteenth notes are counted using 1-ta-la-ta-le-ta. Notice that the syllable "ta" is inserted after each part of the beat (after 1, la, and le) to represent the sixteenth notes. Each eighth note contains two sixteenth notes. Study the following samples.

1 

1 la le 2 la le

2 

1 ta la le 2 la le

3 

1 la le ta 2 la le

4 

1 la ta le 2 la le

5 

1 ta la ta le 2 la le

6 

1 la ta le ta 2 la le

7 

1 ta la ta le ta 2 la le

8 

1 ta la le ta 2 la le

9 

1 (ta, la) ta le 2 la le

Note: The compound time counting system used in this book is called the ***Eastman Counting System*** and was developed by Dr. Allen Irvine McHose during his tenure as professor of music theory at the Eastman School of Music in Rochester, New York.

© 2005. Eric Harris. All Rights Reserved.

Exercise 7.2 - Rhythm Counting Exercise

Directions: Write the counting under each measure of rhythm below. Play the rhythms on your tuning note.

! When counting six-eight time, nine-eight time, and twelve-eight time, look for the triplets. Remember each triplet equals one dotted-quarter note.

1.   2.   3.

4.   5.   6.

7.   8.   9.

10.   11.   12.

13.   14.   15.

16.   17.   18.

19.   20.   21.

22.   23.   24.

25.   26.   27.

© 2005. Eric Harris. All Rights Reserved.

Exercise 7.3 - Rhythm Counting Exercise

Directions: Write the counting under each measure of rhythm below. Play the rhythms on your tuning note.

Exercise 7.4 - Rhythm Counting Exercise

Directions: Write the counting under each measure of rhythm below. Play the rhythms on your tuning note.

© 2005. Eric Harris. All Rights Reserved.

Exercise 7.5 - Rhythm Counting Exercise

Directions: Write the counting under each measure of rhythm below. Play the rhythms on your tuning note.

1.

4.

7.

10.

13.

16.

19.

22.

25.

© 2005. Eric Harris. All Rights Reserved.

Exercise 7.6 - Find The Beat

Directions: Identify the beat or part of the beat to which the arrow points.

Write your answers here.

1.	2.	3.	4.
5. *ta of la of 1*	6.	7.	8.
9.	10.	11.	12.

Exercise 7.7 - Name The Time Signature

Directions: Provide the time signature for each measure below (six-eight, nine-eight, twelve-eight). Remember, beams are typically used to group all of the notes contained within one beat.

© 2005. Eric Harris. All Rights Reserved.

Unit Review Questions

Directions: Answer the questions below.

1. _____ Simple time signatures have a top number of ? (Write all three answers in the blank.)

2. _____ Compound time signatures have a top number of ? (Write all three answers in the blank.)

3. _____ In simple time, each quarter note contains ? eighth notes.

4. _____ In compound time, each dotted-quarter note contains ? eighth notes.

5. _____ In simple time, the beat divides at a ratio of ?

6. _____ In compound time, the beat divides at a ratio of ?

7. _____ In simple time, the ? number of the time signature tells us the total number of beats that will be in each measure.

8. _____ In simple time, the ? number of the time signature is a "code" that tells us which note value will get one beat.

9. _____ The bottom number "code" of 4 means this note value ?

10. _____ The bottom number "code" of 8 means this note value ?

11. _____ In compound time, the top number of the time signature must be ? by three to determine the total number of beats that will be in each measure.

12. _____ In compound time, the note value indicated by the bottom number of the time signature must be ? by three to determine which note value will get one beat.

13. _____ Six-eight time is counted just like ? time with a triplet on each beat.

14. _____ Nine-eight time is counted just like ? time with a triplet on each beat.

15. _____ Twelve-eight time is counted just like ? with a triplet on each beat.

16. _____ In compound time, the whole notes, half notes, and quarter notes are all ? (Look at the chart on page 90 to answer this question.)

17. _____ The ? does not exist naturally in simple time and is borrowed from compound time. (Name it and draw it.)

18. _____ The ? does not exist naturally in compound time and is borrowed from simple time. (Name it and draw it.)

19. _____ This compound time signature requires the use of tied note values to fill an entire measure with sustained sound.

20. _____ Triplets and duplets are called ? divisions.

21. _____ The whole rest is used to fill an entire measure with silence in all time signatures, simple and compound. (True/False)

© 2005. Eric Harris. All Rights Reserved.

LESSON 12: INTRODUCTION TO INTERVALS

1. An **interval** is the distance between two notes (on the staff or on the keyboard).

2. A **harmonic interval** is formed when two notes are played simultaneously (at the same time).

3. A **melodic interval** is formed when two notes are played successively (one after the other). Melodic intervals can be ascending (low to high) or descending (high to low).

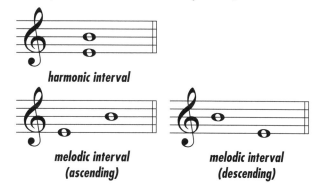

harmonic interval

melodic interval (ascending)   *melodic interval (descending)*

4. The size of an interval is determined by counting the total number of letter names included. When counting letter names for intervals, always begin by calling the lower note in the pair "one." Count all letter names up to and including the top note. Look at the chart below which uses G as the bottom note.

G and G *same pitch* **Unison** (U)	G,A *2 letters* a **Second** (2nd)	G,A,B *3 letters* a **Third** (3rd)	G,A,B,C *4 letters* a **Fourth** (4th)	G,A,B,C,D *5 letters* a **Fifth** (5th)	G,A,B,C, D,E *6 letters* a **Sixth** (6th)	G,A,B,C, D,E,F *7 letters* a **Seventh** (7th)	G,A,B,C, D,E,F,G *8 letters* an **Octave** (Oct.)

5. Intervals are named using ordinal numbers (second, third, fourth, etc.) There are only eight basic intervals: unisons (also called **primes**), seconds, thirds, fourths, fifths, sixths, sevenths, and octaves.

Exercise 8.1 - Review Exercises

Directions: Name the number size of each interval below. Count all letter names included. Watch the clefs!

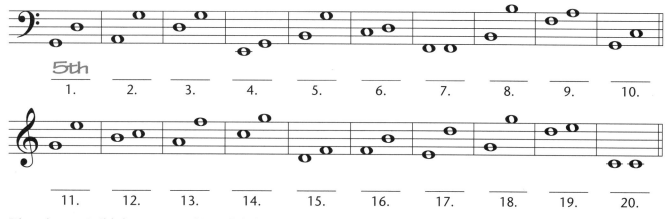

5th

1.	2.	3.	4.	5.	6.	7.	8.	9.	10.

11.	12.	13.	14.	15.	16.	17.	18.	19.	20.

Directions: Build the requested interval above the given pitch.

E

21. a 4th above B	22. a 6th above F	23. a 7th above D	24. a 5th above G	25. a 2nd above E	26. an Octave above A	27. a Unison above C	28. a 3rd above E	29. a 5th above D	30. a 6th above B

© 2005. Eric Harris. All Rights Reserved.

LESSON 13: MAJOR AND PERFECT INTERVALS

1. In addition to determining the size of an interval, we can also determine the **quality** of an interval.

2. To begin this process, we must look at the relationship of the notes in a major scale to the tonic note. In a major scale, certain intervals exist automatically (they are constant). These intervals are shown below in the example from the C major scale. (The notes of the scale are written with blackened note heads; the tonic note – C – is written as a whole note.)

1 and 1 in a major scale	1 to 2 in a major scale	1 to 3 in a major scale	1 to 4 in a major scale	1 to 5 in a major scale	1 to 6 in a major scale	1 to 7 in a major scale	1 to 8 in a major scale
is called a	*is called a*	*is called a*	*is called a*	*is called a*	*is called a*	*is called a*	*is called a*
Perfect* Unison	**Major Second**	**Major Third**	**Perfect* Fourth**	**Perfect* Fifth**	**Major Sixth**	**Major Seventh**	**Perfect* Octave**

3. This pattern of major and perfect intervals remains the same for *all* major scales. Look at the example from the B♭ major scale below. Notice the use of standard abbreviations under each interval.

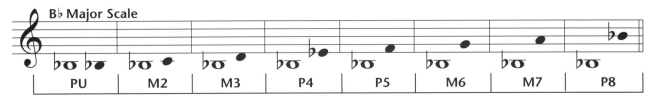

B♭ Major Scale							
PU	M2	M3	P4	P5	M6	M7	P8

MAJOR AND PERFECT INTERVALS

- In a major scale, all seconds, thirds, sixths, and sevenths are *major*.
- In a major scale, all unisons, fourths, fifths, and octaves are *perfect*.

---

4. Perfect seconds, thirds, sixths, and sevenths *do not exist*. Major unisons, fourths, fifths, and octaves also *do not exist*.

5. The intervals that exist in a major scale are said to be **diatonic**. The term diatonic means "related to a scale." Mastery of intervals requires a thorough knowledge of major scales and their key signatures.

IDENTIFYING AND SPELLING MAJOR AND PERFECT INTERVALS

- **To identify a given interval** – call the lower note in the pair "tonic." If the upper note is in the key (scale) of the lower note, the interval is major or perfect. In a major scale, seconds, thirds, sixths, and sevenths are major; unisons, fourths, fifths, and octaves are perfect.

- **To spell a major or perfect interval above a given note** – assume that the given note is the first note of a major scale (tonic). Count up the major scale to the requested interval number.

  Problem: Spell a major sixth above D. The sixth note of the D major scale is B. B is the answer.
  Problem: Spell a perfect fourth above E♭. The fourth note of the E♭ major scale is A♭. A♭ is the answer.

---

*Perfect intervals are called perfect because the upper note is in the major key of the lower note *and* the lower note is in the major key of the upper note. Perfect intervals are the only intervals that behave in this manner.

© 2005. Eric Harris. All Rights Reserved.

Exercise 8.2 - Identifying Major and Perfect Intervals

1 **Directions:** Here are the intervals found in the E♭ major scale. Name each interval.

PU

1.____ 2.____ 3.____ 4.____ 5.____ 6.____ 7.____ 8.____

2 **Directions:** Here are the intervals found in the D major scale. Name each interval.

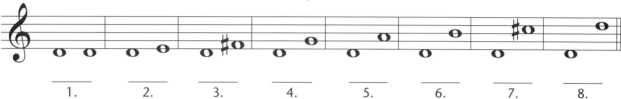

1.____ 2.____ 3.____ 4.____ 5.____ 6.____ 7.____ 8.____

3 **Directions:** Here are the intervals found in the A major scale (which are not in order). Name each interval.

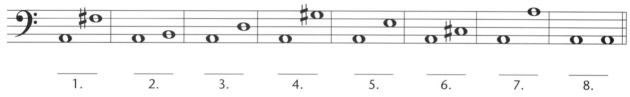

1.____ 2.____ 3.____ 4.____ 5.____ 6.____ 7.____ 8.____

4 **Directions:** Here are the intervals found in the G major scale (which are not in order). Name each interval.

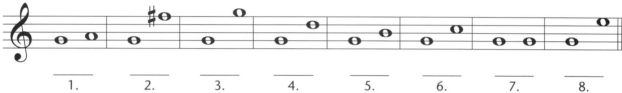

1.____ 2.____ 3.____ 4.____ 5.____ 6.____ 7.____ 8.____

5 **Directions:** Here are the intervals from the F major scale written in different octaves. Name each interval.

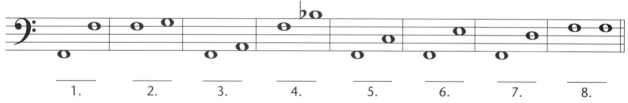

1.____ 2.____ 3.____ 4.____ 5.____ 6.____ 7.____ 8.____

6 **Directions:** Here are the intervals from the D♭ major scale written in different octaves. Name each interval.

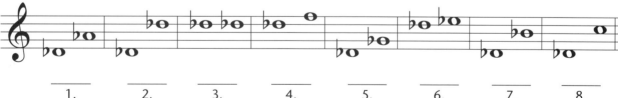

1.____ 2.____ 3.____ 4.____ 5.____ 6.____ 7.____ 8.____

7 **Directions:** Here are the intervals from the C♯ major scale written in different octaves. Name each interval.

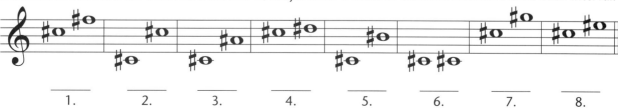

1.____ 2.____ 3.____ 4.____ 5.____ 6.____ 7.____ 8.____

© 2005. Eric Harris. All Rights Reserved.

Exercise 8.3 - Building Major and Perfect Intervals

Directions: Write the requested major scale, ascending, in whole notes (use accidentals, *not* key signatures). Then build the requested Major (M) or Perfect (P) interval above the tonic. Watch the clef!

1 C Major Scale — Intervals: PU · M3 · P5 · M7

2 Gb Major Scale — Intervals: M2 · P4 · M6 · P8

3 Ab Major Scale — Intervals: PU · M3 · P5 · M7

4 Bb Major Scale — Intervals: PU · P4 · P5 · P8

5 E Major Scale — Intervals: M2 · M3 · M6 · M7

6 F# Major Scale — Intervals: PU · M2 · M3 · P4

7 B Major Scale — Intervals: P8 · M7 · M6 · P5

© 2005. Eric Harris. All Rights Reserved.

Exercise 8.4 - Spelling Major and Perfect Intervals

Directions: Build the requested intervals above each given tonic.

1

M3	P4	M6	P5	M2	P8	M7	PU
1.	2.	3.	4.	5.	6.	7.	8.

2

P8	PU	P5	P4	M7	M3	M2	M6
9.	10.	11.	12.	13.	14.	15.	16.

3

M7	P5	M6	P4	M3	P8	M2	PU
17.	18.	19.	20.	21.	22.	23.	24.

4

M2	M3	M6	M7	P4	PU	P5	P8
25.	26.	27.	28.	29.	30.	31.	32.

5 *Check Clef*

P8	M6	PU	M2	P5	M7	P4	M3
33.	34.	35.	36.	37.	38.	39.	40.

6

PU	M2	M3	P4	P5	M6	M7	P8
41.	42.	43.	44.	45.	46.	47.	48.

7

P8	PU	M7	M2	M6	M3	P4	P5
49.	50.	51.	52.	53.	54.	55.	56.

8

PU	M3	M2	P4	P8	M7	P5	M6
57.	58.	59.	60.	61.	62.	63.	64.

© 2005. Eric Harris. All Rights Reserved.

Exercise 8.5 - Spelling Major Seconds

Directions: Build a **major second** above each given pitch. Remember, the given pitch is tonic.

Exercise 8.6 - Spelling Major Thirds

Directions: Build a **major third** above each given pitch. Remember, the given pitch is tonic.

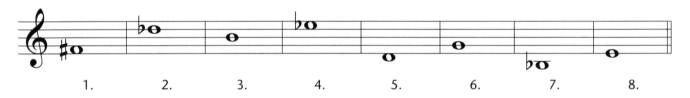

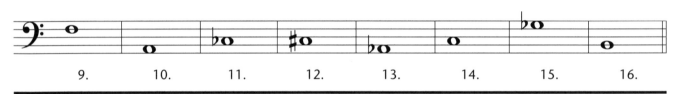

Exercise 8.7 - Spelling Perfect Fourths

Directions: Build a **perfect fourth** above each given pitch. Remember, the given pitch is tonic.

> **THE PERFECT FOURTH RULE**
>
> Most perfect fourths are natural to natural (C to F), sharp to sharp (C# to F#), or flat to flat (Cb to Fb). However, perfect fourths between F and B (F to Bb and F# to B) do not follow this rule. You can now spell perfect fourths above notes that are not the tonics of major scales, (E# to A#, D# to G#, etc.); just maintain the rule.

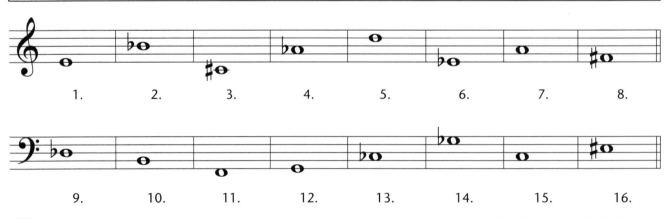

© 2005. Eric Harris. All Rights Reserved.

Exercise 8.8 - Spelling Perfect Fifths

Directions: Build a **perfect fifth** above each given pitch. Remember, the given pitch is tonic.

THE PERFECT FIFTH RULE

Most perfect fifths are natural to natural (C to G), sharp to sharp (C♯ to G♯), or flat to flat (C♭ to G♭). However, perfect fifths between B and F (B♭ to F and B to F♯) do not follow this rule. You can now spell perfect fifths above notes that are not the tonics of major scales, (E♯ to B♯, D♯ to A♯, F♭ to C♭, etc.); just maintain the rule.

Exercise 8.9 - Spelling Major Sixths

Directions: Build a **major sixth** above each given pitch. Remember, the given pitch is tonic.

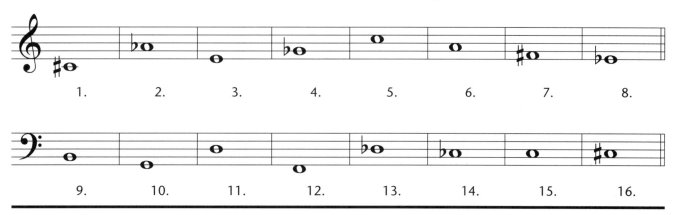

Exercise 8.10 - Spelling Major Sevenths

Directions: Build a **major seventh** above each given pitch. Remember, the given pitch is tonic.

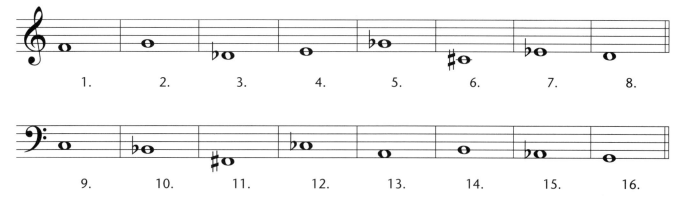

© 2005. Eric Harris. All Rights Reserved.

Exercise 8.11 - Working With Major and Perfect Intervals

Directions: Identify each interval below. Remember to call the lower note tonic. Several items will require that you remember the Rule of Perfect Fourths and the Rule of Perfect Fifths.

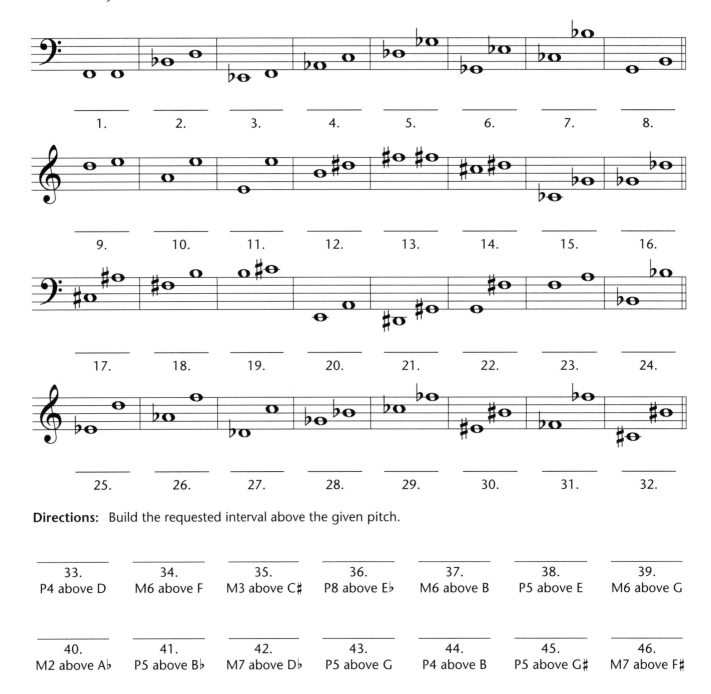

1. 2. 3. 4. 5. 6. 7. 8.

9. 10. 11. 12. 13. 14. 15. 16.

17. 18. 19. 20. 21. 22. 23. 24.

25. 26. 27. 28. 29. 30. 31. 32.

Directions: Build the requested interval above the given pitch.

33.	34.	35.	36.	37.	38.	39.
P4 above D	M6 above F	M3 above C♯	P8 above E♭	M6 above B	P5 above E	M6 above G

40.	41.	42.	43.	44.	45.	46.
M2 above A♭	P5 above B♭	M7 above D♭	P5 above G	P4 above B	P5 above G♯	M7 above F♯

47.	48.	49.	50.	51.	52.	53.
P5 above D	P4 above G♭	M3 above E♭	P8 above C♭	M2 above F♯	M6 above A	M7 above F

54.	55.	56.	57.	58.	59.	60.
M3 above D♭	M2 above B♭	P4 above E	M7 above G	M6 above D♭	P4 above A♯	PU above A

© 2005. Eric Harris. All Rights Reserved.

LESSON 14: MINOR, AUGMENTED, AND DIMINISHED INTERVALS

1. We have learned that major and perfect intervals exist in all major scales. We will now alter major and perfect intervals to make them minor, augmented, and diminished.

2. All intervals can be made larger (expanded) by raising the top note or by lowering the bottom note. (Think of raising the roof or lowering the floor of a room to make it larger.)

3. All intervals can be made smaller (compressed) by lowering the top note or by raising the bottom note. (Think of lowering the roof or raising the floor of a room to make it smaller.)

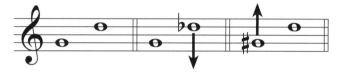

4. When expanding or compressing intervals, changes are most often made to the top note and are made one *chromatic half step* (CHS) at a time.

5. If we expand a major or perfect interval by one chromatic half step, we create an **augmented** (+) interval.

6. If we compress a major interval by one chromatic half step, we create a **minor** (m) interval.

7. If we compress a perfect interval by one chromatic half step, we create a **diminished** (o) interval. Perfect intervals *cannot* become minor.

8. If we compress a major interval by two chromatic half steps, we create a **diminished** (o) interval. Take this one step at a time: first compress the major interval to make it minor. Next compress the minor interval to make it diminished. (You'll eventually be able to skip the first step in many cases.)

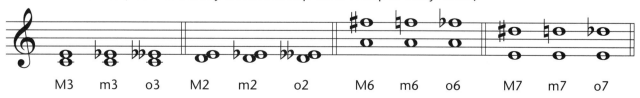

© 2005. Eric Harris. All Rights Reserved.

9. When expanding and compressing intervals, it is important to move the top note by *chromatic* half steps. Let us use the interval C to G (a fifth) as an example. If we wish to expand the interval by raising G a half step, we must say G-sharp, not A-flat. Using the letter A would change the size of the original interval to a sixth. The size of the original interval must remain the same when expanding and compressing intervals.

10. The process of expanding and compressing intervals may at first seem complicated. The chart below helps to summarize the steps required. Memorize this chart and the process will become easy.

Remember the following:
- Major intervals made one CHS larger become augmented intervals.

- Major intervals made one CHS smaller become minor intervals.

- Major intervals made two CHS's smaller become diminished intervals.

- Perfect intervals made one CHS larger become augmented intervals.

- Perfect intervals made one CHS smaller become diminished intervals.

- Perfect intervals never become minor.

11. The following abbreviations are commonly used to indicate the quality of intervals in most theory exercises.

- M, or "Maj." means major.

- m, or m̄, or "min." means minor.

- +, or A, or "Aug." means augmented.

- o, or d, or "dim." means diminished.

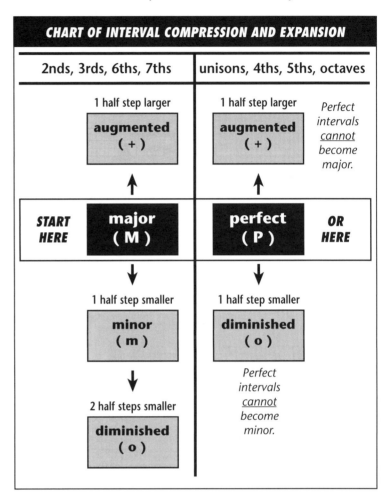

CHART OF INTERVAL COMPRESSION AND EXPANSION

2nds, 3rds, 6ths, 7ths	unisons, 4ths, 5ths, octaves
1 half step larger **augmented (+)**	1 half step larger **augmented (+)** *Perfect intervals cannot become major.*
↑	↑
START HERE **major (M)**	**perfect (P)** *OR HERE*
↓	↓
1 half step smaller **minor (m)**	1 half step smaller **diminished (o)**
↓	*Perfect intervals cannot become minor.*
2 half steps smaller **diminished (o)**	

IDENTIFYING AND SPELLING ALL INTERVAL QUALITIES

- **To identify a given interval** – call the lower note in the pair "tonic." If the upper note is in the key (scale) of the lower note, the interval is major or perfect. If the upper note is **not** in the key of the lower note, determine how many half steps the interval has been expanded or compressed. Follow the chart above to calculate the quality of the given interval.

- **To spell a requested interval** – spell a major or perfect interval above the given note. Raise or lower the top note one chromatic half step (CHS) at a time to arrive at the requested quality.

Problem: Spell an augmented sixth above E♭. First spell a major sixth above E♭, which is C. Raise C a chromatic half step to become C♯. C♯ is the answer.

Problem: Spell a diminished fifth above D. First spell a perfect fifth above D, which is A. Lower A a chromatic half step to become A♭. A♭ is the answer.

© 2005. Eric Harris. All Rights Reserved.

Exercise 8.12 - Review Questions

Directions: Answer the questions below.

1. If F to A is a major third, then:
   F to _____ is a minor third.
   F to _____ is a diminished third.
   F to _____ is an augmented third.

2. If B♭ to F is a perfect fifth, then:
   B♭ to _____ is a diminished fifth.
   B♭ to _____ is an augmented fifth.
   Can there be a minor fifth? _____

3. If D to B is a major sixth, then:
   D to _____ is a minor sixth.
   D to _____ is a diminished sixth.
   D to _____ is an augmented sixth.

4. If E♭ to D is a major seventh, then:
   E♭ to _____ is a minor seventh.
   E♭ to _____ is a diminished seventh.
   E♭ to _____ is an augmented seventh.

5. If A to D is a perfect fourth, then:
   A to _____ is a diminished fourth.
   A to _____ is an augmented fourth.
   Can there be a minor fourth? _____

6. If C♯ to E♯ is a major third, then:
   C♯ to _____ is a minor third.
   C♯ to _____ is a diminished third.
   C♯ to _____ is an augmented third.

7. If A to B is a major second, then:
   A to _____ is a minor second.
   A to _____ is a diminished second.
   A to _____ is an augmented second.

8. If G to D is a perfect fifth, then:
   G to _____ is a diminished fifth.
   G to _____ is an augmented fifth.
   Can there be a minor fifth? _____

9. If E♭ to G♭ is a minor third, then:
   E♭ to _____ is a major third.
   E♭ to _____ is an augmented third.
   E♭ to _____ is a diminished third.

10. If F♯ to C is a diminished fifth, then:
    F♯ to _____ is a perfect fifth.
    F♯ to _____ is an augmented fifth.

11. If E to G𝄪 is an augmented third, then:
    E to _____ is a major third.
    E to _____ is a minor third.
    E to _____ is a diminished third.

12. If B to G♭ is a diminished sixth, then:
    B to _____ is a minor sixth.
    B to _____ is a major sixth.
    B to _____ is an augmented sixth.

13. If D♭ to C♭ is a minor seventh, then:
    D♭ to _____ is a major seventh.
    D♭ to _____ is an augmented seventh.
    D♭ to _____ is a diminished seventh.

14. If A♭ to E is an augmented fifth, then:
    A♭ to _____ is a perfect fifth.
    A♭ to _____ is a diminished fifth.

15. If C to A♭♭ is a diminished sixth, then:
    C to _____ is a minor sixth.
    C to _____ is a major sixth.
    C to _____ is an augmented sixth.

16. If G to B♯ is an augmented third, then:
    G to _____ is a major third.
    G to _____ is a minor third.
    G to _____ is a diminished third.
    Can there be a perfect third? _____

© 2005. Eric Harris. All Rights Reserved.

Exercise 8.13 - Expanding and Compressing Major Intervals

Directions: Build the intervals above the tonic pitches below. Do not alter the bottom note in any way.

© 2005. Eric Harris. All Rights Reserved.

Exercise 8.14 - Expanding and Compressing Perfect Intervals

Directions: Build the intervals above the tonic pitches below. Do not alter the bottom note in any way.

1

P5	+5	o5	P4	+4	o4
1.	2.	3.	4.	5.	6.

2

P8	+8	o8	P5	+5	o5
7.	8.	9.	10.	11.	12.

3

P4	+4	o4	P5	+5	o5
13.	14.	15.	16.	17.	18.

4

P4	+4	o4	P8	+8	o8
19.	20.	21.	22.	23.	24.

5

Check Clef

P5	+5	o5	P5	+5	o5
25.	26.	27.	28.	29.	30.

6

P4	+4	o4	P4	+4	o4
31.	32.	33.	34.	35.	36.

7

P5	+5	o5	P4	+4	o4
37.	38.	39.	40.	41.	42.

8

P4	+4	o4	P8	+8	o8
43.	44.	45.	46.	47.	48.

© 2005. Eric Harris. All Rights Reserved.

Exercise 8.15 - Spelling Minor Intervals

> Remember, major intervals made one chromatic half step smaller become minor. Intervals are most often made smaller by lowering the top note one chromatic half step.

1 **Directions:** Build a **minor second** above each given pitch.

2 **Directions:** Build a **minor third** above each given pitch.

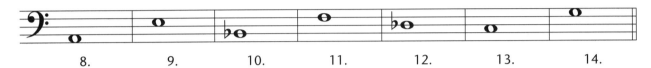

3 **Directions:** Build a **minor sixth** above each given pitch.

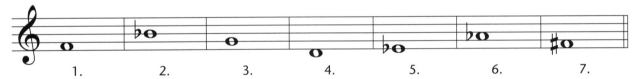

4 **Directions:** Build a **minor seventh** above each given pitch.

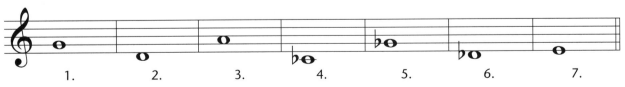

© 2005. Eric Harris. All Rights Reserved.

Exercise 8.16 - Spelling Augmented Intervals

 Remember, perfect intervals made one chromatic half step larger become augmented. Major intervals made one chromatic half step larger also become augmented. Intervals are most often made larger by raising the top note one chromatic half step.

1 **Directions:** Build an **augmented second** above each given pitch.

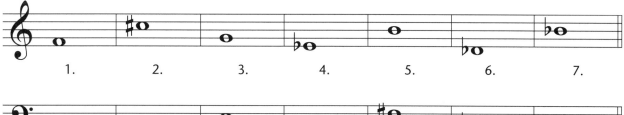

2 **Directions:** Build an **augmented third** above each given pitch.

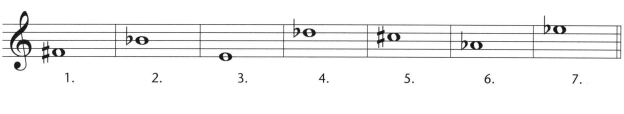

3 **Directions:** Build an **augmented fourth** above each given pitch.

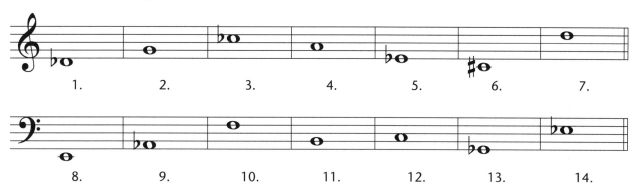

© 2005. Eric Harris. All Rights Reserved.

Exercise 8.17 - Spelling Augmented Intervals

1 **Directions:** Build an **augmented fifth** above each given pitch.

2 **Directions:** Build an **augmented sixth** above each given pitch.

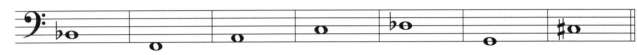

3 **Directions:** Build an **augmented seventh** above each given pitch.

4 **Directions:** Build an **augmented octave** above each given pitch.

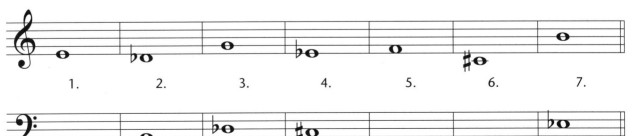

© 2005. Eric Harris. All Rights Reserved.

Exercise 8.18 - Spelling Diminished Intervals

Remember, perfect intervals made one chromatic half step smaller become diminished. Major intervals made two chromatic half steps smaller also become diminished. Minor intervals made one chromatic half step smaller become diminished. Intervals are most often made smaller by lowering the top note one chromatic half step at a time.

1 **Directions:** Build a **diminished second*** above each given pitch.

2 **Directions:** Build a **diminished third** above each given pitch.

3 **Directions:** Build a **diminished fourth** above each given pitch.

*Notice that the diminished second, when spelled correctly, is enharmonic with the given pitch.

© 2005. Eric Harris. All Rights Reserved.

Exercise 8.19 - Spelling Diminished Intervals

1   Directions: Build a **diminished fifth** above each given pitch.

2   Directions: Build a **diminished sixth** above each given pitch.

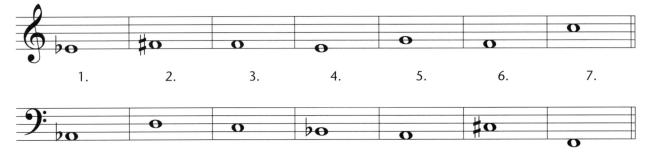

3   Directions: Build a **diminished seventh** above each given pitch.

4   Directions: Build a **diminished octave** above each given pitch.

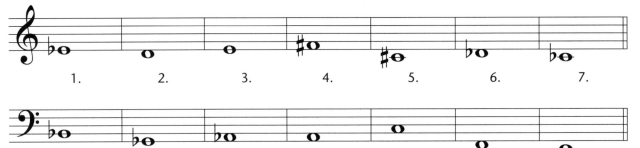

© 2005. Eric Harris. All Rights Reserved.

Exercise 8.20 - Spelling All Interval Qualities

Directions: The tonic note of each major scale is listed across the bottom of the chart. Down the left side are the most common intervals found in music. Build every interval above each tonic. Omit boxes filled with an "X." Why are some of the interval rows highlighted in gray?

	C	G	D	A	E	B	F♯	C♯	F	B♭	E♭	A♭	D♭	G♭	C♭
o8															
+8															
P8															
o7															X
+7															
m7															
M7															
o6													X	X	X
+6															
m6															
M6															
o5															
+5															
P5															
o4															
+4															
P4															
o3														X	X
+3															
m3															
M3															
o2	D♭♭											X	X	X	X
+2	D♯														
m2	D♭														
M2	D														
PU	C														

© 2005. Eric Harris. All Rights Reserved.

Exercise 8.21 - Identifying Intervals

Remember, when identifying an interval, first begin by calling the lower note in the pair "tonic." If the upper note is in the key (scale) of the lower note, the interval is major or perfect. If the upper note is not in the key (scale) of the lower note, determine the number of half steps the interval has been expanded or compressed to determine the interval quality.

Directions: Identify each interval below. Remember to count up from the lower note in each pair.

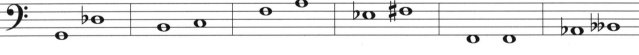

© 2005. Eric Harris. All Rights Reserved.

Exercise 8.22 - Identifying Intervals

Directions: Identify each interval below. Remember to count up from the lower note in each pair.

© 2005. Eric Harris. All Rights Reserved.

LESSON 15: NON-TONIC TONE INTERVALS

1. So far, we have learned to spell intervals above the tonic note of each of the fifteen major scales. There are, however, six additional pitches which are not used as the tonic of any major scale. These pitches are called **non-tonic tones** and are as follows:

2. To spell an interval above a non-tonic tone:
   - Remove the accidental from the given note.
   - Spell the requested interval.
   - Reapply the removed accidental to both notes.

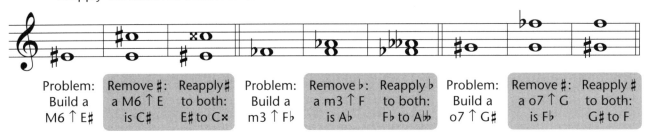

| Problem: Build a M6 ↑ E♯ | Remove ♯: a M6 ↑ E is C♯ | Reapply♯ to both: E♯ to C𝄪 | Problem: Build a m3 ↑ F♭ | Remove ♭: a m3 ↑ F is A♭ | Reapply♭ to both: F♭ to A♭♭ | Problem: Build a o7 ↑ G♯ | Remove ♯: a o7 ↑ G is F♭ | Reapply ♯ to both: G♯ to F |

3. When reapplying accidentals to intervals, use the following chart:

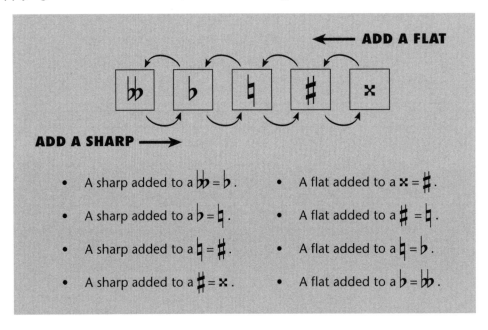

- A sharp added to a 𝄫 = ♭.
- A sharp added to a ♭ = ♮.
- A sharp added to a ♮ = ♯.
- A sharp added to a ♯ = 𝄪.
- A flat added to a 𝄪 = ♯.
- A flat added to a ♯ = ♮.
- A flat added to a ♮ = ♭.
- A flat added to a ♭ = 𝄫.

4. Deductive reasoning can also be used to spell non-tonic tone intervals.
   - If E to G♯ is a major third, E♯ to G𝄪 is also a major third.
   - If A to E is a perfect fifth, A♯ to E♯ is also a perfect fifth.
   - If B to G is a minor sixth, B♯ to G♯ is also a minor sixth.
   - If F to B is an augmented fourth, F♭ to B♭ is also an augmented fourth.

© 2005. Eric Harris. All Rights Reserved.

Exercise 8.23 - Spelling Non-Tonic Tone Intervals

Directions: Build the requested interval above each non-tonic tone given below.

1. P5 ↑ D♯ ____	7. P4 ↑ F♭ ____	13. M2 ↑ B♯ ____	19. m2 ↑ B♯ ____	25. M3 ↑ F♭ ____
2. P5 ↑ E♯ ____	8. P4 ↑ E♯ ____	14. M2 ↑ A♯ ____	20. m2 ↑ A♯ ____	26. M3 ↑ D♯ ____
3. P5 ↑ F♭ ____	9. P4 ↑ D♯ ____	15. M2 ↑ G♯ ____	21. m2 ↑ G♯ ____	27. M3 ↑ E♯ ____
4. P5 ↑ G♯ ____	10. P4 ↑ A♯ ____	16. M2 ↑ F♭ ____	22. m2 ↑ F♭ ____	28. M3 ↑ G♯ ____
5. P5 ↑ A♯ ____	11. P4 ↑ B♯ ____	17. M2 ↑ E♯ ____	23. m2 ↑ E♯ ____	29. M3 ↑ A♯ ____
6. P5 ↑ B♯ ____	12. P4 ↑ G♯ ____	18. M2 ↑ D♯ ____	24. m2 ↑ D♯ ____	30. M3 ↑ B♯ ____
31. m3 ↑ B♯ ____	37. M6 ↑ F♭ ____	43. m6 ↑ B♯ ____	49. M7 ↑ E♯ ____	55. m7 ↑ A♯ ____
32. m3 ↑ A♯ ____	38. M6 ↑ D♯ ____	44. m6 ↑ A♯ ____	50. M7 ↑ G♯ ____	56. m7 ↑ F♭ ____
33. m3 ↑ G♯ ____	39. M6 ↑ E♯ ____	45. m6 ↑ G♯ ____	51. M7 ↑ B♯ ____	57. m7 ↑ D♯ ____
34. m3 ↑ E♯ ____	40. M6 ↑ G♯ ____	46. m6 ↑ E♯ ____	52. M7 ↑ D♯ ____	58. m7 ↑ B♯ ____
35. m3 ↑ D♯ ____	41. M6 ↑ A♯ ____	47. m6 ↑ D♯ ____	53. M7 ↑ F♭ ____	59. m7 ↑ G♯ ____
36. m3 ↑ F♭ ____	42. M6 ↑ B♯ ____	48. m6 ↑ F♭ ____	54. M7 ↑ A♯ ____	60. m7 ↑ E♯ ____

Directions: Build these on the staff. Watch for clef changes.

M6	P5	M3	M2	M7	P4	M2	M3
61.	62.	63.	64.	65.	66.	67.	68.

M7	M3	P5	M6	P8	M3	M2	P5
69.	70.	71.	72.	73.	74.	75.	76.

m3	m7	+6	o7	m2	o5	o4	o8
77.	78.	79.	80.	81.	82.	83.	84.

+6	o3	m7	+4	o5	o6	o7	+3
85.	86.	87.	88.	89.	90.	91.	92.

© 2005. Eric Harris. All Rights Reserved.

Exercise 8.24 - Identifying All Interval Qualities

Directions: Identify each interval below. Watch for clef changes.

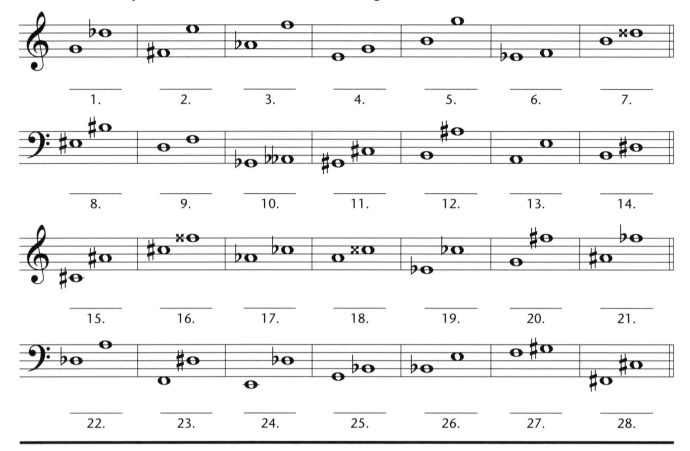

Exercise 8.25 - Spelling All Interval Qualities

Directions: Build the requested interval above each note given below. Watch for clef changes.

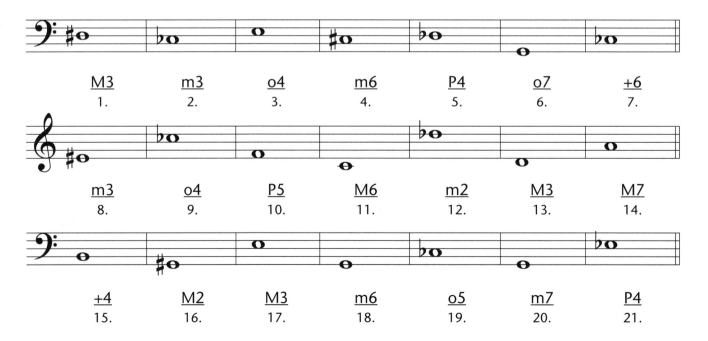

© 2005. Eric Harris. All Rights Reserved.

Exercise 8.26 - Identifying All Interval Qualities

Directions: Circle the letter under each interval who's quality matches that given in the box. More than one answer may be possible for each item. Circle all that apply. Watch for clef changes.

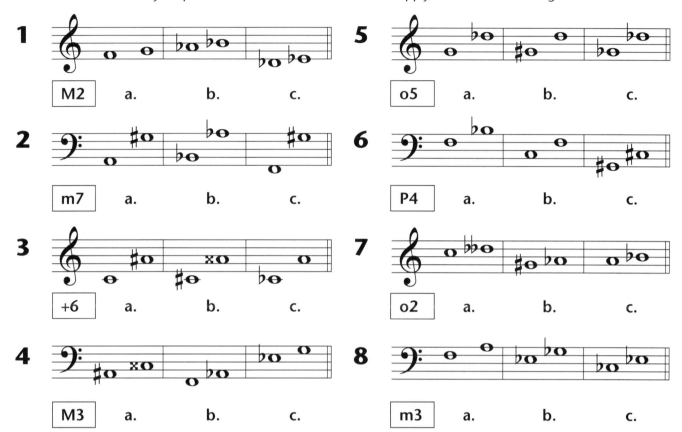

Exercise 8.27 - Spelling All Interval Qualities

Directions: Build the requested interval above each note given below. Watch for clef changes.

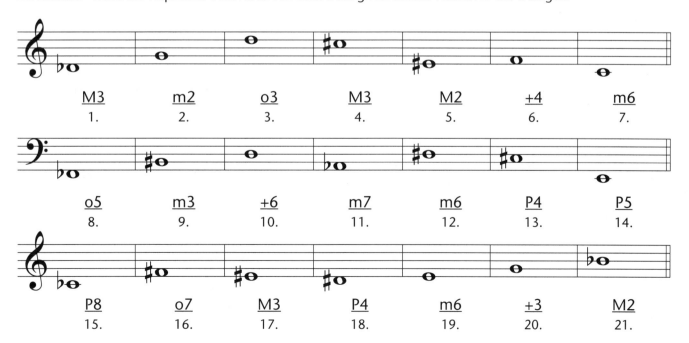

© 2005. Eric Harris. All Rights Reserved.

LESSON 16: INVERTING INTERVALS

1. All intervals can be turned upside down. This process is called **inversion**.

2. Inversion is accomplished by taking the lower note in an interval and making it the higher note (by writing it one octave higher).

 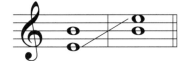

3. We can also invert by taking the higher note in an interval and making it the lower note (by writing it one octave lower).

 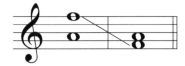

4. When intervals invert, the size changes. An interval plus its inversion will always equal nine. This phenomenon is called the **rule of nine**.

> Unisons invert to become octaves..........C and C = Unison; C to C = Octave....... 1 + 8 = 9
> Seconds invert to become sevenths.......C to D = Second; D to C = Seventh....... 2 + 7 = 9
> Thirds invert to become sixths.............C to E = Third; E to C = Sixth................. 3 + 6 = 9
> Fourths invert to become fifths.............C to F = Fourth; F to C = Fifth............... 4 + 5 = 9
> Fifths invert to become fourths.............C to G = Fifth; G to C = Fourth............. 5 + 4 = 9
> Sixths invert to become thirds.............C to A = Sixth; A to C = Third.............. 6 + 3 = 9
> Sevenths invert to become seconds.......C to B = Seventh; B to C = Second.........7 + 2 = 9
> Octaves invert to become unisons........ C to C = Octave; C and C = Unison....... 8 + 1 = 9

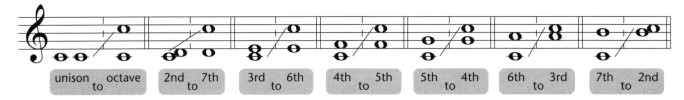

| unison to octave | 2nd to 7th | 3rd to 6th | 4th to 5th | 5th to 4th | 6th to 3rd | 7th to 2nd |

5. Qualifiers invert too:
> Perfect intervals invert to become perfect.
> > C to F = Perfect Fourth; F to C = Perfect Fifth.
> Major intervals invert to become minor.
> > C to A = Major Sixth; A to C = Minor Third.
> Minor intervals invert to become major.
> > C to E♭ = Minor Third; E♭ to C = Major Sixth.
> Augmented intervals invert to become diminished.
> > C to F♯ = Augmented Fourth; F♯ to C = Diminished Fifth.
> Diminished intervals invert to become augmented.
> > C to G♭ = Diminished Fifth; G♭ to C = Augmented Fourth.

Staff Examples of Qualifier Inversions

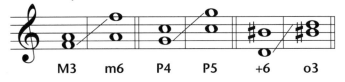

M3   m6   P4   P5   +6   o3

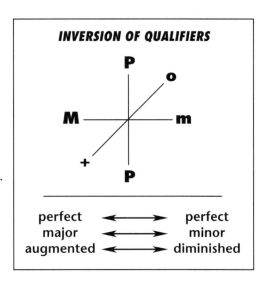

INVERSION OF QUALIFIERS

perfect	⟷	perfect
major	⟷	minor
augmented	⟷	diminished

© 2005. Eric Harris. All Rights Reserved.

Exercise 8.28 - Inverting Intervals

Directions: Provide the inversion for each interval below. You may use abbreviations in your answer.

1. A minor third inverts to become a _____.

2. An augmented fifth inverts to become a _____.

3. A major seventh inverts to become a _____.

4. A perfect fourth inverts to become a _____.

5. An augmented second inverts to become a _____.

6. A minor seventh inverts to become a _____.

7. A diminished third inverts to become a _____.

8. A diminished seventh inverts to become a _____.

9. A diminished fourth inverts to become a _____.

10. A minor second inverts to become a _____.

11. A diminished fifth inverts to become a _____.

12. An augmented third inverts to become a _____.

13. A diminished sixth inverts to become a _____.

14. A perfect fifth inverts to become a _____.

15. An augmented fourth inverts to become a _____.

16. A major second inverts to become a _____.

17. A minor sixth inverts to become a _____.

18. A major third inverts to become a _____.

19. An augmented sixth inverts to become a _____.

20. A major sixth inverts to become a _____.

Exercise 8.29 - Inverting Intervals

Directions: Name each interval, then invert it (by making the lower note the higher note); name the inversion.

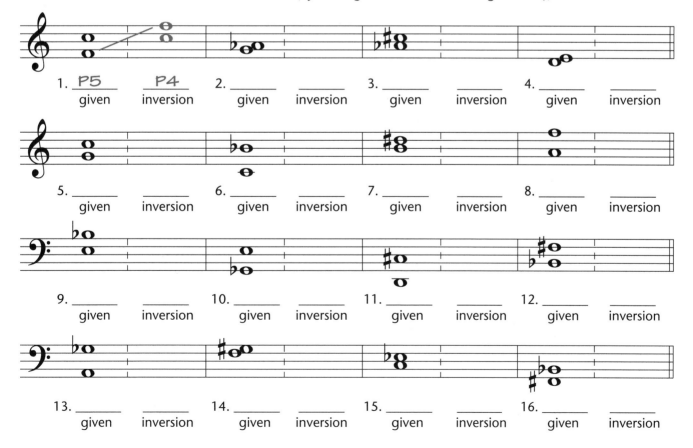

1. P5 (given) / P4 (inversion)

© 2005. Eric Harris. All Rights Reserved.

LESSON 17: DESCENDING INTERVALS

1. We can use our knowledge of interval inversion to help us build descending intervals.

2. To build a descending interval:

    *   Invert the question.
    *   Spell the inverted interval above the given note.
    *   Drop the answer one octave so it is written below the given note.

    Look at the following examples.

Problem: Build a m3 ↓ A♭.
Invert the question: (M6 ↑ A♭) = F.
Drop the answer one octave (so F is written below A♭).

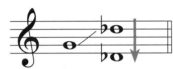

Problem: Build an +4 ↓ G.
Invert the question: (o5 ↑ G) = D♭.
Drop the answer one octave (so D♭ is written below G).

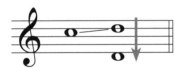

Problem: Build a m7 ↓ C.
Invert the question: (M2 ↑ C) = D.
Drop the answer one octave (so D is written below C).

Problem: Build a P5 ↓ B.
Invert the question: (P4 ↑ B) = E.
Drop the answer one octave (so E is written below B).

Problem: Build a o3 ↓ F.
Invert the question, (+6 ↑ F) = D♯.
Drop the answer one octave (so D♯ is written below F).

Problem: Build a m2 ↓ B♭.
Invert the question, (M7 ↑ B♭) = A.
Drop the answer one octave (so A is written below B♭).

3. With fill-in-the-blank questions, there is no need to drop the answer an octave (because of the absence of a staff). Just invert the question, solve, and write the answer. Look at the examples below:

    *   M3 ↓ B♭ = (m6 ↑ B♭) = G♭

    *   o5 ↓ A = (+4 ↑ A) = D♯

    *   o7 ↓ B = (+2 ↑ B) = C⨯

    *   m6 ↓ D♭ = (M3 ↑ D♭) = F

    *   +4 ↓ E♭ = (o5 ↑ E♭) = B♭♭

> ### TO CHECK THE SPELLING OF DESCENDING INTERVALS
>
> Students can check the spelling of any descending interval by building up from the newly-created bottom note. If the spelling matches the original problem, the answer is correct.
>
> Example: Build a M3 below B♭. The answer is G♭. Is G♭ up to B♭ a M3? Yes – so the answer is correct.

© 2005. Eric Harris. All Rights Reserved.

Exercise 8.30 - Spelling Descending Intervals

Directions: Using your knowledge of inversions, build the descending intervals below.

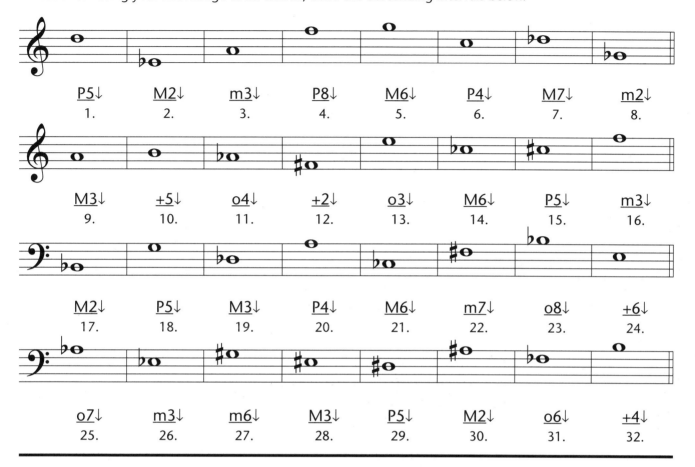

P5↓	M2↓	m3↓	P8↓	M6↓	P4↓	M7↓	m2↓
1.	2.	3.	4.	5.	6.	7.	8.

M3↓	+5↓	o4↓	+2↓	o3↓	M6↓	P5↓	m3↓
9.	10.	11.	12.	13.	14.	15.	16.

M2↓	P5↓	M3↓	P4↓	M6↓	m7↓	o8↓	+6↓
17.	18.	19.	20.	21.	22.	23.	24.

o7↓	m3↓	m6↓	M3↓	P5↓	M2↓	o6↓	+4↓
25.	26.	27.	28.	29.	30.	31.	32.

Exercise 8.31 - Identifiying Intervals In Melodies

Directions: Identify the intervals between the notes of the melodies below. Remember to count up from the lower note in the pair, and don't forget to apply the key signature!

Anonymous

1
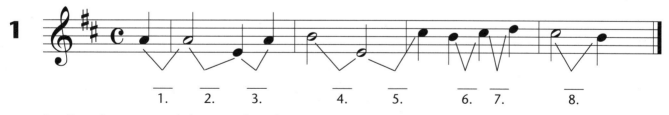

 1. 2. 3.   4.   5.   6. 7.   8.

For Fun: Can you name the tune above? _____

James Pierpont

2
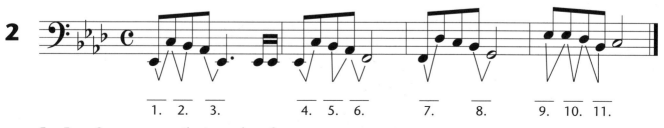

 1. 2. 3.   4. 5. 6.   7.   8.   9. 10. 11.

For Fun: Can you name the tune above? _____

© 2005. Eric Harris. All Rights Reserved.

Exercise 8.32 - Final Interval Review

Directions: Build the requested intervals below. All types, including major, minor, augmented, diminished, ascending, descending, and non-tonic tone, are included.

© 2005. Eric Harris. All Rights Reserved.

Unit Review Questions

Directions: Answer the questions below.

1. _____ The distance between two notes (on the staff or on the keyboard) is called an ?

2. _____ When two notes are played simultaneously (at the same time) a ? interval is formed.

3. _____ When two notes are played successively (one after the other) a ? interval is formed.

4. _____ The size of an interval is determined by counting the ? number of letter names included.

5. _____ Intervals are named using ? numbers (second, third, fourth, etc.)

6. _____ There are eight basic intervals: unisons (also called ?), seconds, thirds, fourths, fifths, sixths, sevenths, and octaves.

7. _____ A melodic interval played low to high is said to be ? (ascending or descending).

8. _____ A melodic interval played high to low is said to be ? (ascending or descending).

9. _____ When determining the size of an interval, count up from the ? note in the pair.

10. _____ In addition to determining the size of an interval, we can also determine the ?.

11. _____ If we look at the relationship of each note in a major scale to the tonic note, we will find that certain intervals exist ? (they are constant).

12. _____ 1 to 1 in a major scale is called a ? (Use the standard abbreviation.)

13. _____ 1 to 2 in a major scale is called a ? (Use the standard abbreviation.)

14. _____ 1 to 3 in a major scale is called a ? (Use the standard abbreviation.)

15. _____ 1 to 4 in a major scale is called a ? (Use the standard abbreviation.)

16. _____ 1 to 5 in a major scale is called a ? (Use the standard abbreviation.)

17. _____ 1 to 6 in a major scale is called a ? (Use the standard abbreviation.)

18. _____ 1 to 7 in a major scale is called a ? (Use the standard abbreviation.)

19. _____ 1 to 8 in a major scale is called an ? (Use the standard abbreviation.)

20. _____ The pattern of major and perfect intervals is the same for all major scales. (True/False)

21. _____ In a major scale, all seconds, thirds, sixths, and sevenths are ?

22. _____ In a major scale, all unisons, fourths, fifths, and octaves are ?

23. _____ The intervals that exist in a major scale are said to be ?. This term means "related to a scale."

© 2005. Eric Harris. All Rights Reserved.

24. _____ Most perfect fourths are sharp to sharp, flat to flat, or natural to natural. The exception is perfect fourths between ? and ? (Write both answers in the blank).

25. _____ Most perfect fifths are sharp to sharp, flat to flat, or natural to natural. The exception is perfect fifths between ? and ? (Write both answers in the blank).

26. _____ All intervals can be made larger by raising the ? note or lowering the bottom note.

27. _____ All intervals can be made smaller by lowering the ? note or raising the bottom note.

28. _____ When expanding or compressing intervals, changes are most often made to the top note and are made one ? half step at a time.

29. _____ If we expand a major or perfect interval by one chromatic half step, we create an ? interval.

30. _____ If we compress a major interval by one chromatic half step, we create a ? interval.

31. _____ If we compress a perfect interval by one chromatic half step, we create a ? interval.

32. _____ If we compress a major interval by two chromatic half steps, we create a ? interval.

33. _____ If we compress a minor interval by one chromatic half step, we create a ? interval.

34. _____ Write the abbreviations used to indicate "major."

35. _____ Write the abbreviations used to indicate "minor."

36. _____ Write the abbreviations used to indicate "augmented."

37. _____ Write the abbreviations used to indicate "diminished."

38. _____ The ? of the interval must remain the same when expanding and compressing intervals. *Do not change the letter names.*

39. _____ To identify a given interval, call the lower note in the pair "tonic." If the higher note is in the ? of the lower note, the interval is perfect or major.

40. _____ If the upper note of an interval is not in the key (scale) of the lower note, determine how many half steps the interval has been ? or ? to calculate the quality. (Write both answers in the blank.)

41. _____ To spell a requested interval, spell a major or perfect interval above the given note and then raise or lower the top note one ? half step at a time to arrive at the requested quality.

42. _____ Can there be major unisons, fourths, fifths, or octaves?

43. _____ Can there be perfect seconds, thirds, sixths, or sevenths?

© 2005. Eric Harris. All Rights Reserved.

44. _____ Notes which are not used as the tonic of a major scale are called ? tones.

45. _____ To spell an interval above a non-tonic tone, ? the accidental from the given note, spell the requested interval, and then reapply the removed accidental to both notes.

46. _____ Inversion is accomplished by taking the lower note in a pair and making it the ? note in the pair (by writing it one octave higher).

47. _____ Inversion can also be accomplished by taking the higher note in a pair and making it the ? note in the pair (by writing it one octave lower).

48. _____ An interval plus its inversion will always equal ?

49. _____ Unisons invert to become ?

50. _____ Seconds invert to become ?

51. _____ Thirds invert to become ?

52. _____ Fourths invert to become ?

53. _____ Fifths invert to become ?

54. _____ Sixths invert to become ?

55. _____ Sevenths invert to become ?

56. _____ Octaves invert to become ?

57. _____ Perfect intervals invert to become ?

58. _____ Major intervals invert to become ?

59. _____ Minor intervals invert to become ?

60. _____ Augmented intervals invert to become ?

61. _____ Diminished intervals invert to become ?

62. _____ We can use our knowledge of interval inversion to help us build ? intervals.

63. _____ To build a descending interval: ? the question, spell the inverted interval above the given note, then drop the answer one octave so it is written below the given note.

© 2005. Eric Harris. All Rights Reserved.

LESSON 18: RELATIVE MINOR

1. Each major scale has a **minor scale** contained within it. The minor scale begins on the sixth note of the major scale, follows the musical alphabet for one octave, and uses the same key signature. When two scales (a major scale and a minor scale) share the same key signature, they are said to be **relative**. Look at the relative scales below.

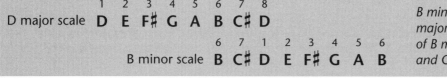

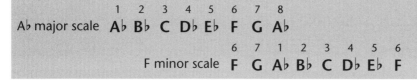

2. Relative major and minor scales are separated by the interval of a minor third. Look at the examples below.

| F minor and A♭ major are relative | E minor and G major are relative | C♯ minor and E major are relative |

3. When given the major key and asked to determine the relative minor, simply count up to the sixth note of the major scale – this will reveal the name of the relative minor. You can also count down three half steps (a m3). Problem: Find the relative minor for D major. Count up to the sixth note of the D major scale = B. B minor is the relative minor for D major. (You could have also counted down three half steps from D = B.)

4. When given the minor key and asked to determine the relative major, simply count up three half steps (a m3) – this will reveal the name of the relative major. Problem: Find the relative major for G minor. Count up three half steps (a m3) from G = B♭. B♭ major is the relative major for G minor.

5. Below is the chart of fifths with relative minors shown. Note that the names of minor keys are sometimes written in lowercase letters. This is especially true if the key name is not followed by the word "minor" or the lowercase letter "m."

C Major (a minor) – no sharps; no flats	
F Major (d minor) – 1 flat	G Major (e minor) – 1 sharp
B♭ Major (g minor) – 2 flats	D Major (b minor) – 2 sharps
E♭ Major (c minor) – 3 flats	A Major (f♯ minor) – 3 sharps
A♭ Major (f minor) – 4 flats	E Major (c♯ minor) – 4 sharps
D♭ Major (b♭ minor) – 5 flats	B Major (g♯ minor) – 5 sharps
G♭ Major (e♭ minor) – 6 flats	F♯ Major (d♯ minor) – 6 sharps
C♭ Major (a♭ minor) – 7 flats	C♯ Major (a♯ minor) – 7 sharps

© 2005. Eric Harris. All Rights Reserved.

Exercise 9.1 - Find The Relative Minor

Directions: Write the name of the relative minor for each major key given below.

1. F major _____ minor
2. G major _____ minor
3. B♭ major _____ minor
4. D major _____ minor
5. E♭ major _____ minor

6. A major _____ minor
7. A♭ major _____ minor
8. E major _____ minor
9. D♭ major _____ minor
10. B major _____ minor

11. G♭ major _____ minor
12. F♯ major _____ minor
13. C major _____ minor
14. C♯ major _____ minor
15. C♭ major _____ minor

Exercise 9.2 - Find The Relative Major

Directions: Write the name of the relative major for each minor key given below.

1. e minor _____ major
2. d minor _____ major
3. b minor _____ major
4. g minor _____ major
5. f♯ minor _____ major

6. c minor _____ major
7. c♯ minor _____ major
8. f minor _____ major
9. g♯ minor _____ major
10. e♭ minor _____ major

11. d♯ minor _____ major
12. b♭ minor _____ major
13. a minor _____ major
14. a♯ minor _____ major
15. a♭ minor _____ major

Exercise 9.3 - Name the Relatives

Directions: You are given the number and type of accidentals found in the key signature. Provide the name of the major key and the relative minor key.

1. six sharps _____major _____ minor
2. seven flats _____major _____ minor
3. three sharps _____major _____ minor
4. one sharp _____major _____ minor
5. three flats _____major _____ minor
6. four flats _____major _____ minor
7. two sharps _____major _____ minor

8. two flats _____major _____ minor
9. five sharps _____major _____ minor
10. five flats _____major _____ minor
11. seven sharps _____major _____ minor
12. one flat _____major _____ minor
13. six flats _____major _____ minor
14. four sharps _____major _____ minor

© 2005. Eric Harris. All Rights Reserved.

Exercise 9.4 - Identifying Minor Key Signatures

Directions: Identify the minor key signatures given below. You know the name of the major key. *Go down a minor third (three half steps) to determine the name of the relative minor.*

1. _____ minor   2. _____ minor   3. _____ minor   4. _____ minor

5. _____ minor   6. _____ minor   7. _____ minor   8. _____ minor

9. _____ minor   10. _____ minor   11. _____ minor   12. _____ minor

13. _____ minor   14. _____ minor   15. _____ minor   16. _____ minor

17. _____ minor   18. _____ minor   19. _____ minor   20. _____ minor

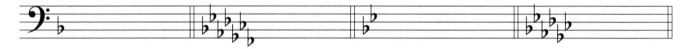

21. _____ minor   22. _____ minor   23. _____ minor   24. _____ minor

25. _____ minor   26. _____ minor   27. _____ minor   28. _____ minor

29. _____ minor   30. _____ minor   31. _____ minor   32. _____ minor

© 2005. Eric Harris. All Rights Reserved.

Exercise 9.5 - Identifying Minor Key Signatures

Directions: Identify the minor key signatures given below. You know the name of the major key. *Go down a minor third (three half steps) to determine the name of the relative minor.*

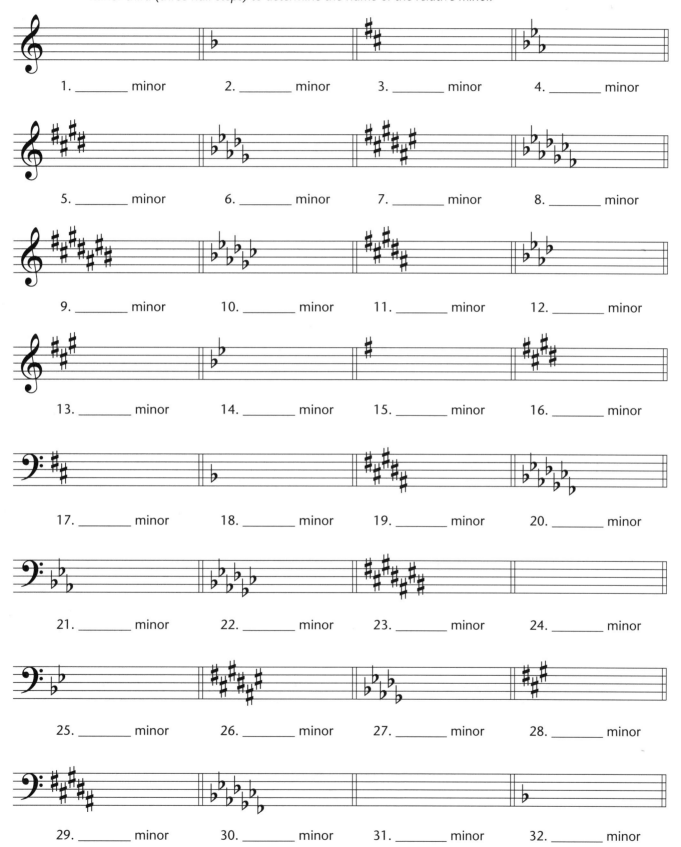

1. _____ minor 2. _____ minor 3. _____ minor 4. _____ minor

5. _____ minor 6. _____ minor 7. _____ minor 8. _____ minor

9. _____ minor 10. _____ minor 11. _____ minor 12. _____ minor

13. _____ minor 14. _____ minor 15. _____ minor 16. _____ minor

17. _____ minor 18. _____ minor 19. _____ minor 20. _____ minor

21. _____ minor 22. _____ minor 23. _____ minor 24. _____ minor

25. _____ minor 26. _____ minor 27. _____ minor 28. _____ minor

29. _____ minor 30. _____ minor 31. _____ minor 32. _____ minor

© 2005. Eric Harris. All Rights Reserved.

Exercise 9.6 - Identifying Minor Key Signatures

Directions: Identify the minor key signatures given below. You know the name of the major key. *Go down a minor third (three half steps) to determine the name of the relative minor.*

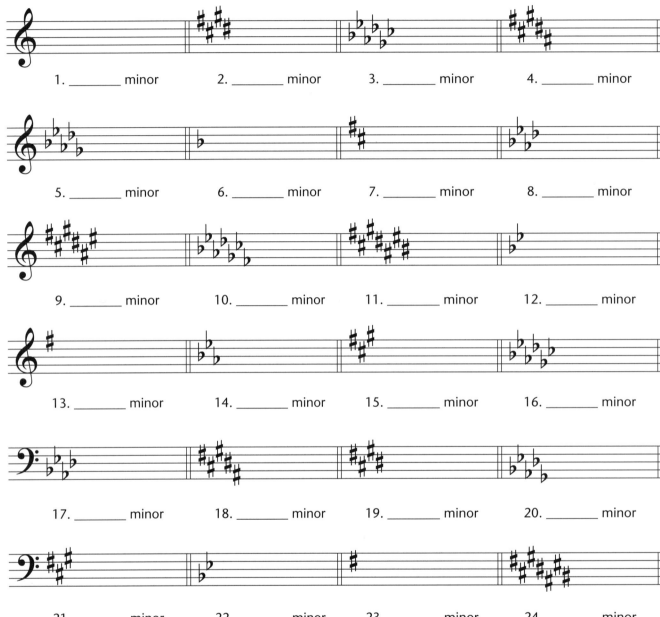

1. _____ minor   2. _____ minor   3. _____ minor   4. _____ minor

5. _____ minor   6. _____ minor   7. _____ minor   8. _____ minor

9. _____ minor   10. _____ minor   11. _____ minor   12. _____ minor

13. _____ minor   14. _____ minor   15. _____ minor   16. _____ minor

17. _____ minor   18. _____ minor   19. _____ minor   20. _____ minor

21. _____ minor   22. _____ minor   23. _____ minor   24. _____ minor

25. _____ minor   26. _____ minor   27. _____ minor   28. _____ minor

29. _____ minor   30. _____ minor   31. _____ minor   32. _____ minor

© 2005. Eric Harris. All Rights Reserved.

Exercise 9.7 - Writing Minor Key Signatures

Directions: Write the requested minor key signatures. *Go up a minor third to determine the relative major key signature; write that key signature on the staff.*

1. A♯ minor
2. D♯ minor
3. G♯ minor
4. B♭ minor

5. E minor
6. F minor
7. E♭ minor
8. C minor

9. D minor
10. D♯ minor
11. F minor
12. B♭ minor

13. B minor
14. B♭ minor
15. E minor
16. G minor

Clef Change

17. D♯ minor
18. D minor
19. G♯ minor
20. G minor

21. C minor
22. C♯ minor
23. F minor
24. F♯ minor

25. E minor
26. E♭ minor
27. A minor
28. A♭ minor

29. G♯ minor
30. B♭ minor
31. C♯ minor
32. E♭ minor

© 2005. Eric Harris. All Rights Reserved.

Exercise 9.8 - Writing Minor Key Signatures

Directions: Write the requested minor key signatures. *Go up a minor third to determine the relative major key signature; write that key signature on the staff.*

1. D minor   2. E minor   3. G minor   4. F♯ minor

5. B minor   6. B♭ minor   7. C♯ minor   8. F minor

9. E♭ minor   10. D♯ minor   11. C minor   12. A♯ minor

13. E minor   14. G minor   15. B minor   16. F minor

Clef Change

17. B♭ minor   18. F♯ minor   19. A♭ minor   20. C♯ minor

21. G♯ minor   22. G minor   23. G♯ minor   24. E♭ minor

25. A♭ minor   26. D♯ minor   27. G minor   28. A♯ minor

29. F minor   30. C minor   31. B minor   32. A♭ minor

© 2005. Eric Harris. All Rights Reserved.

Exercise 9.9 - Writing Minor Key Signatures

Directions: Write the requested minor key signatures. *Go up a minor third to determine the relative major key signature; write that key signature on the staff.*

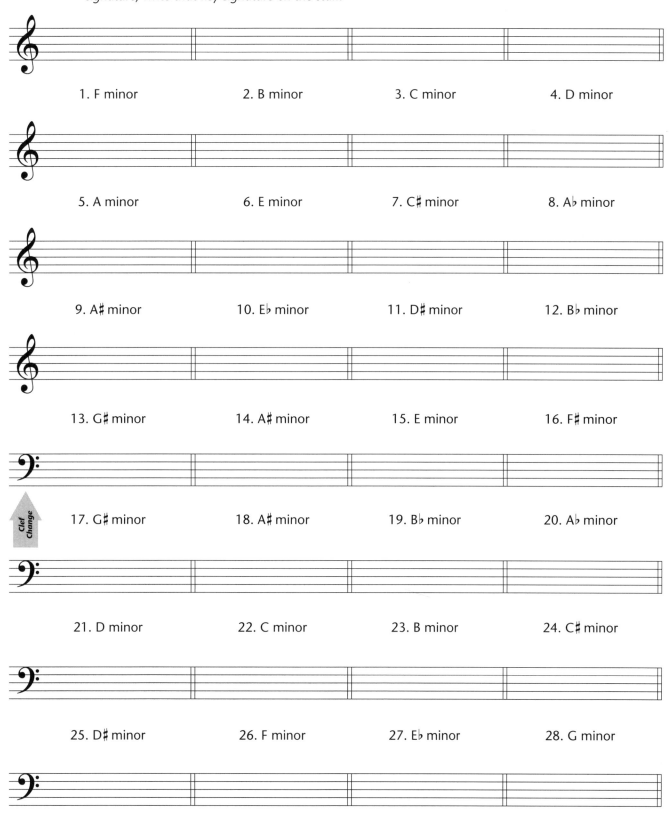

1. F minor   2. B minor   3. C minor   4. D minor

5. A minor   6. E minor   7. C♯ minor   8. A♭ minor

9. A♯ minor   10. E♭ minor   11. D♯ minor   12. B♭ minor

13. G♯ minor   14. A♯ minor   15. E minor   16. F♯ minor

17. G♯ minor   18. A♯ minor   19. B♭ minor   20. A♭ minor

21. D minor   22. C minor   23. B minor   24. C♯ minor

25. D♯ minor   26. F minor   27. E♭ minor   28. G minor

29. F minor   30. C minor   31. B minor   32. A♭ minor

© 2005. Eric Harris. All Rights Reserved.

LESSON 19: MINOR SCALES

1. Each major scale has a minor scale contained within it. The **pure minor*** (sometimes called **natural minor**) scale begins on the sixth scale degree of the relative major scale, follows the musical alphabet pattern for one octave and uses the same key signature. Notice that the sixth note of the major scale becomes the first note of the related pure minor scale.

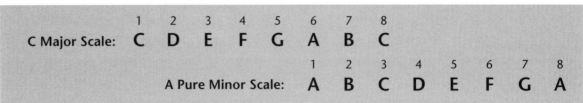

	1	2	3	4	5	6	7	8		
C Major Scale:	C	D	E	F	G	A	B	C		
						1	2	3	4	5	6	7	8
A Pure Minor Scale:						A	B	C	D	E	F	G	A

2. The pure minor scale can also be written using the following step pattern: (W = whole step, H = half step). Notice that half steps occur between 2 and 3 and between 5 and 6.

1	2	3	4	5	6	7	8
A	B	C	D	E	F	G	A
	W	H	W	W	H	W	W

3. The **harmonic minor** scale is a pure minor scale with the seventh scale degree raised one chromatic half step (CHS).

	1	2	3	4	5	6	7	8
C Major Scale:	C	D	E	F	G	A	B	C

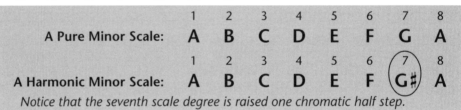

	1	2	3	4	5	6	7	8
A Pure Minor Scale:	A	B	C	D	E	F	G	A
A Harmonic Minor Scale:	A	B	C	D	E	F	G♯	A

Notice that the seventh scale degree is raised one chromatic half step.

4. The harmonic minor scale can also be written using the following step pattern: (W = whole step, H = half step). Notice that a step and a half now exists between 6 and 7.

1	2	3	4	5	6	7	8
A	B	C	D	E	F	G♯	A
	W	H	W	W	H	1 1/2	W

5. The **melodic minor** scale is a pure minor scale with the sixth *and* seventh scale degrees each raised one chromatic half step (CHS).

	1	2	3	4	5	6	7	8
C Major Scale:	C	D	E	F	G	A	B	C

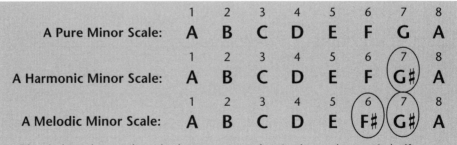

	1	2	3	4	5	6	7	8
A Pure Minor Scale:	A	B	C	D	E	F	G	A
A Harmonic Minor Scale:	A	B	C	D	E	F	G♯	A
A Melodic Minor Scale:	A	B	C	D	E	F♯	G♯	A

The sixth and seventh scale degrees are each raised one chromatic half step.

*Note: The pure minor scale is the same as the aeolian mode. The pure minor scale is sometimes called the aeolian minor scale.

© 2005. Eric Harris. All Rights Reserved.

6. The melodic minor scale can also be written using the following step pattern: (W = whole step, H = half step). Notice that the last four notes of the melodic minor scale follow the same step pattern as the last four notes of a major scale!

     1   2   3   4   5   6   7   8

A   B   C   D   E   F♯ G♯ A

   W   H   W   W   W   W   H

7. The melodic minor scale has an ascending pattern and a descending pattern. The descending melodic minor scale is the same as the descending pure minor scale.

8. The following procedure should be used when students are asked to write any minor scale.

WRITING MINOR SCALES – SUMMARY OF THE PROCESS

- **Determine the relative major key for the requested minor scale.** Do this by building a minor third above the tonic of the requested minor scale.

     Problem: Write a G minor scale.

     Solution: Build a minor third above G to find the major key signature you will use.

     Answer: A minor third above G is B♭. You will use the B♭ major key signature to write the requested scale. It contains two flats – B♭ and E♭.

- **Write the basic alphabet pattern** that will be needed to create the minor scale. The G minor scale will use the G to G alphabet pattern.

     G   A   B   C   D   E   F   G

- **Apply the accidentals from the relative major key signature.** (Remember you determined this information in step one.) For the G minor scale, the relative key signature of B♭ major will be used. Add B♭ and E♭ to the G to G basic pattern.

     G   A   B♭   C   D   E♭   F   G

- **If the harmonic form is requested. Raise the seventh scale degree one chromatic half step (CHS).** *Please note that a mixture of sharps and flats is acceptable in harmonic and melodic minor scales.*

     G   A   B♭   C   D   E♭   (F♯)   G

- **If the melodic form is requested** check to see which pattern (ascending or descending) is requested. If no pattern is specified, **write the ascending form of the scale by raising the sixth and seventh scale degrees of the pure minor scale each one chromatic half step (CHS).** *Please notice that E natural is required to raise the sixth scale degree a half step. Simply writing an E in the scale is acceptable, but the addition of a natural sign (called a "courtesy accidental") is preferred.*

     G   A   B♭   C   D   (E♮)   (F♯)   G

---

9. The term **mode** is often used when referring to scales or keys. You may hear another musician say, "This piece is in the minor mode," meaning that the piece is written using minor scales, or, "This piece is in the major mode," meaning that the piece is written using a major scale. The term "mode" means "scale" or "key."

© 2005. Eric Harris. All Rights Reserved.

Exercise 9.10 - Scale Spell

Directions: Write the requested major and relative minor scales.

1

Major Scale   KEY OF: **C MAJOR**   KEY OF: _____ **minor** (Name the relative minor.)

Pure Minor Scale   (Built on the 6th scale degree of the relative major – uses the same key signature.)

Harmonic Minor Scale   (Same as pure minor with the 7th scale degree raised one CHS.)

Melodic Minor Scale–Ascending   (Same as pure minor with the 6th and 7th scale degrees each raised one CHS.)

2

Major Scale   KEY OF: **D MAJOR**   KEY OF: _____ **minor** (Name the relative minor.)

Pure Minor Scale   (Built on the 6th scale degree of the relative major – uses the same key signature.)

Harmonic Minor Scale   (Same as pure minor with the 7th scale degree raised one CHS.)

Melodic Minor Scale–Ascending   (Same as pure minor with the 6th and 7th scale degrees each raised one CHS.)

3

Major Scale   KEY OF: **F MAJOR**   KEY OF: _____ **minor** (Name the relative minor.)

Pure Minor Scale   (Built on the 6th scale degree of the relative major – uses the same key signature.)

Harmonic Minor Scale   (Same as pure minor with the 7th scale degree raised one CHS.)

Melodic Minor Scale–Ascending   (Same as pure minor with the 6th and 7th scale degrees each raised one CHS.)

© 2005. Eric Harris. All Rights Reserved.

Exercise 9.11 - Scale Spell

Directions: Write the requested major and relative minor scales.

1

Major Scale   KEY OF: **G MAJOR**   KEY OF: _____ **minor** (Name the relative minor.)

Pure Minor Scale   (Built on the 6th scale degree of the relative major – uses the same key signature.)

Harmonic Minor Scale   (Same as pure minor with the 7th scale degree raised one CHS.)

Melodic Minor Scale–Ascending   (Same as pure minor with the 6th and 7th scale degrees each raised one CHS.)

2

Major Scale   KEY OF: **A♭ MAJOR**   KEY OF: _____ **minor** (Name the relative minor.)

Pure Minor Scale   (Built on the 6th scale degree of the relative major – uses the same key signature.)

Harmonic Minor Scale   (Same as pure minor with the 7th scale degree raised one CHS.)

Melodic Minor Scale–Ascending   (Same as pure minor with the 6th and 7th scale degrees each raised one CHS.)

3

Major Scale   KEY OF: **F♯ MAJOR**   KEY OF: _____ **minor** (Name the relative minor.)

Pure Minor Scale   (Built on the 6th scale degree of the relative major – uses the same key signature.)

Harmonic Minor Scale   (Same as pure minor with the 7th scale degree raised one CHS.)

Melodic Minor Scale–Ascending   (Same as pure minor with the 6th and 7th scale degrees each raised one CHS.)

© 2005. Eric Harris. All Rights Reserved.

Exercise 9.12 - Scale Spell

Directions: Write the requested major and relative minor scales.

1

Major Scale KEY OF: **C♭ MAJOR** KEY OF: _____ **minor** (Name the relative minor.)

Pure Minor Scale (Built on the 6th scale degree of the relative major – uses the same key signature.)

Harmonic Minor Scale (Same as pure minor with the 7th scale degree raised one CHS.)

Melodic Minor Scale–Ascending (Same as pure minor with the 6th and 7th scale degrees each raised one CHS.)

2

Major Scale KEY OF: **E MAJOR** KEY OF: _____ **minor** (Name the relative minor.)

Pure Minor Scale (Built on the 6th scale degree of the relative major – uses the same key signature.)

Harmonic Minor Scale (Same as pure minor with the 7th scale degree raised one CHS.)

Melodic Minor Scale–Ascending (Same as pure minor with the 6th and 7th scale degrees each raised one CHS.)

3

Major Scale KEY OF: **B♭ MAJOR** KEY OF: _____ **minor** (Name the relative minor.)

Pure Minor Scale (Built on the 6th scale degree of the relative major – uses the same key signature.)

Harmonic Minor Scale (Same as pure minor with the 7th scale degree raised one CHS.)

Melodic Minor Scale–Ascending (Same as pure minor with the 6th and 7th scale degrees each raised one CHS.)

© 2005. Eric Harris. All Rights Reserved.

Exercise 9.13 - Scale Spell

Directions: Write the requested major and relative minor scales.

1

Major Scale   KEY OF: **D♭ MAJOR**   KEY OF: _____ **minor** (Name the relative minor.)

Pure Minor Scale   (Built on the 6th scale degree of the relative major – uses the same key signature.)

Harmonic Minor Scale   (Same as pure minor with the 7th scale degree raised one CHS.)

Melodic Minor Scale–Ascending   (Same as pure minor with the 6th and 7th scale degrees each raised one CHS.)

2

Major Scale   KEY OF: **A MAJOR**   KEY OF: _____ **minor** (Name the relative minor.)

Pure Minor Scale   (Built on the 6th scale degree of the relative major – uses the same key signature.)

Harmonic Minor Scale   (Same as pure minor with the 7th scale degree raised one CHS.)

Melodic Minor Scale–Ascending   (Same as pure minor with the 6th and 7th scale degrees each raised one CHS.)

3

Major Scale   KEY OF: **C♯ MAJOR**   KEY OF: _____ **minor** (Name the relative minor.)

Pure Minor Scale   (Built on the 6th scale degree of the relative major – uses the same key signature.)

Harmonic Minor Scale   (Same as pure minor with the 7th scale degree raised one CHS.)

Melodic Minor Scale–Ascending   (Same as pure minor with the 6th and 7th scale degrees each raised one CHS.)

© 2005. Eric Harris. All Rights Reserved.

Exercise 9.14 - Scale Spell

Directions: Write the requested major and relative minor scales.

1

Major Scale   KEY OF: **G♭ MAJOR**   KEY OF: _____ **minor** (Name the relative minor.)

Pure Minor Scale   (Built on the 6th scale degree of the relative major – uses the same key signature.)

Harmonic Minor Scale   (Same as pure minor with the 7th scale degree raised one CHS.)

Melodic Minor Scale–Ascending   (Same as pure minor with the 6th and 7th scale degrees each raised one CHS.)

2

Major Scale   KEY OF: **B MAJOR**   KEY OF: _____ **minor** (Name the relative minor.)

Pure Minor Scale   (Built on the 6th scale degree of the relative major – uses the same key signature.)

Harmonic Minor Scale   (Same as pure minor with the 7th scale degree raised one CHS.)

Melodic Minor Scale–Ascending   (Same as pure minor with the 6th and 7th scale degrees each raised one CHS.)

3

Major Scale   KEY OF: **E♭ MAJOR**   KEY OF: _____ **minor** (Name the relative minor.)

Pure Minor Scale   (Built on the 6th scale degree of the relative major – uses the same key signature.)

Harmonic Minor Scale   (Same as pure minor with the 7th scale degree raised one CHS.)

Melodic Minor Scale–Ascending   (Same as pure minor with the 6th and 7th scale degrees each raised one CHS.)

© 2005. Eric Harris. All Rights Reserved.

LESSON 20: USE OF THE MINOR SCALE

1. Each version of the minor scale (pure, harmonic, melodic) has a special purpose which has evolved over hundreds of years of music history.

2. The pure minor scale is actually a mode – the aeolian mode. Both the aeolian mode and the natural minor scale can be created by playing a major scale from scale degree six to scale degree six (keeping the key signature of course). In G major this would be: E, F♯, G, A, B, C, D, E. (6 to 6)

   E Aeolian Mode   **E F♯ G A B C D E**

   E Pure Minor   **E F♯ G A B C D E**

3. The harmonic form of the minor scale (as its name implies) is used for harmonies and chord patterns. Chords are created by stacking pitches one over the other. The music below is a chorale written by J.S. Bach and is in the key of E minor. Notice the appearance of D♯ in the shaded boxes – indicating the use of the harmonic form of the scale. The D♮ in measure two is being used melodically.

   E Harmonic Minor   **E F♯ G A B C D♯ E**   (Notice the raised seventh scale degree: D♯)

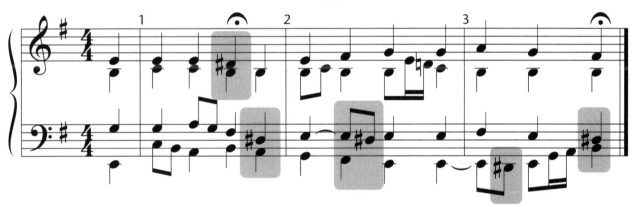

4. The melodic form of the minor scale (as its name implies) is used for melodies. The ascending form of the scale (with its raised sixth and seventh scale degrees) sounds like the last four notes of the major scale and allows the leading tone to move smoothly up a half step to tonic (unlike the harmonic form which has three half steps between scale degrees six and seven). When the melody line descends, the scale returns to its pure form creating a unique major/minor sound that no other scale can provide. Look at the Bach melody shown below. Notice that when the melody ascends, the sixth and seventh scale degrees are raised (C♯ and D♯). But when the melody descends, they are lowered (C♮ and D♮).

   E Melodic Minor–
   Ascending   **E F♯ G A B C♯ D♯ E**   (Notice the raised sixth and seventh scale degrees: C♯ and D♯)

   E Melodic Minor–
   Descending   **E D C B A G F E**

5. It is important for students to understand that the accidentals required to create the harmonic and melodic (ascending) forms of the minor scale will not appear in the key signature. They appear, where needed, in individual measures. Since major and relative minor keys share the same key signature, these accidentals can often be a good clue as to whether the piece is written in major or minor. A careful look at the last note of the piece and also "giving it a listen" are other good ways to determine this information.

© 2005. Eric Harris. All Rights Reserved.

Exercise 9.15 - Writing Minor Scales On The Staff

Directions: Write the requested minor scales, ascending and descending, on the staves provided below. (Space your notes evenly across the staff as in the example below.) Finally, try playing these scales on the piano or on your instrument. Watch for clef changes.

D Pure Minor

1

C Harmonic Minor

2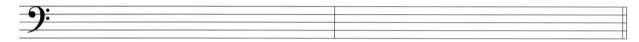

A♭ Pure Minor

3

F♯ Melodic Minor

4

B Harmonic Minor

5

A Pure Minor

6

E♭ Melodic Minor

7

© 2005. Eric Harris. All Rights Reserved.

Exercise 9.16 - Writing Minor Scales On The Staff

Directions: Write the requested minor scales, ascending and descending, on the staves provided below. You pick the octave. Finally, try playing these scales on the piano or on your instrument. Watch for clef changes.

1 Bb Pure Minor

2 E Harmonic Minor

3 F Melodic Minor

4 G# Pure Minor

5 Bb Harmonic Minor

6 Ab Melodic Minor

7 F Pure Minor

© 2005. Eric Harris. All Rights Reserved.

Exercise 9.17 - Writing Minor Scales On The Staff

Directions: Write the requested minor scales, ascending and descending, on the staves provided below. You pick the octave. Finally, try playing these scales on the piano or on your instrument. Watch for clef changes.

F# Harmonic Minor

1

G Melodic Minor

2

G# Melodic Minor

3

A# Pure Minor

4

Eb Harmonic Minor

5

C Melodic Minor

6

D# Pure Minor

7

© 2005. Eric Harris. All Rights Reserved.

Exercise 9.18 - Writing Minor Scales On The Staff

Directions: Write the requested minor scales, ascending and descending, on the staves provided below. You pick the octave. Finally, try playing these scales on the piano or on your instrument. Watch for clef changes.

A♯ Melodic Minor

1

B Pure Minor

2

C Pure Minor

3

G♯ Harmonic Minor

4

B♭ Melodic Minor

5

D Harmonic Minor

6

F♯ Pure Minor

7

© 2005. Eric Harris. All Rights Reserved.

Exercise 9.19 - Writing Minor Scales On The Staff

Directions: Write the requested minor scales, ascending and descending, on the staves provided below. You pick the octave. Finally, try playing these scales on the piano or on your instrument. Watch for clef changes.

A♯ Harmonic Minor

1

A Harmonic Minor

2

G Pure Minor

3

D♯ Melodic Minor

4

A♭ Harmonic Minor

5

E Pure Minor

6

C♯ Harmonic Minor

7

© 2005. Eric Harris. All Rights Reserved.

Exercise 9.20 - Writing Minor Scales On The Staff

Directions: Write the requested minor scales, ascending and descending, on the staves provided below. You pick the octave. Finally, try playing these scales on the piano or on your instrument. Watch for clef changes.

D Melodic Minor

1

C♯ Melodic Minor

2

G Harmonic Minor

3

F Harmonic Minor

4

E Melodic Minor

5

D♯ Harmonic Minor

6

E♭ Pure Minor

7

© 2005. Eric Harris. All Rights Reserved.

Exercise 9.21 - Identifying Major and Minor Scales

Directions: Name the tonic and type (major, pure minor, harmonic minor, or melodic minor) for each scale given below. Watch for clef changes.

1. _____ 2. _____

3. _____ 4. _____

5. _____ 6. _____

7. _____ 8. _____

9. _____ 10. _____

11. _____ 12. _____

13. _____ 14. _____

15. _____ 16. _____

© 2005. Eric Harris. All Rights Reserved.

LESSON 21: PARALLEL MINOR

1. Major and minor scales that share the same tonic* are called **parallel** scales. C major and C minor are parallel. (C major is the parallel major of C minor; C minor is the parallel minor of C major.)

2. To transform any major scale into its parallel minor, use the following procedure:

    *   Write the major scale:

1	2	3	4	5	6	7	8
C	D	E	F	G	A	B	C

    *   To create pure minor, lower scale degrees 3, 6, and 7 each one chromatic half step.

1	2	3	4	5	6	7	8
C	D	Eb	F	G	Ab	Bb	C

    *   To create harmonic minor, lower scale degrees 3 and 6 each one chromatic half step.

1	2	3	4	5	6	7	8
C	D	Eb	F	G	Ab	B	C

    *   To create melodic minor (ascending form), lower scale degree 3 one chromatic half step. This example shows clearly an important point: the last four notes of the melodic minor scale are the same as the last four notes of the parallel major scale.

1	2	3	4	5	6	7	8
C	D	Eb	F	G	A	B	C

Exercise 9.22 - Parallel Major and Minor Scales

Directions: You are given the major scale. Name the parallel minor scale.

1. G M	2. F M	3. Bb M	4. E M	5. B M	6. Db M	7. Ab M

Directions: Take the major scales below and lower the required notes to create the requested form of the parallel minor. Write the requested parallel minor scale in the blanks provided.

1. A B C# D E F# G# A
    Convert to A Pure Minor

    ___ ___ ___ ___ ___ ___ ___ ___

2. Eb F G Ab Bb C D Eb
    Convert to Eb Pure Minor

    ___ ___ ___ ___ ___ ___ ___ ___

3. Bb C D Eb F G A Bb
    Convert to Bb Harmonic Minor

    ___ ___ ___ ___ ___ ___ ___ ___

4. G A B C D E F# G
    Convert to G Harmonic Minor

    ___ ___ ___ ___ ___ ___ ___ ___

5. F# G# A# B C# D# E# F#
    Convert to F# Melodic Minor

    ___ ___ ___ ___ ___ ___ ___ ___

6. D E F# G A B C# D
    Convert to D Harmonic Minor

    ___ ___ ___ ___ ___ ___ ___ ___

---

* Proper scale degree names for notes in the minor scale are the same as those in the major scale. Two exceptions, however, do exist. In pure minor, the seventh scale degree is called the **subtonic** – because is lies a whole step below tonic (unlike the leading tone which lies a half step below tonic). Finally, the sixth scale degree in melodic minor ascending is called the raised **submediant**.

© 2005. Eric Harris. All Rights Reserved.

Unit Review Questions

Directions: Answer the questions below.

1. _____ Each major scale shares its key signature with a ? scale.

2. _____ Scales that share key signatures are said to be ?

3. _____ If we are given the name of a major scale or key, we can find the name of the relative minor by counting down a ?

4. _____ The sixth note of the major scale is also the ? note of the relative minor scale.

5. _____ If we are given the name of a minor scale or key, we can find the name of the relative major by counting up a ?

6. _____ The letter names of ? keys are sometimes written in lowercase.

7. _____ This form of the minor scale begins on the sixth note of the relative major, and uses the same key signature.

8. _____ This form of the minor scale is the same as pure minor with the seventh scale degree raised one chromatic half step.

9. _____ This form of the minor scale is the same as pure minor with the sixth and seventh scale degrees each raised one chromatic half step.

10. _____ The melodic form of the minor scale has two patterns: ascending and ?

11. _____ Descending melodic minor and descending ? are the exact same scale.

12. _____ This form of the minor scale uses a step and a half (three half steps) between scale degrees 6 and 7.

13. _____ This form of the minor scale uses a step pattern for the last four notes that is the same as the step pattern for the last four notes of the major scale.

14. _____ This form of the minor scale is the same as the aeolian mode.

15. _____ This form of the minor scale is used for harmonies and chord patterns.

16. _____ This form of the minor scale is used for melodies.

17. _____ The accidentals required for the harmonic and melodic forms of the minor scale (will/will not) appear in the key signature.

18. _____ When a major scale and a minor scale share the same tonic they are said to be ?

19. _____ To convert a major scale to its parallel pure form, lower scale degrees ?, ?, and ? each one chromatic half step.

20. _____ To convert a major scale to its parallel harmonic form, lower scale degrees ? and ? each one chromatic half step.

21. _____ To convert a major scale to its parallel melodic form, lower scale degree ? one chromatic half step.

© 2005. Eric Harris. All Rights Reserved.

LESSON 22: THREE-EIGHT TIME

1. Three-eight time is classified as a simple time signature and may be counted as such. The counting sample below shows the same method used for three-four time. The only difference is the beat value, which in this case is the eighth note (three eighth notes in each measure).

Three-Eight Time – Simple Time Counting Method

2. However, many students find it easier to count three-eight time like a half measure of six-eight time using the 1-la-le system. This is especially true when this meter is played at faster tempos. Compare the following three-eight sample with the six-eight sample placed below it.

Three-Eight Time – Compound Time Counting Method

3. Three-eight time can be counted just like six-eight time. The only difference is the total number of beats in each measure. In six-eight time, there are two beats (two dotted-quarter notes) in each measure. In three-eight time, there is one beat (one dotted-quarter note) in each measure.

4. When counting three-eight time like a compound meter, each measure will only contain one beat – other beat numbers will not appear (like 2, 3, or 4). For this reason, counting three-eight time in this manner is called "counting in one" – because there is only one complete beat counted in each measure.

Exercise 10.1 - Counting Exercise

Directions: Write the counting under each measure of rhythm below. Use the counting method preferred by your teacher.

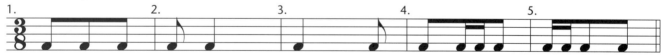

© 2005. Eric Harris. All Rights Reserved.

LESSON 23: TWO-TWO (CUT) TIME

1. Two-two time is also known as **cut-time** and is indicated with 𝄵 written in place of the time signature.

2. In two-two time, there are two beats in each measure and the half note gets one beat.
    Two-two time looks exactly like four-four time, but the counting (and playing) is very different.

3. In two-two time, notes receive half the number of beats they normally receive in four-four time.
    The values have been "cut" in half, hence the nickname "cut-time." Study the chart below.

whole note	𝅝	gets **2 beats**	(Counted like a half note in four-four time.)
half note	𝅗𝅥	gets **1 beat**	(Counted like a quarter note in four-four time.)
quarter note	𝅘𝅥	gets **1/2 beat**	(Counted like an eighth note in four-four time.)
eighth note	𝅘𝅥𝅮	gets **1/4 beat**	(Counted like a sixteenth note in four-four time.)

4. Study the following rhythm figures. Each is shown in two-two time and two-four time for comparison.
    Each pair will sound and be played exactly alike – the only difference is the notation.

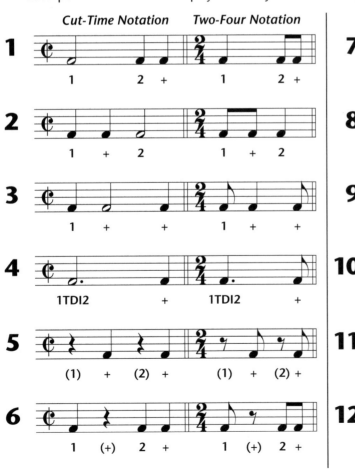

© 2005. Eric Harris. All Rights Reserved.

Exercise 10.2 - Counting Exercise

Directions: Write the counting under each measure of rhythm below. Several of these are tricky. Be careful!

LESSON 24: THREE-TWO & FOUR-TWO TIME

1. Three-two and four-two time are counted just like two-two (cut) time. The only difference is the number of beats in each measure.

2. Each measure of two-two (cut) time will contain two half notes or some combination of notes and rests that equals two half notes. Each measure of three-two time will contain three half notes or some combination of notes and rests that equals three half notes. Each measure of four-two time will contain four half notes or some combination of notes and rests that equals four half notes.

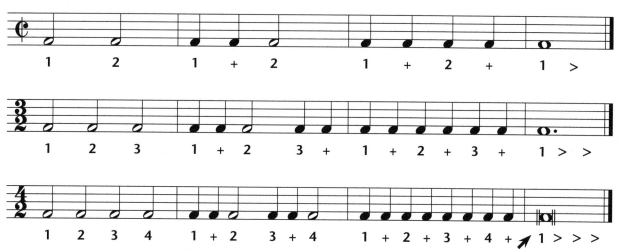

*This rare note value is called a **breve** or **double whole note**.*
It equals two whole notes (or four half notes).

© 2005. Eric Harris. All Rights Reserved.

LESSON 25: FIVE-EIGHT & SEVEN-EIGHT TIME

1. Simple meter contains groups or divisions of two. Compound meter contains groups or divisions of three.

2. **Hybrid meter*** contains elements which are simple (a group of two) and elements which are compound (a group of three). Five-eight and seven-eight time are examples of hybrid meter.

3. In five-eight time, there will be a group of two eighth notes (or some notational equivalent) and a group of three eighth notes (or some notational equivalent). The groupings in five-eight time can be (2 + 3) or (3 + 2).

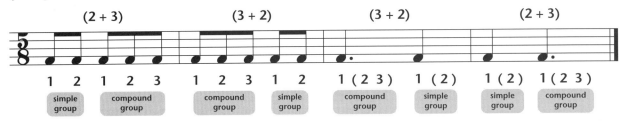

4. In seven-eight time, there will be *two* groups of two eighth notes (or some notational equivalent) and a group of three eighth notes (or some notational equivalent). The groupings in seven-eight time can be (2 + 2 + 3), (3 + 2 + 2), or (2 + 3 + 2).

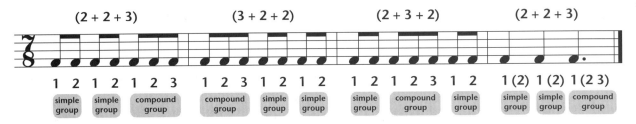

5. Counting rhythms in five-eight and seven-eight can be accomplished in two ways:

   • by counting pairs (or notes which represent pairs) as "one-two;" and by counting triplets (or notes which represent triplets) as "one-two-three." This is the most common approach.

   • by counting pairs (or notes which represent pairs) as "one-and;" and by counting triplets (or notes which represent triplets) as "1-la-le." This method follows the counting system students have already learned.

6. Borrowed divisions do not exist in hybrid meter. Both simple and compound elements exist in *every* measure of hybrid meter.

*Hybrid meter can also be called irregular meter or asymmetrical meter.

© 2005. Eric Harris. All Rights Reserved.

Exercise 10.3 - Funky Rhythm Review I

Directions: Many previously learned rhythms are included in this exercise. Write the counting under each measure. Then try playing the rhythms on your tuning note.

© 2005. Eric Harris. All Rights Reserved.

Exercise 10.4 - Funky Rhythm Review II

Directions: Many previously learned rhythms are included in this exercise. Write the counting under each measure. Then try playing the rhythms on your tuning note.

© 2005. Eric Harris. All Rights Reserved.

Exercise 10.5 - Funky Rhythm Review III

Directions: Many previously learned rhythms are included in this exercise. Write the counting under each measure. Then try playing the rhythms on your tuning note.

© 2005. Eric Harris. All Rights Reserved.

LESSON 26: FIVE-FOUR & SEVEN-FOUR TIME

1. Five-four time is considered a hybrid meter because of its groups of two quarter notes and three quarter notes.

2. Five-four time can be counted like alternating measures of two-four and three-four time. The groupings can be (2 + 3) or (3 + 2). Five-four can also be counted with five independent beats in each measure (like a measure of four-four with one extra beat). Both counting methods are shown below.

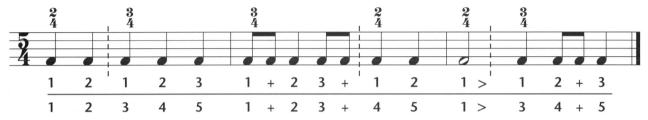

3. Seven-four time is also considered to be a hybrid meter because it contains groups of three quarter notes and groups of two quarter notes (two groups of two create the group of four).

4. Seven-four time is very rare and is used when composers wish to avoid constant changes between three-four and four-four time. Seven-four is counted just like alternating measures of three-four and four-four time. The groupings can be (3 + 4) or (4 + 3). Only one counting method is used for seven-four time.

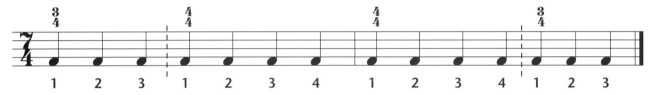

Note: An excellent example of seven-four time, and one that is easily playable by most high school bands, occurs in Clifton Williams' *Dedicatory Overture*. Each measure of seven-four includes dotted lines showing the division of three and four beats. Students will quickly understand this meter concept if the introduction of this lesson is followed by a short reading session of this excellent work.

LESSON 27: COUNTING THIRTY-SECOND NOTES

1. Thirty-second notes are found in more difficult band literature and are counted by adding the syllable "ta" after each of the sixteenth note syllables: **1** - **ta** - **e** - **ta** - **+** - **ta** - **a** - **ta**.

2. Remember that thirty-second notes use three beams (or three flags) and that two thirty-second notes equal one sixteenth note. Thirty-second rests also have three flags.

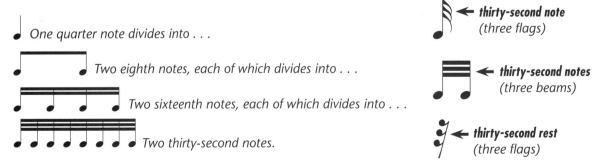

One quarter note divides into . . .

Two eighth notes, each of which divides into . . .

Two sixteenth notes, each of which divides into . . .

Two thirty-second notes.

← thirty-second note (three flags)

← thirty-second notes (three beams)

← thirty-second rest (three flags)

© 2005. Eric Harris. All Rights Reserved.

LESSON 28: COMPARING METERS

1. The chart below shows most of the simple and compound time signatures that students might encounter. Notice that the beat value and division value are given for each time signature. Notice the 2:1 division values in simple time and the 3:1 division values in compound time.

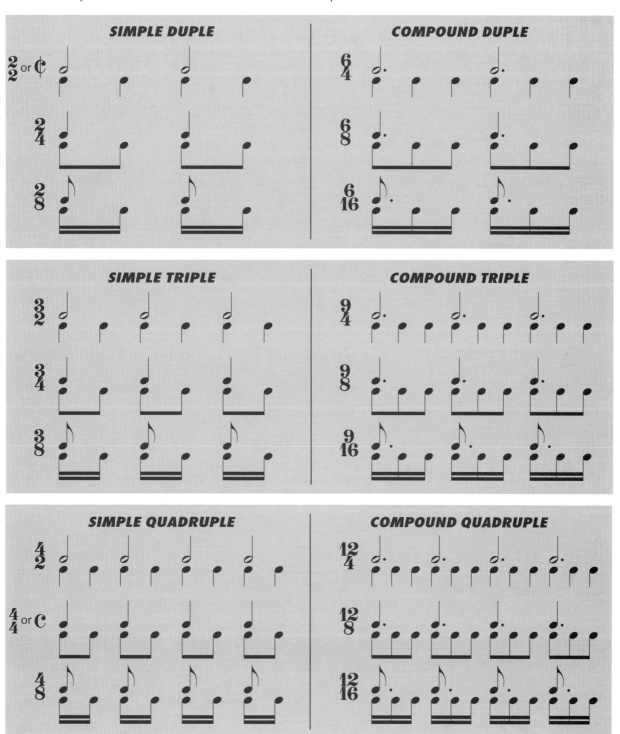

2. By applying the counting systems used for 2/4, 3/4, and 4/4 time and the counting system used for 6/8, 9/8, and 12/8 time, students should be able to count basic rhythms in any of the meters shown above.

© 2005. Eric Harris. All Rights Reserved.

LESSON 29: TRIPLET GROUPINGS

1. We have learned to count triplets using the 1-la-le method. Students must realize, however, that triplets do not always appear in neat groups of three. Sometimes rests are used and sometimes other note values can be included. Look at the examples below. These are the six most common types of triplet groupings.

1 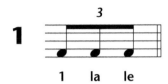   Three of a note value written in the same time/space as two is the most common triplet grouping and the one that you learned first.

2    Here the beat number is replaced with a rest. Brackets are used when triplet groups begin or end with a rest.

3    Here "Le" is replaced with a rest. Again, notice the use of the bracket to clearly indicate the triplet group.

4    Here "La" is replaced with a rest. No bracket is needed – just the number. The beam is sufficient to clarify the triplet group.

5    Here the last two eighth notes are combined into a single quarter note. This is counted just like the compound time figure you've seen many times before (only without the bracket).

6    Here the first two eighth notes are combined into a single quarter note. Again, this is counted just like the compound time figure you've seen many times before (only without the bracket).

2. Remember, triplets are borrowed from compound time, so all the figures above should be very familiar to you. Study the counting sample below.

© 2005. Eric Harris. All Rights Reserved.

Unit Review Questions

Directions: Answer the questions below.

1. _____ Three-eight time is classified as a simple time signature but can be counted like a ? time signature.

2. _____ Three-eight time looks (and can be counted) like a half measure of ? time.

3. _____ When counting three-eight time using the 1-la-le method, there is only one beat in each measure. For this reason, counting three-eight time in this manner is called counting in ?

4. _____ Two-two time is also known as ? time.

5. _____ Cut-time is indicated with a large ? written in place of the time signature. (Draw the symbol in the blank.)

6. _____ In two-two (cut) time, there are two beats in each measure and the ? note gets one beat.

7. _____ Two-two (cut) time looks like four-four time but the ? (and playing) is different.

8. _____ In two-two (cut) time, notes receive ? the number of beats they normally receive in four-four time.

9. _____ In two-two (cut) time, a whole note gets ? beats.

10. _____ In two-two (cut) time, a half note gets ? beat.

11. _____ In two-two (cut) time, a quarter note gets ? beat.

12. _____ In two-two (cut) time, an eighth note gets ? beat.

13. _____ Three-two time and four-two time are counted just like two-two (cut) time, the only difference is the total number of ? in each measure.

14. _____ In four-two time, this single note value is used to fill an entire measure with sound. (Name it and draw it.)

15. _____ Hybrid meters have features which are both ? and ? (Write both answers in blank.)

16. _____ Write the two possible groupings for five-eight time. (Write the answers one above the other in the blank.)

17. _____ Write the three possible groupings for seven-eight time.

18. _____ Borrowed divisions (do/do not) exist in hybrid meter.

19. _____ Five-four time is counted just like alternating measures of ? and ? time.

20. _____ Seven-four time is counted just like alternating measures of ? and ? time.

21. _____ Thirty-second notes have ? flags (or beams).

22. _____ Two thirty-second notes equal one ? note.

© 2005. Eric Harris. All Rights Reserved.

LESSON 30: TRIADS

1. A **chord** is a musical structure that is created when three or more notes are played simultaneously (at the same time).

2. A **triad** is a three note chord.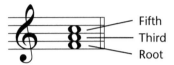

3. Each note in a triad has a functional name in addition to a pitch name.
    The **root** is the fundamental pitch on which the triad is built. It gives the chord its name.
    The **third** is the middle pitch in a triad. It is named such because it is built a third above the root.
    The **fifth** is the top pitch in a triad. It is named such because it is built a fifth above the root.

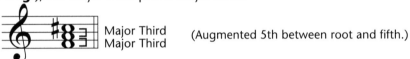

4. There are four types of triads used in most Western* music. Also shown are abbreviations for each quality.
    An **augmented** triad (**+ or aug.**), is a Major third plus a Major third.

    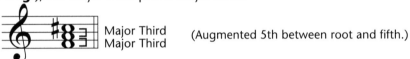 Major Third / Major Third   (Augmented 5th between root and fifth.)

    A **major** triad (**M or maj.**), is a major third plus a minor third.

     Minor Third / Major Third   (Perfect 5th between root and fifth.)

    A **minor** triad (**m or min.**), is a minor third plus a major third.

     Major Third / Minor Third   (Perfect 5th between root and fifth.)

    A **diminished** triad (**o or dim.**), is a minor third plus a minor third.

    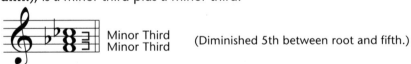 Minor Third / Minor Third   (Diminished 5th between root and fifth.)

5. If we look at the interval construction of triads, we can see that the augmented triad is the largest because it contains a major third plus a major third. A diminished triad is the smallest because it contains a minor third plus a minor third. To avoid confusion in remembering interval combinations for major and minor triads (because they both contain a major third and a minor third) just remember the interval on the bottom determines the quality of the triad. A major triad has a major third on the bottom. A minor triad has a minor third on the bottom.

6. Many musicians use the major scale to help them spell triads. For example:
    A major triad is the first, third, and fifth note of the major scale. (C-E-G)
    A minor triad is a major triad with the third lowered one chromatic half step. (C-E♭-G)
    An augmented triad is a major triad with the fifth raised one chromatic half step. (C-E-G♯)
    A diminished triad is a major triad with the third and fifth each lowered one chromatic half step. (C-E♭-G♭)

*The term "Western Music" is used to refer to music of the European and North American continents written between 1600 and 1950. Western Music is **tertian** (which means made of thirds – look at the triads above). Our scales are based on the whole step and half step. Music from other cultures often uses a much different set of "building blocks." Music of the Middle East, for example, uses quarter tones (half of a half step). The fundamentals you are learning in this series are the fundamentals of Western Music. These concepts are so important they are studied not only by musicians from Europe and North America but also from many other countries around the world.

168

© 2005. Eric Harris. All Rights Reserved.

7. When spelling major triads it is important to remember the following:
   Major triads built on C, F, and G will have the same accidental or lack thereof on each note in the chord.

C-E-G	F-A-C	G-B-D
C♯-E♯-G♯	F♯-A♯-C♯	G♯-B♯-D♯
C♭-E♭-G♭	F♭-A♭-C♭	G♭-B♭-D♭

Major triads built on D, E, and A will have a third that is one accidental higher than the root or fifth.

D-F♯-A	E-G♯-B	A-C♯-E	→ *The sharp is higher than the natural.*
D♭-F-A♭	E♭-G-B♭	A♭-C-E♭	→ *The natural is higher than the flat.*
D♯-F𝄪-A♯	E♯-G𝄪-B♯	A♯-C𝄪-E♯	→ *The double sharp is higher than the sharp.*

Major triads built on B will have a third and fifth that are one accidental higher than the root.

B-D♯-F♯ → *The sharp is higher than the natural.*
B♭-D-F → *The natural is higher than the flat.*
B♯-D𝄪-F𝄪 → *The double sharp is higher than the sharp.*
B♭♭-D♭-F♭ → *The flat is higher than the double flat.*

8. All triads are written on consecutive lines (line, line, line) or consecutive spaces (space, space, space). As such, they will always use skipped letter names. Below are all of the basic triad spellings. All other triads are spelled by adding sharps, flats, double sharps, or double flats to these basic spellings. Other clefs and other octaves may, of course, be used.

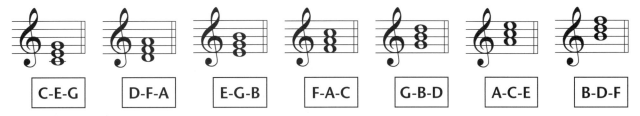

| C-E-G | D-F-A | E-G-B | F-A-C | G-B-D | A-C-E | B-D-F |

9. If asked to spell a triad above a non-tonic tone, remove the accidental from the root, spell the triad, and re-apply the removed accidental to all chord tones (root, third, and fifth).

Problem:	Spell a major triad above E♯.
Solution:	Remove the sharp from the root. Spell a major triad above E: E-G♯-B
	Re-apply the removed accidental to all chord tones: E♯-G𝄪-B♯
	Notice that G♯ becomes G𝄪 when the removed sharp is re-applied to all chord tones.

Problem:	Spell a diminished triad above B♯.
Solution:	Remove the sharp from the root. Spell a diminished triad above B: B-D-F
	Reapply the removed accidental to all chord tones: B♯-D♯-F♯

SPELLING TRIADS – A SUMMARY OF THE MOST COMMON PROCESS (THE EASY WAY)

- Begin by spelling a major triad (the first, third, and fifth note of a major scale). Lower the third a chromatic half step to make it minor; lower the third and fifth a chromatic half step to make it diminished; or raise the fifth a chromatic half step to make it augmented.

- If the given root is not a tonic tone, remove the accidental, spell the triad, then re-apply the removed accidental to each note in the chord (all chord tones).

© 2005. Eric Harris. All Rights Reserved.

Exercise 11.1 - Spelling Major Triads

Directions: Using the first, third, and fifth notes of the major scale, spell the requested major triads below. You may also choose to spell them using interval construction (M3 + m3).

1. C major

   Root   Third   Fifth

2. F major

   Root   Third   Fifth

3. G major

   Root   Third   Fifth

4. D major

   Root   Third   Fifth

5. E major

   Root   Third   Fifth

6. A major

   Root   Third   Fifth

7. B major

   Root   Third   Fifth

8. Db major

   R   3   5

9. F# major

   R   3   5

10. Eb major

   R   3   5

11. Gb major

   R   3   5

12. C# major

   R   3   5

13. Bb major

   R   3   5

14. Ab major

   R   3   5

Exercise 11.2 - Spelling Minor Triads

Directions: Look at the major triads written in exercise 11.1. Lower the third of each triad one chromatic half step to make the minor triads requested below. You may also choose to spell them using interval construction (m3 + M3).

1. C minor

   Root   Third   Fifth

2. F minor

   Root   Third   Fifth

3. G minor

   Root   Third   Fifth

4. D minor

   Root   Third   Fifth

5. E minor

   Root   Third   Fifth

6. A minor

   Root   Third   Fifth

7. B minor

   Root   Third   Fifth

8. Db minor

   R   3   5

9. F# minor

   R   3   5

10. Eb minor

   R   3   5

11. Gb minor

   R   3   5

12. C# minor

   R   3   5

13. Bb minor

   R   3   5

14. Ab minor

   R   3   5

© 2005. Eric Harris. All Rights Reserved.

Exercise 11.3 - Spelling Diminished Triads

Directions: Look at the major triads written in exercise 11.1. Lower the third and fifth of each triad one chromatic half step to make the diminished triads requested below. You may also choose to spell them using interval construction (m3 + m3).

1. C diminished ___ ___ ___
   Root Third Fifth

2. F diminished ___ ___ ___
   Root Third Fifth

3. G diminished ___ ___ ___
   Root Third Fifth

4. D diminished ___ ___ ___
   Root Third Fifth

5. E diminished ___ ___ ___
   Root Third Fifth

6. A diminished ___ ___ ___
   Root Third Fifth

7. B diminished ___ ___ ___
   Root Third Fifth

8. D♭ diminished ___ ___ ___
   R 3 5

9. F♯ diminished ___ ___ ___
   R 3 5

10. E♭ diminished ___ ___ ___
    R 3 5

11. G♭ diminished ___ ___ ___
    R 3 5

12. C♯ diminished ___ ___ ___
    R 3 5

13. B♭ diminished ___ ___ ___
    R 3 5

14. A♭ diminished ___ ___ ___
    R 3 5

Exercise 11.4 - Spelling Augmented Triads

Directions: Look at the major triads written in exercise 11.1. Raise the fifth of each triad one chromatic half step to make the augmented triads requested below. You may also choose to spell them using interval construction (M3 + M3).

1. C augmented ___ ___ ___
   Root Third Fifth

2. F augmented ___ ___ ___
   Root Third Fifth

3. G augmented ___ ___ ___
   Root Third Fifth

4. D augmented ___ ___ ___
   Root Third Fifth

5. E augmented ___ ___ ___
   Root Third Fifth

6. A augmented ___ ___ ___
   Root Third Fifth

7. B augmented ___ ___ ___
   Root Third Fifth

8. D♭ augmented ___ ___ ___
   R 3 5

9. F♯ augmented ___ ___ ___
   R 3 5

10. E♭ augmented ___ ___ ___
    R 3 5

11. G♭ augmented ___ ___ ___
    R 3 5

12. C♯ augmented ___ ___ ___
    R 3 5

13. B♭ augmented ___ ___ ___
    R 3 5

14. A♭ augmented ___ ___ ___
    R 3 5

© 2005. Eric Harris. All Rights Reserved.

Exercise 11.5 - Spelling Triads On The Piano Keyboard

Directions: Spell the requested triad, then mark the corresponding piano keys with dots.

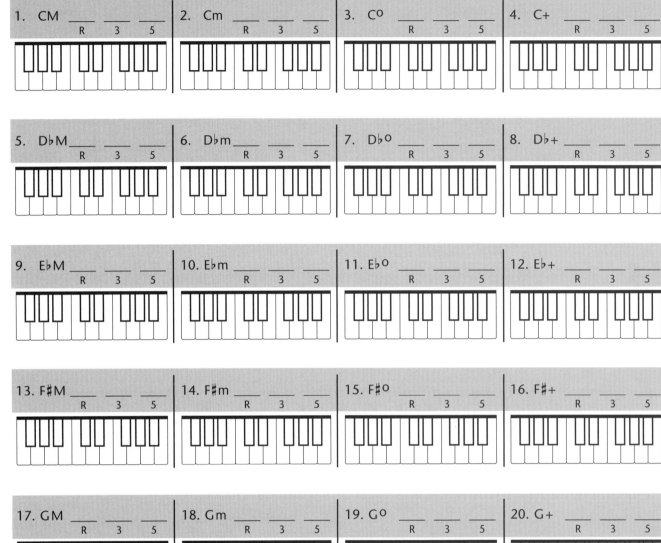

1. CM ___ ___ ___
   R   3   5

2. Cm ___ ___ ___
   R   3   5

3. C° ___ ___ ___
   R   3   5

4. C+ ___ ___ ___
   R   3   5

5. D♭M ___ ___ ___
   R   3   5

6. D♭m ___ ___ ___
   R   3   5

7. D♭° ___ ___ ___
   R   3   5

8. D♭+ ___ ___ ___
   R   3   5

9. E♭M ___ ___ ___
   R   3   5

10. E♭m ___ ___ ___
   R   3   5

11. E♭° ___ ___ ___
   R   3   5

12. E♭+ ___ ___ ___
   R   3   5

13. F♯M ___ ___ ___
   R   3   5

14. F♯m ___ ___ ___
   R   3   5

15. F♯° ___ ___ ___
   R   3   5

16. F♯+ ___ ___ ___
   R   3   5

17. GM ___ ___ ___
   R   3   5

18. Gm ___ ___ ___
   R   3   5

19. G° ___ ___ ___
   R   3   5

20. G+ ___ ___ ___
   R   3   5

21. A♭M ___ ___ ___
   R   3   5

22. A♭m ___ ___ ___
   R   3   5

23. A♭° ___ ___ ___
   R   3   5

24. A♭+ ___ ___ ___
   R   3   5

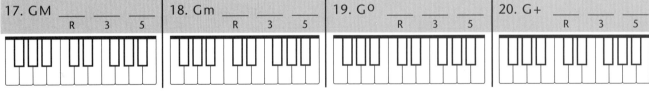

25. BM ___ ___ ___
   R   3   5

26. Bm ___ ___ ___
   R   3   5

27. B° ___ ___ ___
   R   3   5

28. B+ ___ ___ ___
   R   3   5

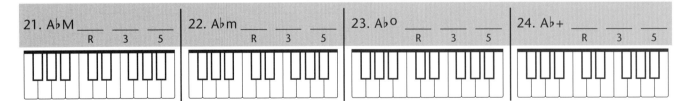

© 2005. Eric Harris. All Rights Reserved.

Exercise 11.6 - Spelling Major Triads

> Remember, major triads are built using the first, third, and fifth notes of a major scale.

Directions: You are given the root of the chord. Spell the major triad *vertically*. Remember to think major scales!

5															
3	↑	↑	↑												
R	C	E♭	B	G♭	A♭	D	G	C♭	F	D♭	A	E	B♭	C♯	F♯
	1.	2.	3.	4.	5.	6.	7.	8.	9.	10.	11.	12.	13.	14.	15.

Directions: You are given the third of the chord. Spell the major triad *vertically*. **Do not alter the given pitch.**

5															
3	D♯	C	E♭	G	F♯	B♭	C♯	B	F	E♯	A	D	E	A♯	G♯
R															
	16.	17.	18.	19.	20.	21.	22.	23.	24.	25.	26.	27.	28.	29.	30.

Directions: You are given the fifth of the chord. Spell the major triad *vertically*. **Do not alter the given pitch.**

5	B	F	E♭	G	B♭	E	A♭	C	D	F♯	G♭	D♭	C♯	A	G♯
3															
R															
	31.	32.	33.	34.	35.	36.	37.	38.	39.	40.	41.	42.	43.	44.	45.

Directions: Answer the following questions.

1. The first note of a major scale is used as the _____ of a major triad.

2. The third note of a major scale is used as the _____ of a major triad.

3. The fifth note of a major scale is used as the _____ of a major triad.

4. Major triads built on _____, _____, and _____ have a third that is one accidental higher than the other chord tones.

5. Major triads built on _____ have a third and fifth that are each one accidental higher than the root.

6. Major triads built on _____, _____, and _____ have the same accidental (or lack thereof) on each chord tone.

© 2005. Eric Harris. All Rights Reserved.

Exercise 11.7 - Spelling Minor Triads

! Remember, to spell a minor triad, first spell a major triad, then lower the third one chromatic half step.

Directions: You are given the root of the chord. Spell the minor triad *vertically*.

5															
3															
R	C	E♭	B	G♭	A♭	D	G	C♭	F	D♭	A	E	B♭	C♯	F♯
	1.	2.	3.	4.	5.	6.	7.	8.	9.	10.	11.	12.	13.	14.	15.

Directions: You are given the third of the chord. Spell the minor triad *vertically*. **Do not alter the given pitch.**

5															
3	A♭	C	E♭	D♭	F	G♭	C♭	B♭	D	E	B♭♭	E♭♭	A	G	F♭
R															
	16.	17.	18.	19.	20.	21.	22.	23.	24.	25.	26.	27.	28.	29.	30.

Directions: You are given the fifth of the chord. Spell the minor triad *vertically*. **Do not alter the given pitch.**

5	B	F	E♭	G	B♭	E	A♭	C	D	F♯	G♭	D♭	C♯	A	G♯
3															
R															
	31.	32.	33.	34.	35.	36.	37.	38.	39.	40.	41.	42.	43.	44.	45.

Directions: Answer the following questions.

1. A major third plus a major third equals an _____ triad.

2. A minor third plus a major third equals a _____ triad.

3. A minor third plus a minor third equals a _____ triad.

4. A major third plus a minor third equals a _____ triad.

5. Major and minor triads have the interval of a _____ between the root and fifth of the chord.

6. Augmented triads have the interval of a _____ between the root and fifth of the chord.

7. Diminished triads have the interval of a _____ between the root and fifth of the chord.

© 2005. Eric Harris. All Rights Reserved.

Exercise 11.8 - Spelling Augmented Triads

! Remember, to spell an augmented triad, first spell a major triad, then raise the fifth one chromatic half step.

Directions: You are given the root of the chord. Spell the augmented triad *vertically*.

5															
3															
R	C	E♭	B	G♭	A♭	D	G	C♭	F	D♭	A	E	B♭	C#	F#
	1.	2.	3.	4.	5.	6.	7.	8.	9.	10.	11.	12.	13.	14.	15.

Directions: You are given the third of the chord. Spell the augmented triad *vertically*.

5															
3	D#	C	E♭	G	F#	B♭	C#	B	F	E#	A	D	E	A#	G#
R															
	16.	17.	18.	19.	20.	21.	22.	23.	24.	25.	26.	27.	28.	29.	30.

Exercise 11.9 - Spelling Diminished Triads

! Remember, to spell a diminished triad, first spell a major triad, then lower the third and the fifth each one chromatic half step.

Directions: You are given the root of the chord. Spell the diminished triad *vertically*.

5															
3															
R	C	E♭	B	G♭	A♭	D	G	C♭	F	D♭	A	E	B♭	C#	F#
	1.	2.	3.	4.	5.	6.	7.	8.	9.	10.	11.	12.	13.	14.	15.

© 2005. Eric Harris. All Rights Reserved.

Exercise 11.10 - Spelling Non-Tonic Tone Triads

 Remember, to spell a non-tonic tone triad: remove the accidental from the root; spell the requested triad type; and then re-apply the removed accidental to each note in the chord.

Directions: Spell the non-tonic tone triads below. Several tonic-tone triads *are* included in this exercise.

1. D♯M	2. E♯M	3. F♭M	4. A♯M	5. B♯M	6. G♯M	7. B♭♭M	8. A♭♭M	9. G♭♭M	10. D♭♭M
5	5	5	5	5	5	5	5	5	5
3	3	3	3	3	3	3	3	3	3
R	R	R	R	R	R	R	R	R	R

11. C𝄪M	12. C♭♭M	13. A♭M	14. F𝄪M	15. EM	16. G𝄪M	17. B♭M	18. DM	19. E♭♭M	20. F♭♭M
5	5	5	5	5	5	5	5	5	5
3	3	3	3	3	3	3	3	3	3
R	R	R	R	R	R	R	R	R	R

21. D♯m	22. E♯m	23. F♭m	24. A♯m	25. B♯m	26. G♯m	27. C𝄪m	28. A♭♭m	29. B♭♭m	30. E♭♭m
5	5	5	5	5	5	5	5	5	5
3	3	3	3	3	3	3	3	3	3
R	R	R	R	R	R	R	R	R	R

31. A♯o	32. E♯o	33. F♭o	34. D♯o	35. G♯o	36. G♯+	37. A♯+	38. D♭♭+	39. B♭♭+	40. E♯+
5	5	5	5	5	5	5	5	5	5
3	3	3	3	3	3	3	3	3	3
R	R	R	R	R	R	R	R	R	R

© 2005. Eric Harris. All Rights Reserved.

Exercise 11.11 - Triad Analysis

Directions: Name the root and type of each triad given below. Watch for clef changes.

© 2005. Eric Harris. All Rights Reserved.

Exercise 11.12 - Writing Triads on the Staff

Directions: Write the requested triads on the staff below. If necessary, offset the accidentals to prevent crowding.

1. E♭M   2. Dm   3. B°   4. A+   5. G♭m

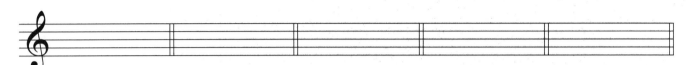

6. F°   7. Cm   8. E+   9. B♭M   10. D♯M

11. Fm   12. G♯M   13. G+   14. A♭m   15. C♭+

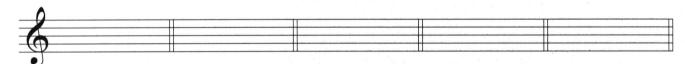

16. D+   17. B♭+   18. FM   19. E♭°   20. AM

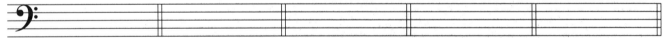

21. C♯M   22. G♭+   23. A♭M   24. EM   25. F♯+

26. D♭M   27. B♭m   28. CM   29. A♯M   30. Em

31. F♯M   32. Gm   33. D♭+   34. BM   35. C♯m

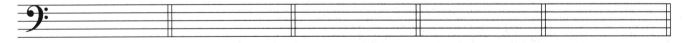

36. C°   37. A♭+   38. F♯°   39. E♭m   40. D♭°

© 2005. Eric Harris. All Rights Reserved.

LESSON 31: DIATONIC TRIADS

1. Triads can be built above each note of a major scale. These triads are called **diatonic triads**.

2. Only the notes of the major scale are used as roots, and only the notes from the major scale are used as the upper triad tones (third and fifth). Look at the B♭ major scale and its diatonic triads below. Notice how the notes of the B♭ scale are used as the roots for each triad. Now look closer and you will see that only notes from the scale are used as the third or fifth of each triad.

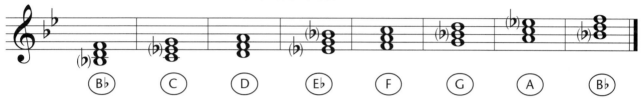

3. It is important to remember to apply the accidentals from the key signature when building diatonic triads. The chart below shows the triads from the B♭ major scale spelled-out. Notice the appearance of B♭ and E♭ in the triads throughout the scale. These accidentals are a result of the key signature.

fifth	F	G	A	B♭	C	D	E♭	F
third	D	E♭	F	G	A	B♭	C	D
root (the scale)	B♭	C	D	E♭	F	G	A	B♭
scale degree	1	2	3	4	5	6	7	8 (1)
quality	M	m	m	M	M	m	o	M

4. When triads are built above the notes of a major scale, specific qualitites appear as a result of the key signature. These triad qualitites are the same for *all* major scales. Look at the F major scale example below.

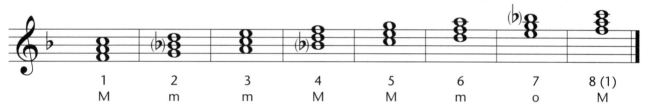

| 1 | 2 | 3 | 4 | 5 | 6 | 7 | 8 (1) |
| M | m | m | M | M | m | o | M |

*   Triads built on the first, fourth, and fifth scale degrees of every major scale will be major (M).
*   Triads built on the second, third, and sixth scale degrees of every major scale will be minor (m).
*   Triads built on the seventh scale degree of every major scale will be diminished (o).

5. When we identify triads associated with a key we use Roman numerals. These numerals indicate the scale degree on which the triad is built *and* the quality of the triad. This process is called **Roman Numeral Analysis** (RNA). The basic procedure is as follows:

*   Capital numerals are used to designate major triads (I, IV, and V).
*   Lowercase numerals are used to designate minor triads (ii, iii, and vi).
*   Lowercase numerals with a superscript "o" are used to designate diminished triads (vii^o).
*   Augmented triads do not appear diatonically in a major key.

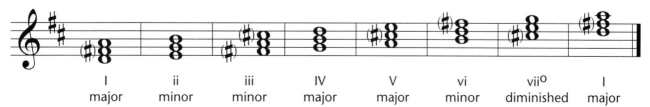

| I | ii | iii | IV | V | vi | vii^o | I |
| major | minor | minor | major | major | minor | diminished | major |

© 2005. Eric Harris. All Rights Reserved.

6. Diatonic triads can also be named using the proper degree names of the scale degree on which they are built: Tonic (I), Supertonic (ii), Mediant (iii), Subdominant (IV), Dominant (V), Submediant (vi), Leading Tone (vii°), and Tonic (I).

7. When analyzing diatonic triads, use the following procedure:
   - Determine the major key.
   - Determine which scale degree is used as the root of the triad.
   - Supply the appropriate Roman numeral for that scale degree/triad.

   Study the following examples.

   1)
   The key is D major (indicated by a capital "D" followed by a colon).
   The root of the triad is G.
   G is the fourth note of the D major scale.
   Write the capital Roman numeral IV under the chord. (IV is major).
   (Make sure the quality of the numeral matches the quality of the triad.)

   2)
   The key is A♭ major (indicated by a capital "A♭" followed by a colon).
   The root of the triad is F.
   F is the sixth note of the A♭ major scale.
   Write the lowercase Roman numeral vi under the chord. (vi is minor).

   3)
   The key is G major (indicated by a capital "G" followed by a colon).
   The root of the triad is F♯.
   F♯ is the seventh note of the G major scale.
   Write the lowercase Roman numeral vii° under the chord. (vii° is diminished).

8. When spelling diatonic triads, use the following procedure:
   - Go to the scale degree indicated by the Roman numeral (in the given major key).
   - Spell a basic triad.
   - Apply the accidentals from the key signature.
   - Check the quality of your answer against the triad quality indicated by the Roman numeral.
     (If the numeral indicates major, did you spell a major triad?)

   Study the following examples. (Don't forget to apply the key signature of the major scale.)

   1) E♭: IV   The fourth note of the E♭ major scale is A♭.
   The basic triad built on A is A-C-E.
   Apply the E♭ major key signature: A♭-C-E♭.
   The capital IV indicates a major triad;
   A♭-C-E♭ is a major triad; the answer is correct.

   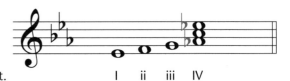

   2) B: vi   The sixth note of the B major scale is G♯.
   The basic triad built on G is G-B-D.
   Apply the B major key signature: G♯-B-D♯.
   The lower case vi indicates a minor triad;
   G♯-B-D♯ is a minor triad; the answer is correct.

   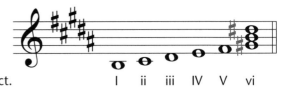

   3) D♭: iii   The third note of the D♭ major scale is F.
   The basic triad built on F is F-A-C.
   Apply the D♭ major key signature: F-A♭-C.
   The lower case iii indicates a minor triad;
   F-A♭-C is a minor triad; the answer is correct.

© 2005. Eric Harris. All Rights Reserved.

Exercise 11.13 - Roman Numeral Analysis

1 **Directions:** Here are the diatonic triads from the C major scale. Provide the correct Roman numerals.

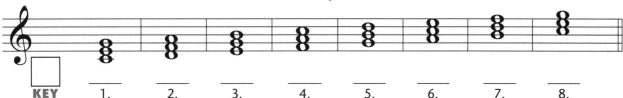

KEY   1.   2.   3.   4.   5.   6.   7.   8.

2 **Directions:** Here are the diatonic triads from the D major scale. Provide the correct Roman numerals.

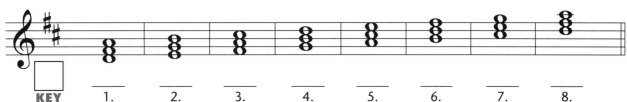

KEY   1.   2.   3.   4.   5.   6.   7.   8.

3 **Directions:** Here are the diatonic triads from the E♭ major scale. Provide the correct Roman numerals.

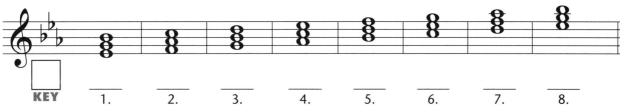

KEY   1.   2.   3.   4.   5.   6.   7.   8.

4 **Directions:** Here are the diatonic triads from the G major scale. Provide the correct Roman numerals.

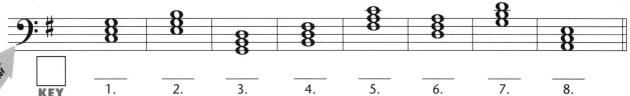

Check Clef

KEY   1.   2.   3.   4.   5.   6.   7.   8.

5 **Directions:** Here are the diatonic triads from the B♭ major scale. Provide the correct Roman numerals.

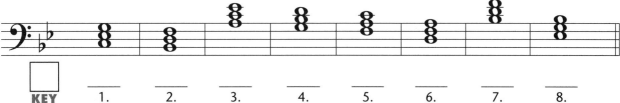

KEY   1.   2.   3.   4.   5.   6.   7.   8.

6 **Directions:** Here are the diatonic triads from the A major scale. Provide the correct Roman numerals.

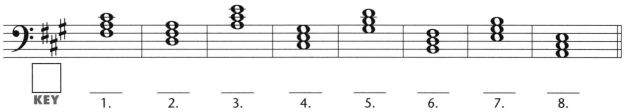

KEY   1.   2.   3.   4.   5.   6.   7.   8.

7 **Directions:** Here are the diatonic triads from the A♭ major scale. Provide the correct Roman numerals.

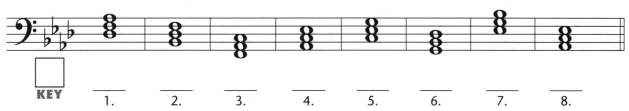

KEY   1.   2.   3.   4.   5.   6.   7.   8.

© 2005. Eric Harris. All Rights Reserved.

Exercise 11.14 - Roman Numeral Analysis

Directions: Each measure below contains a key signature and a diatonic triad. Name the major key and supply the correct Roman numeral under the given chord.

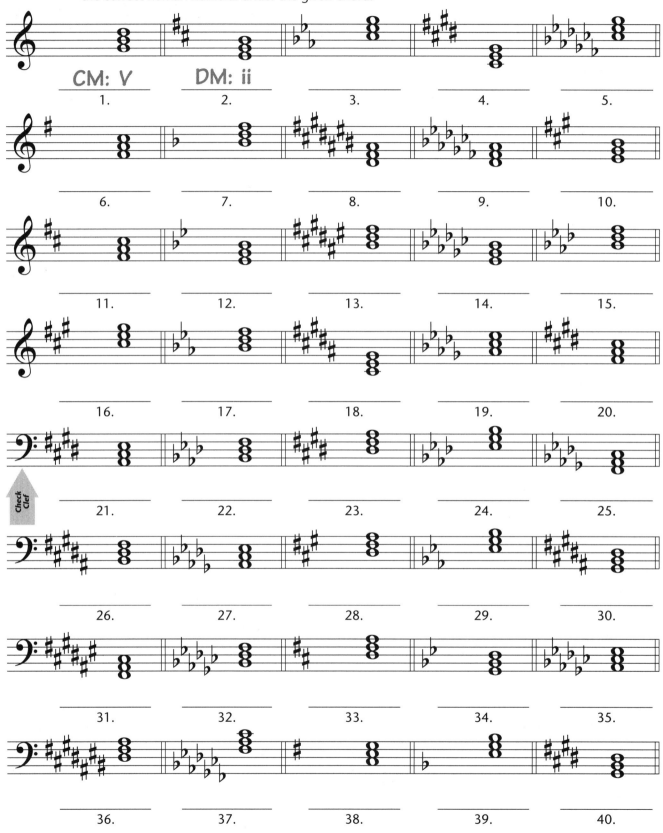

CM: V   DM: ii

© 2005. Eric Harris. All Rights Reserved.

Exercise 11.15 - Spelling Diatonic Triads

Directions: You are given a major key and a Roman numeral. Spell the matching diatonic triad.

1. AM: IV   D   F♯   A
2. B♭M: ii _____ _____ _____
3. EM: V _____ _____ _____
4. FM: iii _____ _____ _____
5. GM: vii° _____ _____ _____
6. D♭M: I _____ _____ _____
7. CM: iii _____ _____ _____
8. GM: V _____ _____ _____
9. A♭M: ii _____ _____ _____
10. BM: vii° _____ _____ _____
11. EM: I _____ _____ _____
12. FM: vi _____ _____ _____
13. C♯M: IV _____ _____ _____
14. G♭M: ii _____ _____ _____
15. E♭M: vi _____ _____ _____
16. BM: iii _____ _____ _____
17. DM: vi _____ _____ _____
18. GM: ii _____ _____ _____
19. F♯M: V _____ _____ _____
20. E♭M: iii _____ _____ _____
21. CM: IV _____ _____ _____
22. D♭M: vi _____ _____ _____
23. C♭M: I _____ _____ _____
24. DM: ii _____ _____ _____
25. CM: V _____ _____ _____

26. FM: vii° _____ _____ _____
27. AM: iii _____ _____ _____
28. C♯M: vi _____ _____ _____
29. E♭M: V _____ _____ _____
30. F♯M: ii _____ _____ _____
31. DM: IV _____ _____ _____
32. AM: V _____ _____ _____
33. D♭M: iii _____ _____ _____
34. FM: ii _____ _____ _____
35. DM: vii° _____ _____ _____
36. A♭M: V _____ _____ _____
37. E♭M: ii _____ _____ _____
38. AM: vi _____ _____ _____
39. GM: I _____ _____ _____
40. A♭M: iii _____ _____ _____
41. FM: V _____ _____ _____
42. DM: iii _____ _____ _____
43. B♭M: vi _____ _____ _____
44. C♭M: vii° _____ _____ _____
45. G♭M: I _____ _____ _____
46. A♭M: vii° _____ _____ _____
47. B♭M: iii _____ _____ _____
48. C♯M: ii _____ _____ _____
49. BM: V _____ _____ _____
50. CM: ii _____ _____ _____

51. EM: iii _____ _____ _____
52. AM: ii _____ _____ _____
53. CM: I _____ _____ _____
54. D♭M: ii _____ _____ _____
55. BM: IV _____ _____ _____
56. E♭M: vii° _____ _____ _____
57. G♭M: V _____ _____ _____
58. F♯M: IV _____ _____ _____
59. EM: vi _____ _____ _____
60. DM: I _____ _____ _____
61. A♭M: vi _____ _____ _____
62. F♯M: vii° _____ _____ _____
63. EM: IV _____ _____ _____
64. GM: iii _____ _____ _____
65. CM: vi _____ _____ _____
66. A♭M: IV _____ _____ _____
67. BM: vi _____ _____ _____
68. DM: V _____ _____ _____
69. A♭M: I _____ _____ _____
70. BM: ii _____ _____ _____
71. GM: IV _____ _____ _____
72. C♯M: iii _____ _____ _____
73. B♭M: V _____ _____ _____
74. EM: vii° _____ _____ _____
75. G♭M: iii _____ _____ _____

© 2005. Eric Harris. All Rights Reserved.

LESSON 32: TRIADS IN INVERSION – PART I

1. When triads are written with the root as the lowest note, the triad is said to be in **root position**. Triads written in root position will resemble "snowmen" and will always appear on consecutive lines (line-line-line) or consecutive spaces (space-space-space) of the staff. The basic triads shown below (and all the triads we have written in this book thus far) are in root position.

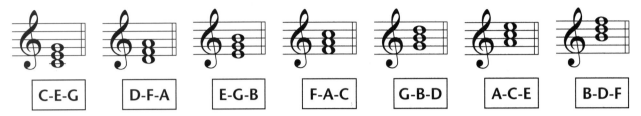

C-E-G   D-F-A   E-G-B   F-A-C   G-B-D   A-C-E   B-D-F

2. In actual music, triads seldom appear in such neat configurations like those shown above. They are often "scrambled" with sometimes the third appearing as the lowest note or even the fifth appearing as the lowest note. Sometimes they are written on the grand staff and have notes that are **doubled** (appear more than once).

G MAJOR TRIADS

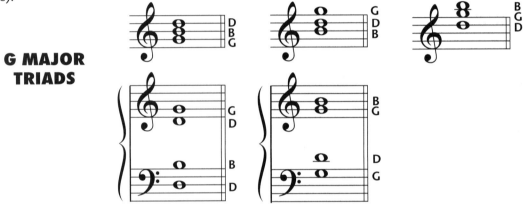

3. It is important to know that a triad keeps its root and quality regardless of the order in which the notes appear on the staff. All of the chords above are G major triads. All contain at least one G, one B, and one D. Doubled notes have no effect on the root or quality of a triad. The order in which notes appear on the staff has no effect on the root or quality of a triad.

4. When a chord is "scrambled," it is said to be **inverted**.

5. Music students must be able to "unscramble" an inverted triad and determine the root and the quality of the chord. This process is accomplished by using the following procedure:

PROCEDURE FOR "UNSCRAMBLING" INVERTED TRIADS

*   Name each note in the chord (feel free to write the letter names beside each note if necessary – as in the examples above).

*   Rearrange the notes into one of the basic alphabet patterns (C-E-G, D-F-A, E-G-B, F-A-C, G-B-D, A-C-E, B-D-F). This is called **third order** because the notes are stacked a third apart. Triads written in third order will look like "snowmen."

*   Remember that doubled notes count only once and have no impact on the root or quality of the triad.

*   Determine the quality.

© 2005. Eric Harris. All Rights Reserved.

Exercise 11.16 - Unscrambling Inverted Triads

Directions: Take the inverted triads below and and rewrite them in their root position ("snowman") form. Name the root and quality of each chord.

© 2005. Eric Harris. All Rights Reserved.

Exercise 11.17 - Analyzing Inverted Triads

Directions: Determine the root and quality of each triad below. You may wish to write letter names beside each chord tone to help with this process.

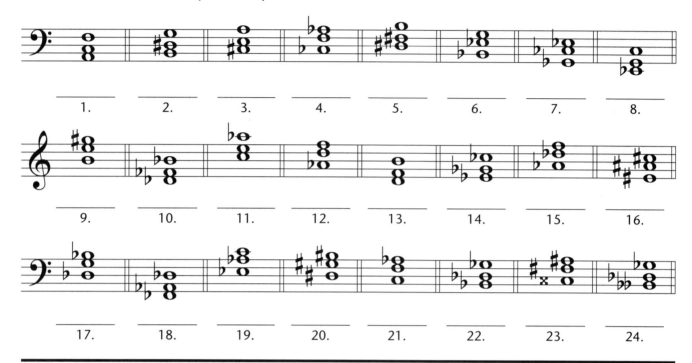

1. 2. 3. 4. 5. 6. 7. 8.

9. 10. 11. 12. 13. 14. 15. 16.

17. 18. 19. 20. 21. 22. 23. 24.

Exercise 11.18 - Analyzing Triads on the Grand Staff

Directions: Determine the root and quality (M,m,+,o) of each triad below. Doubled notes only count once!

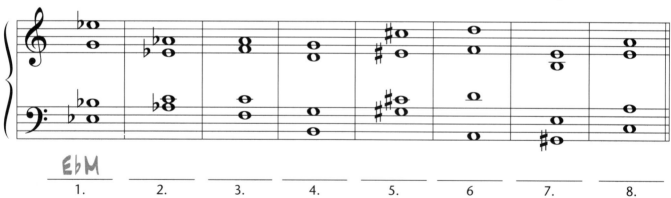

EbM

1. 2. 3. 4. 5. 6 7. 8.

9. 10. 11. 12. 13. 14. 15. 16.

© 2005. Eric Harris. All Rights Reserved.

LESSON 33: TRIADS IN INVERSION – PART II

1. If a triad is written with the root as the lowest note, the triad is said to be in **root position** (F-A-C).
   If a triad is written with the third as the lowest note, the triad is said to be in **first inversion** (A-C-F).
   If a triad is written with the fifth as the lowest note, the triad is said to be in **second inversion** (C-F-A).

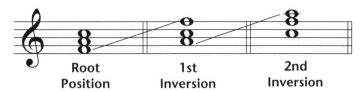

2. Small Arabic numerals are used to indicate the inversion of a triad. These numbers are called **figured bass** and are left over from an old form of keyboard notation. Here are the numbers we use today:

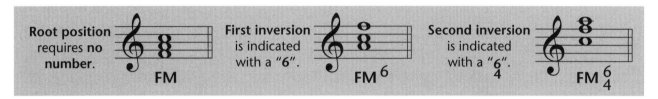

3. Hundreds of years ago, keyboard players were given a bass line with numbers under it. The numbers told the player which intervals to build above a **bass note***. The numbers were the actual intervals needed to build the chord. The numbers used today are just a simplified version of the old system.

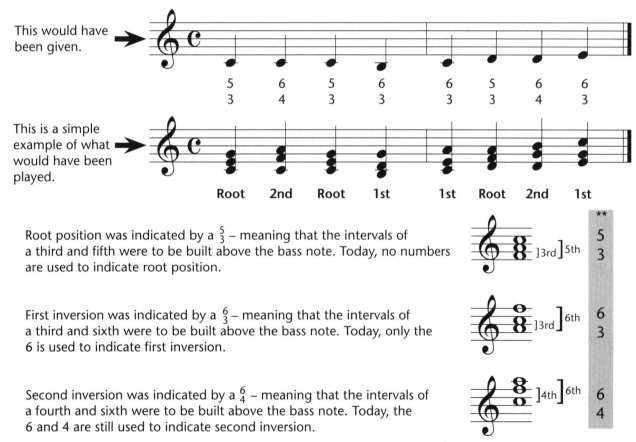

This would have been given.

| | 5 | 6 | 5 | 6 | 6 | 5 | 6 | 6 |
| | 3 | 4 | 3 | 3 | 3 | 3 | 4 | 3 |

This is a simple example of what would have been played.

Root 2nd Root 1st 1st Root 2nd 1st

Root position was indicated by a $\frac{5}{3}$ – meaning that the intervals of a third and fifth were to be built above the bass note. Today, no numbers are used to indicate root position.

First inversion was indicated by a $\frac{6}{3}$ – meaning that the intervals of a third and sixth were to be built above the bass note. Today, only the 6 is used to indicate first inversion.

Second inversion was indicated by a $\frac{6}{4}$ – meaning that the intervals of a fourth and sixth were to be built above the bass note. Today, the 6 and 4 are still used to indicate second inversion.

* Note: It is important to understand that the term "bass note" does not necessarily mean a low note written in the bass clef. In any chord, the lowest note written (or sounding) is called the bass note – regardless of the clef or octave in which it is written.

** Note: The smaller interval (always found on the bottom of the chord) is always indicated by the bottom number. The larger interval (always found on the "outside" of the chord) is always indicated by the top number.

© 2005. Eric Harris. All Rights Reserved.

Exercise 11.19 - Analyzing Triads Using Figured Bass Numerals

Directions: Write the root, quality, and inversion symbol for each chord given below.

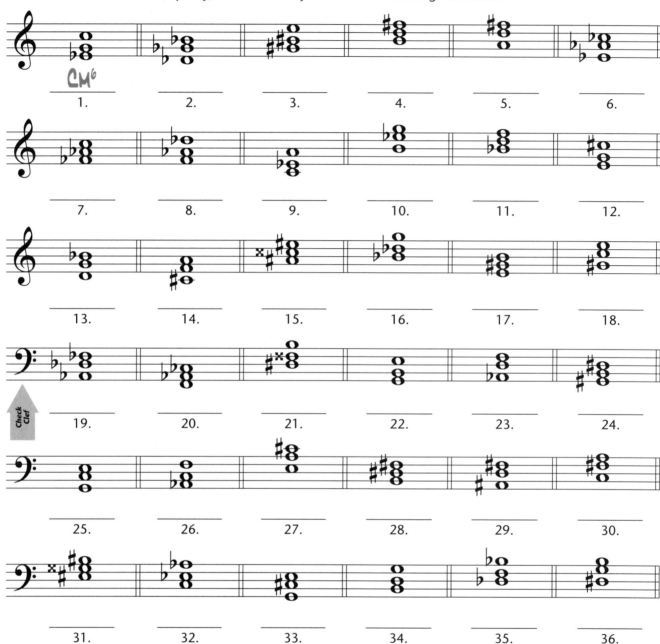

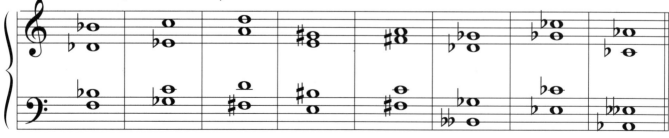

Remember, the inversion is determined by the lowest note in the chord. The arrangement of upper notes is irrelevant! Also remember, doubled notes only count once!

© 2005. Eric Harris. All Rights Reserved.

LESSON 34: DIATONIC TRIADS IN INVERSION

1. Figured bass can also be used with Roman numerals to indicate the inversions of diatonic triads. The chart below shows all of the diatonic triads from the C major scale – in root position, first inversion, and second inversion. Roman numerals with the correct figured bass notation are also shown.

ROOT POSITION

| I | ii | iii | iv | V | vi | vii° | I |

FIRST INVERSION

| I⁶ | ii⁶ | iii⁶ | iv⁶ | V⁶ | vi⁶ | vii°⁶ | I⁶ |

$I^6 \quad ii^6 \quad iii^6 \quad iv^6 \quad V^6 \quad vi^6 \quad vii^{o6} \quad I^6$

SECOND INVERSION

$I^6_4 \quad ii^6_4 \quad iii^6_4 \quad IV^6_4 \quad V^6_4 \quad vi^6_4 \quad vii^{o6}_4 \quad I^6_4$

2. Many rules exist which dictate the use of inverted diatonic triads in music. There are also rules that govern chord progressions (which chords can follow which chords). Such rules, however, are beyond the scope of this book and are covered in all beginning harmony textbooks.

Exercise 11.20 - Diatonic RNA With Inversions

Directions: Here are diatonic triads from the D major scale. They are out of order, and some are inverted. Provide the correct Roman numeral *and* the figured bass notation for the given inversion. The accidentals from the key signature have been written beside the note heads to assist you.

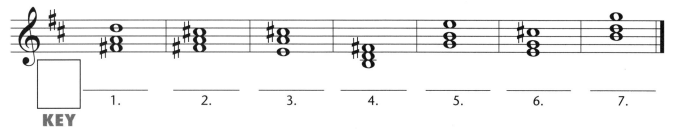

KEY   1.   2.   3.   4.   5.   6.   7.

Directions: Here are diatonic triads from the A♭ major scale. They are out of order, and some are inverted. Provide the correct Roman numeral *and* the figured bass notation for the given inversion. The accidentals from the key signature have been written beside the note heads to assist you.

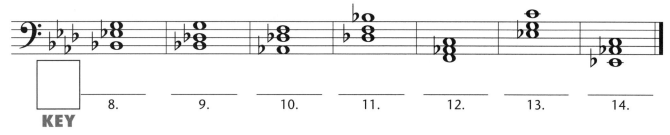

KEY   8.   9.   10.   11.   12.   13.   14.

© 2005. Eric Harris. All Rights Reserved.

Unit Review Questions

Directions: Answer the questions below.

1. _____ A ? is a musical structure that is created when three or more notes are played simultaneously.

2. _____ A ? is a three-note chord.

3. _____ The fundamental pitch on which a triad is built is called the ?

4. _____ The middle pitch in a triad is called the ?

5. _____ The top pitch in a triad is called the ?

6. _____ The third of a triad is built an interval of a ? above the root.

7. _____ The fifth of a triad is built an interval of a ? above the root.

8. _____ There are ? types of triads.

9. _____ An ? triad is a major third plus a major third.

10. _____ A ? triad is a major third plus a minor third.

11. _____ A ? triad is a minor third plus a major third.

12. _____ A ? triad is a minor third plus a minor third.

13. _____ A major triad has a ? third on the bottom.

14. _____ A minor triad has a ? third on the bottom.

15. _____ An augmented triad has the interval of an ? between the root and fifth.

16. _____ A major triad has the interval of a ? between the root and fifth.

17. _____ A minor triad has the interval of a ? between the root and fifth.

18. _____ A diminished triad has the interval of a ? between the root and fifth.

19. _____ A ? triad is the first, third, and fifth note of the major scale.

20. _____ A ? triad is the same as a major triad with the third lowered one chromatic half step.

21. _____ An ? triad is the same as a major triad with the fifth raised one chromatic half step.

22. _____ A ? triad is the same as a major triad with the third and fifth lowered each one chromatic half step.

23. _____ This term means, "made of thirds."

24. _____ Major triads built on ?, ? and ? will have the same accidental or lack thereof on each note of the chord.

© 2005. Eric Harris. All Rights Reserved.

25. _____ Major triads built on <u>?</u>, <u>?</u>, and <u>?</u> will have a third that is one accidental higher than the root or fifth.

26. _____ Major triads built on <u>?</u> will have a third and fifth that are one accidental higher than the root.

27. _____ One accidental higher that a natural is a <u>?</u>

28. _____ One accidental higher than a sharp is a <u>?</u>

29. _____ One accidental higher than a flat is a <u>?</u>

30. _____ One accidental higher than a double flat is a <u>?</u>

31. _____ If asked to spell a triad above a non-tonic tone, <u>?</u> the accidental, spell the requested triad, then re-apply the removed accidental to all chord tones.

32. _____ Triads built above each note of a major scale are called <u>?</u> triads.

33. _____ Triads built on the first, fourth, and fifth notes of a major scale will be <u>?</u> (quality).

34. _____ Triads built on the second, third, and sixth notes of a major scale will be <u>?</u>

35. _____ Triads built on the seventh note of a major scale will be <u>?</u>

36. _____ When we identify chords associated with a key we use <u>?</u> numerals.

37. _____ Capital numerals are used to indicate <u>?</u> triads.

38. _____ Lowercase numerals are used to indicate <u>?</u> triads.

39. _____ Lowercase numerals with a superscript "o" are used to indicate <u>?</u> triads.

40. _____ Augmented triads (do/do not) exist diatonically in major scales.

41. _____ Triads can also be named using the proper degree names of the scale degree on which the triad is built. (True/False)

42. _____ Triads written with the root as the lowest note are said to be in <u>?</u> position.

43. _____ Triads written with the third as the lowest note are said to be in <u>?</u> inversion.

44. _____ Triads written with the fifth as the lowest note are said to be in <u>?</u> inversion.

45. _____ A triad retains its root and quality regardless of the arrangement of the notes on the staff. (True/False)

46. _____ Doubled notes (do/do not) affect the root and quality of a triad.

47. _____ Small Arabic numerals used to indicate the inversion of a triad are called <u>?</u> bass.

48. _____ What figured bass is used to indicate root position?

49. _____ What figured bass is used to indicate first inversion?

50. _____ What figured bass is used to indicate second inversion?

© 2005. Eric Harris. All Rights Reserved.

LESSON 35: THE MOVEABLE C CLEF

1. The C clef is the third and final clef that will be introduced in this series. The C clef is sometimes called the "moveable" or "floating" clef because it can be centered on different lines of the staff.

2. The C clef is an old form of the letter C.

3. When centered on line three of the staff, the C clef is called the **alto clef**. The alto clef is used in viola music.

4. When centered on line four of the staff, the C clef is called the **tenor clef**. The tenor clef is sometimes used in music written for bassoon and trombone.

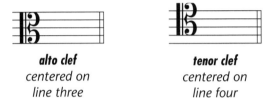

alto clef
*centered on
line three*

tenor clef
*centered on
line four*

5. The indent in the clef identifies the location of middle C.

alto clef

tenor clef

6. If we know the location of C, we can count up or down the musical alphabet to name the remaining lines and spaces of each staff.

    The lines and spaces of the alto clef are:

ALTO CLEF LINES

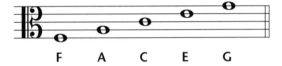

F   A   C   E   G

ALTO CLEF SPACES

G   B   D   F

The lines and spaces of the tenor clef are:

TENOR CLEF LINES

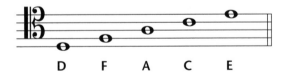

D   F   A   C   E

TENOR CLEF SPACES

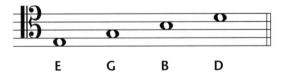

E   G   B   D

7. To draw the alto or tenor clef, draw two straight lines and attach two backward "c's."
    Trace the examples below.

8. Ledger lines may be used with alto and tenor clef; just continue to follow the musical alphabet (forward when going up, and backward when going down).

© 2005. Eric Harris. All Rights Reserved.

Exercise 12.1 - Alto Clef Note Identification

Directions: Name the notes below.

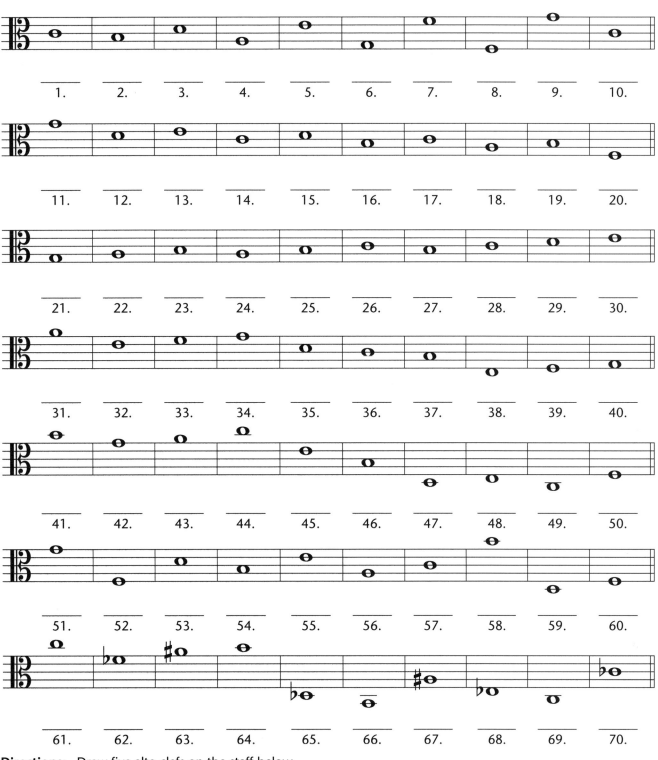

Directions: Draw five alto clefs on the staff below.

© 2005. Eric Harris. All Rights Reserved.

Exercise 12.2 - Tenor Clef Note Identification

Directions: Name the notes below.

1.   2.   3.   4.   5.   6.   7.   8.   9.   10.

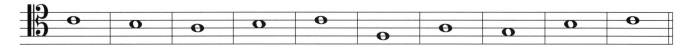

11.   12.   13.   14.   15.   16.   17.   18.   19.   20.

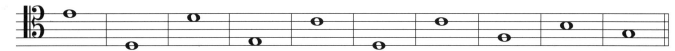

21.   22.   23.   24.   25.   26.   27.   28.   29.   30.

31.   32.   33.   34.   35.   36.   37.   38.   39.   40.

41.   42.   43.   44.   45.   46.   47.   48.   49.   50.

51.   52.   53.   54.   55.   56.   57.   58.   59.   60.

61.   62.   63.   64.   65.   66.   67.   68.   69.   70.

Directions: Draw five tenor clefs on the staff below.

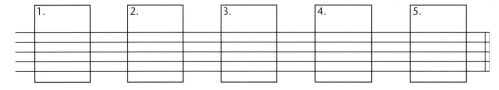

© 2005. Eric Harris. All Rights Reserved.

Unit Review Questions

Directions: Answer the questions below.

1. _____ This clef is sometimes called the "moveable" or "floating" clef. (Name it and draw it.)

2. _____ When centered on line three of the staff, the C clef can also be called the ? clef.

3. _____ When centered on line four of the staff, the C clef can also be called the ? clef.

4. _____ The lines of the alto clef are ? (Write all five answers in the blank.)

5. _____ The spaces of the alto clef are ? (Write all four answers in the blank.)

6. _____ The lines of the tenor clef are ? (Write all five answers in the blank.)

7. _____ The spaces of the tenor clef are ? (Write all four answers in the blank.)

8. _____ The alto clef is used by this instrument.

9. _____ The tenor clef is sometimes used by bassoon and ?

10. _____ The indent in the C clef indentifies the location of middle ?

11. _____ Ledger lines can be used with the alto and tenor clef. (True/False)

12. _____ This clef assigns the names E, G, B, D, F to the lines of the staff.

13. _____ This clef assigns the names G, B, D, F, A to the lines of the staff.

14. _____ This clef assigns the names A, C, E, G to the spaces of the staff.

15. _____ This clef assigns the names F, A, C, E to the spaces of the staff.

16. _____ The alto clef and tenor clef are an old form of the letter ?

17. _____ The treble clef is an old form of the letter ?

18. _____ The bass clef is an old form of the letter ?

Directions: Name the notes below.

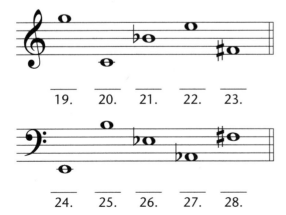

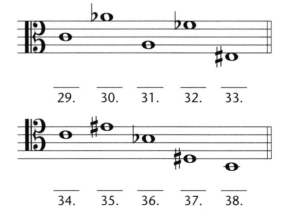

© 2005. Eric Harris. All Rights Reserved.

LESSON 36: ESSENTIAL TERMS & SYMBOLS

I. TERMS WHICH INDICATE TEMPO
(Arranged from slowest to fastest.)

slowest

grave – very slow and solemn.
largo – slow and broad.
lento – slow.
adagio – slow (at rest).
andante – a leisurely walking pace.
moderato – moderately.
allegretto – slightly slower than allegro.
allegro – quick and lively.
vivace – quickly.
presto – very fast.
prestissimo – as fast as possible.

fastest

II. TERMS WHICH INDICATE TEMPO CHANGE

accelerando (accel.) – gradually faster.
allargando (allarg.) – gradually slower and broader.
a tempo – return to the original tempo (usually follows a tempo change).
con moto – with motion; faster.
meno mosso – less motion; slower.
non troppo – not too much; such as *allegro non troppo* – quick and lively but not too fast.
più mosso – more motion; faster.
rallentando (rall.) – gradually slower.
ritardando (rit.) – gradually slower.
ritenuto – held back at a slower speed.
rubato – robbed tempo; speeding up and slowing down as the performer or conductor sees fit.
stringendo – pressing on; hurrying.
tempo primo – return to the original tempo.

III. DYNAMICS – VOLUME LEVELS
(Arranged from softest to loudest.)

softest

pp	pianissimo.......	very soft.
p	piano..............	soft.
mp	mezzo piano...	moderately soft.
mf	mezzo forte....	moderately loud.
f	forte...............	loud.
ff	fortissimo........	very loud.

loudest

IV. TERMS & SYMBOLS WHICH INDICATE DYNAMIC CHANGE

crescendo (cresc.) – gradually louder. **decrescendo** (decresc.) or **diminuendo** (dim.) – gradually softer.

morendo – dying away.
perdendosi – dying away.
subito – suddenly; often combined with dynamic terms (such as *subito piano*) to indicate an instant change.

V. ARTICULATION SYMBOLS & TERMS

 long accent – "dah" with emphasis placed on the "d."

 short accent (sometimes called a "roof-top" accent) – "dot" with emphasis placed on the "t."

 fermata – long hold or pause. In an ensemble, hold until the conductor releases you. In solo work, the note value shown is typically doubled.

 staccato – short, separated, detached. Staccato notes are usually played for half the original value.

 tenuto – full value. Usually follows other markings like staccato to indicate that marked notes are to be played full value. May be stretched by conductors.

fp **fortepiano** – loud, then suddenly soft. Much like the effect of saying, "Boo!"

sfz **sforzando** – heavy and sudden sustained accent, with a "surprise" effect. Longer than the long accent.

VI. TERMS CONCERNING MUTES

The Italian term for mute is **sordino**.
Con sordino means, "with mute."
Senza sordino means, "without mute."

© 2005. Eric Harris. All Rights Reserved.

VII. TERMS WHICH INDICATE STYLE

agitato – agitated; rapid.

alla marcia – in a march style.

amore, con* – with love or tenderness.

anima, con – with spirit.

animato – spirited.

appassionato – with passion.

bellicoso – warlike; military.

bravura, con – bravely; with skill (a difficult part).

brilliante – brilliantly.

brio, con – with brilliance; with spirit.

calando – gradually softer <u>and</u> slower.

cantabile – in a singing style.

dolce – sweetly.

doloroso – painfully; with sorrow.

drammatico – dramatic.

energico – with energy.

espressivo – with expression and emotion.

forza, con – with force.

fuoco, con – with fire.

furioso – furiously.

giocoso – joyfully.

giusto – with precise, steady tempo.
  (also appears as *tempo giusto.*)

grandioso – in a grand or noble style.

grazia, con – with grace; with elegance.

grazioso – gracefully.

lacrimoso – with tears; full of sorrow.

largamente – with dignity.

legato – smooth and connected.

leggiero (also "leggero") – light; nimble; quick.

l'istesso tempo – maintain the same tempo
  (usually into the next movement or section).

lustig – merrily; with joy.

maestoso – majestically; regally.

marcato – marked; with emphasis; accented.

marziale – martial; regal; march style.

misterioso – mysteriously.

nobile, con – with nobility; with dignity.

nobilmente – with nobility; with dignity.

pesante – heavily; with emphasis; burdened.

pomposo – pompously; with arrogance.

religioso – in a solemn, reverent style.

scherzo – playfully; jokingly.

semplice – simply.

serioso – seriously.

sostenuto – sustained.

sotto voce – in a hushed whisper.

spirito, con – with spirit.

strepitoso – noisy; furious.

tranquillo – tranquil; peaceful; calm.

* The Italian word *con* means, "with."

** The Italian word *ben* means, "well," and is sometimes used
  with other words (*ben strepitoso*) for added emphasis.

VIII. TERMS & SYMBOLS WHICH INDICATE DIRECTION

Measure repeat – repeat the previous measure.

Internal repeat – repeat the music between the bars.

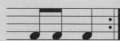

End repeat – return to the beginning.

Coda Sign – skip to the section marked CODA. This section is usually found at the end of a piece.

D.S. **Dal Segno** – "the sign" (𝄋). Repeat from the sign.

D.C. **Da Capo** – "the head." Repeat from the beginning of the piece.

D.S. al Coda **Dal Segno al Coda** – Repeat from the sign (𝄋). When you see the coda sign (⊕), skip to the section marked CODA at the end of the piece.

D.C. al Coda **Da Capo al Coda** – Repeat from the beginning. When you see the coda sign (⊕), skip to the section marked CODA at the end of the piece.

D.S. al Fine **Dal Segno al Fine** – Repeat from the sign (𝄋). Play to the Fine (the end).

D.C. al Fine **Da Capo al Fine** – Repeat from the beginning. Play to the Fine.

First and Second Endings

Play through the first ending. Repeat the passage a second time. Skip the first ending. Play the second ending.

© 2005. Eric Harris. All Rights Reserved.

Unit Review Questions

Directions: Provide the Italian term and the English meaning for each dynamic abbreviation shown below.

Italian Word	1.	2.	3.	4.	5.	6.
Abbreviation	*pp*	*p*	*mp*	*mf*	*f*	*ff*
English Meaning	7.	8.	9.	10.	11.	12.

Directions: Identify each term or symbol shown below.

1. maestoso	6. rubato	11. 
2. con sordino	7. diminuendo (dim.)	12. 
3. ritardando (rit.)	8. con fuoco	13. *fp*
4. allegro	9. l'istesso tempo	14. 
5. legato	10. D.C. al fine	15. 

Directions: Complete the crossword puzzle on the next page. The clues are given below.

CROSSWORD CLUES (FOR NEXT PAGE)

ACROSS
1. very soft
2. full value
3. suddenly; instantly
4. slow (at rest)
5. gradually slower
6. expressive
7. loud
8. very fast
9. pressing on; hurrying
10. sweetly
11. quickly
12. slow
13. return to the original tempo

DOWN
1. more motion; faster
2. moderately
3. noisy; furious
4. a leisurely walking pace
5. very slow and solemn
6. gradually louder
7. in a singing style
8. marked; with emphasis; accented
9. less motion; slower
10. with love or tenderness
11. soft
12. playfully; jokingly
13. with spirit

© 2005. Eric Harris. All Rights Reserved.

BIG CROSSWORD PUZZLE

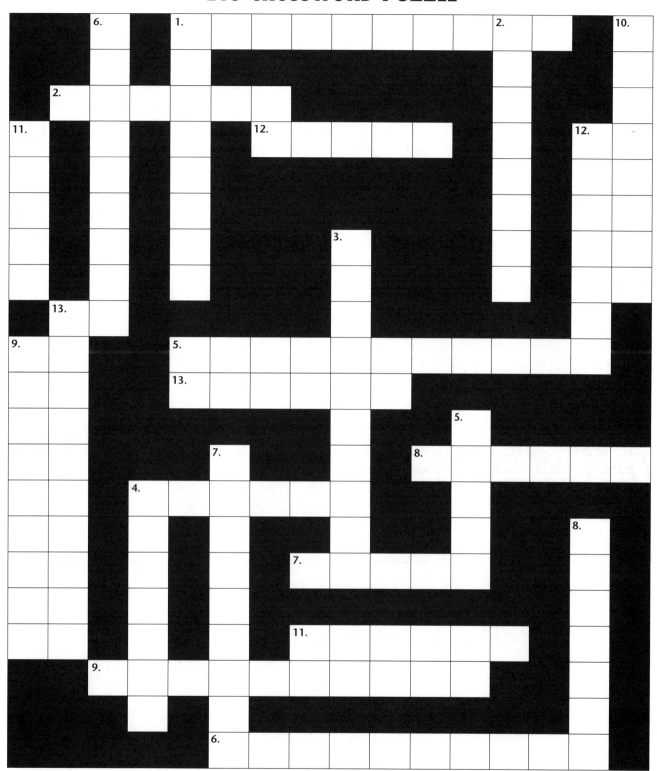

TEACHER'S NOTE:

To assist students with learning the terms and symbols found on pages 196 and 197, it is suggested that teachers assign one box (or half a box) of terms or symbols each week for memorization. A short quiz can be given at the end of the week to ensure students have completed the assignment.

Congratulations! You've finished the third and final book in the series!

© 2005. Eric Harris. All Rights Reserved.

BOOK THREE • MASTERY TEST

Part 1 • Name the notes.

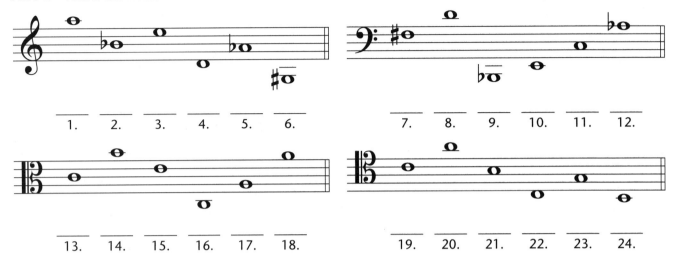

| 1. | 2. | 3. | 4. | 5. | 6. | | 7. | 8. | 9. | 10. | 11. | 12. |

| 13. | 14. | 15. | 16. | 17. | 18. | | 19. | 20. | 21. | 22. | 23. | 24. |

Part 2 • Provide the enharmonic spelling for each pitch given below (no doubles).

1. D♭   2. C   3. E♭   4. F   5. B♭   6. B   7. G♭   8. E   9. A♭

Part 3 • Name each key marked below. If two blanks are provided, give two names (no doubles).

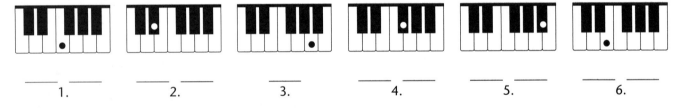

1.   2.   3.   4.   5.   6.

Part 4 • Mark the pitch with a dot on the corresponding piano key.

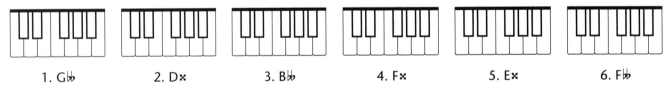

1. G♭♭   2. D𝄪   3. B♭♭   4. F𝄪   5. E𝄪   6. F♭♭

Part 5 • Build a chromatic half step (CHS), diatonic half step (DHS), or whole step (WS) above or below the given pitch as indicated.

1.	2.	3.	4.	5.	6.
CHS above F	CHS above D♭	CHS above E	CHS below G♯	CHS below D♭	CHS below B

7.	8.	9.	10.	11.	12.
DHS above C	DHS above B	DHS above A♯	DHS below E	DHS below F♭	DHS below A

13.	14.	15.	16.	17.	18.
WS above D♭	WS above G♯	WS above E♯	WS below C♭	WS below C♯	WS below F

© 2005. Eric Harris. All Rights Reserved.

Part 6 • Name the major and minor key for each signature given below.

1. Three Flats	2. One Sharp	3. Seven Flats	4. Six Sharps	5. Two Flats
___ ___ major minor	___ ___ major minor	___ ___ major minor	___ ___ major minor	___ ___ major minor

6. Four Flats	7. Five Sharps	8. No Sharps or Flats	9. Five Flats	10. Four Sharps
___ ___ major minor	___ ___ major minor	___ ___ major minor	___ ___ major minor	___ ___ major minor

11. Two Sharps	12. Six Flats	13. Seven Sharps	14. One Flat	15. Three Sharps
___ ___ major minor	___ ___ major minor	___ ___ major minor	___ ___ major minor	___ ___ major minor

Part 7 • Provide the matching pitch name for each.

_____ Tonic: E♭M 1.	_____ Mediant: G♭M 2.	_____ Submediant: F♯M 3.	_____ Dominant: BM 4.	_____ Subdominant: D♭M 5.
_____ Supertonic: AM 6.	_____ Leading Tone: C♯M 7.	_____ Fa: FM 8.	_____ Mi: DM 9.	_____ Re: AM 10.
_____ Ti: GM 11.	_____ Do: EM 12.	_____ Sol: FM 13.	_____ La: A♭M 14.	_____ Mediant: C♭M 15.
_____ Dominant: B♭M 16.	_____ Supertonic: CM 17.	_____ Ti: DM 18.	_____ Sol: E♭M 19.	_____ Submediant: GM 20.

Part 8 • Write the requested scale; ascending only.

1. ___ ___ ___ ___ ___ ___ ___ ___
   B♭ minor (pure)

2. ___ ___ ___ ___ ___ ___ ___ ___
   E minor (melodic)

3. ___ ___ ___ ___ ___ ___ ___ ___
   F minor (harmonic form)

4. ___ ___ ___ ___ ___ ___ ___ ___
   G♯ minor (melodic form)

5. ___ ___ ___ ___ ___ ___ ___ ___
   A minor (harmonic form)

6. ___ ___ ___ ___ ___ ___ ___ ___
   C minor (harmonic form)

7. ___ ___ ___ ___ ___ ___ ___ ___
   B minor (melodic form)

8. ___ ___ ___ ___ ___ ___ ___ ___
   F♯ minor (pure form)

9. ___ ___ ___ ___ ___ ___ ___ ___
   A♭ minor (harmonic form)

10. ___ ___ ___ ___ ___ ___ ___ ___
   C♯ minor (melodic form)

11. ___ ___ ___ ___ ___ ___ ___ ___
   G♭ major

12. ___ ___ ___ ___ ___ ___ ___ ___
   E major

© 2005. Eric Harris. All Rights Reserved.

Part 9 • Write the requested mode; ascending only.

1. ___ ___ ___ ___ ___ ___ ___ ___
   B Phrygian

2. ___ ___ ___ ___ ___ ___ ___ ___
   C Mixolydian

3. ___ ___ ___ ___ ___ ___ ___ ___
   A Locrian

4. ___ ___ ___ ___ ___ ___ ___ ___
   Db Lydian

5. ___ ___ ___ ___ ___ ___ ___ ___
   F# Dorian

6. ___ ___ ___ ___ ___ ___ ___ ___
   Eb Ionian

7. ___ ___ ___ ___ ___ ___ ___ ___
   G Lydian

8. ___ ___ ___ ___ ___ ___ ___ ___
   E Locrian

9. ___ ___ ___ ___ ___ ___ ___ ___
   Bb Dorian

10. ___ ___ ___ ___ ___ ___ ___ ___
    D# Phrygian

11. ___ ___ ___ ___ ___ ___ ___ ___
    C Aeolian

12. ___ ___ ___ ___ ___ ___ ___ ___
    F Mixolydian

Part 10 • Write the counting under each measure of rhythm below. Write the meter classification for each example under the time signature: simple time (S), compound time (C), hybrid meter (H).

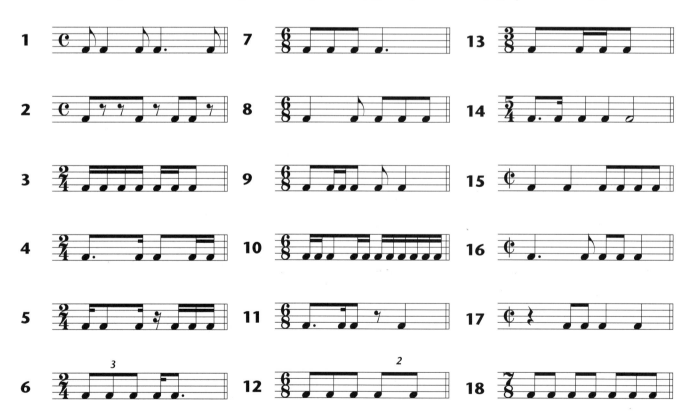

© 2005. Eric Harris. All Rights Reserved.

Part 11 • Write one note in the blank that is equal to the notes in the equation.

1. ♩. + ♪ = _____

2. 𝅗𝅥. + ♩ = _____

3. ♪. + ♬ = _____

4. ♩ + ♩ + ♩ = _____

5. ♩ + ♪ + ♪ = _____

6. ♬ + ♬ + ♬ = _____

7. ♪ + ♬ + ♩ + ♬ = _____

8. 𝅝 – 𝅗𝅥. = _____

9. ♪ + ♪ + ♪ = _____

10. ♬ + ♬ + ♬ + ♬ + 𝅗𝅥. = _____

11. ♪. – ♬ = _____

12. 𝅗𝅥 – ♪ = _____

Part 12 • Identify the given interval. Remember to count up from the lower note in the pair. **Check the clef!**

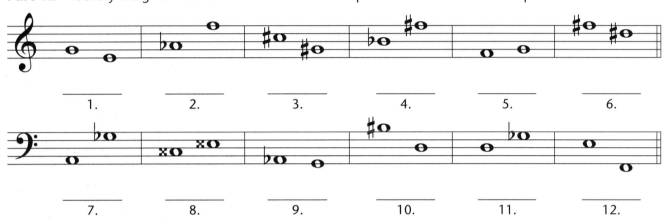

1. _____ 2. _____ 3. _____ 4. _____ 5. _____ 6. _____

7. _____ 8. _____ 9. _____ 10. _____ 11. _____ 12. _____

Part 13 • Spell the requested interval above or below as indicated.

1. M6 above E♭ _____

2. P4 above G♯ _____

3. m3 above F♭ _____

4. m7 above B _____

5. M3 above A♭ _____

6. m2 above D _____

7. +5 above C♯ _____

8. +6 below D♭ _____

9. o7 below G _____

10. M3 below F♯ _____

11. M2 below A _____

12. P5 below C _____

13. +4 below E♭ _____

14. m3 below B♭ _____

15. m2 below D _____

16. M7 below B _____

17. +6 above F♯ _____

18. P5 below F♭ _____

19. o3 above A♯ _____

20. o6 below C _____

Part 14 • Build the requested triad. The root and quality are given.

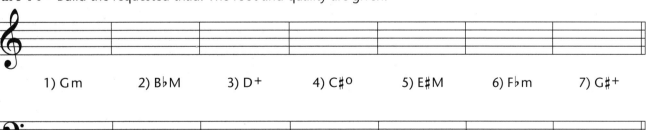

1) Gm   2) B♭M   3) D+   4) C♯o   5) E♯M   6) F♭m   7) G♯+

8) F♯+   9) Do   10) E♭m   11) B♯o   12) A♯M   13) Cm   14) E♯M

© 2005. Eric Harris. All Rights Reserved.

Part 15 • Name the key and provide the correct Roman Numerals for the diatonic triads below.

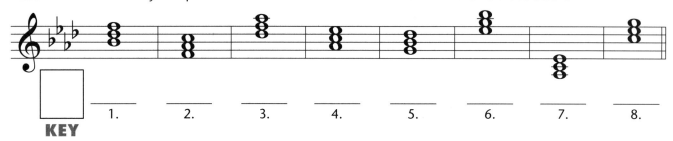

KEY [ ]

____ ____ ____ ____ ____ ____ ____ ____
1.   2.   3.   4.   5.   6.   7.   8.

Part 16 • Spell the requested diatonic triads.

1. A♭M: iii   ____ ____ ____
                  R   3   5

2. GM: IV   ____ ____ ____
                  R   3   5

3. FM: vi   ____ ____ ____
                  R   3   5

4. G♭M: vii°   ____ ____ ____
                  R   3   5

5. C♯M: ii   ____ ____ ____
                  R   3   5

6. D♭M: V   ____ ____ ____
                  R   3   5

7. BM: I   ____ ____ ____
                  R   3   5

8. AM: IV   ____ ____ ____
                  R   3   5

9. E♭M: V   ____ ____ ____
                  R   3   5

Part 17 • Name the root, quality, and inversion symbol for each triad below. **No Roman Numerals!**

____ ____ ____ ____ ____ ____
1.   2.   3.   4.   5.   6.

Part 18 • Identify and/or explain the meaning of each. (If a note is shown, identify the symbol above the note.)

1.	*maestoso*	7.	*più mosso*	13.	*dolce*
2.	*andante*	8.	*diminuendo (dim.)*	14.	
3.	*rallentando (rall.)*	9.	*a tempo*	15.	
4.	*allegro*	10.	*accelerando*	16.	*fp*
5.	*legato*	11.	*adagio*	17.	
6.	*meno mosso*	12.	*l'istesso tempo*	18.	

© 2005. Eric Harris. All Rights Reserved.

GLOSSARY OF TERMS
(WITH INDEX PAGE NUMBERS)

A

Accidentals – symbols used to raise or lower the sound of notes; includes sharps, flats, naturals, double sharps, and double flats. (p25)

Aeolian Mode – one of the seven church modes; follows the same pattern as the major scale played from scale degree six to scale degree six; same as a natural minor scale. (p86)

Alto Clef – the moveable C clef centered on the third line of the staff. (p192)

Anacrusis – a note or notes that come before the first full measure of music; also called pick-up notes. (p49)

And – the second eighth note in each pair. (p46)

Augmented – a quality created when a major or perfect interval is expanded by one chromatic half step; a quality created when the fifth of a major triad is raised one chromatic half step. (p107 & p168)

Augmented Triad – chord consisting of a major third plus a major third. (p168)

B

Bar Lines – vertical lines used to divide the staff into measures. (p5)

Bass Clef – also called the F clef; identifies line number four of the staff and calls it "F." (p6)

Bass Note – the lowest note written (sounding) in any chord. (p187)

Beams – heavy lines used in place of flags; one beam equals one flag, two beams equals two flags, etc. (p18)

Beat Number – number assigned to each beat in a measure (usually 1, 2, 3, or 4). (p46)

Beat Value – the note value indicated by the bottom number of the time signature in simple time; the note value derived when the note value indicated by the bottom number of the time signature is multiplied by three in compound time. (p43)

Borrowed Division – a duplet appearing in compound time (borrowed from simple time); a triplet appearing in simple time (borrowed from compound time). (p92)

Breve – a double whole note. (p159)

C

Chart of Fifths – a vertical chart which shows all of the major key signatures – flats in the left column, sharps in the right column, and enharmonic keys connected with dotted lines across the bottom. (p63)

Chord – a musical structure created when three or more notes are played simultaneously. (p168)

Chromatic Half Step – two notes a half step apart which share the same letter name – C to C♯ for example. (p26)

Circle of Fifths – a clock-like device which shows all of the major key signatures – flats to the left, sharps to the right, and enharmonic keys crossing at the bottom. (p63)

Classic Beams – eighth notes beamed in sets of four or six instead of in pairs. (p46)

Clefs – special symbols used to assign letter names to the lines and spaces of the staff. (p5-6)

Common Time – four-four time. (p43)

Compound Duple Meter – 6/2, 6/4, or 6/8 time. (p90)

Compound Quadruple Meter – 12/2, 12/4, or 12/8 time. (p90)

Compound Time – time signatures with a top number of six, nine, or twelve. (p89)

Compound Triple Meter – 9/2, 9/4, or 9/8 time. (p90)

Counting – the process of numbering each beat in each measure of music; used to help musicians learn, recognize, and accurately perform rhythms. (p46)

Cut Time – two-two time. (p158)

D

Degree Number – Arabic number (1 – 8) assigned to one of eight notes of the major scale. (p80)

Diatonic – related to a scale; used to refer to intervals and triads. (p100 & p179)

Diatonic Half Step – two notes a half step apart which have different (but consecutive) letter names – C to D♭ for example. (p26)

Diatonic Triad – triads built above the scale degrees of a major or minor scale. (p179)

Diminished – a quality created when a minor interval is compressed a chromatic half step; a quality created when the third and fifth of a major triad are each lowered a chromatic half step. (p107 & p168)

Diminished Triad – chord consisting of a minor third plus a minor third. (p168)

Division Value – in simple time, the two notes into which each beat note divides; in compound time, the three notes into which each beat note divides. (p43)

Dorian Mode – one of the seven church modes; follows the same step pattern as a major scale played from scale degree two to scale degree two. (p86)

Dot – increases the value of a note by one half of its original value. (p19)

Double Bar Line – used to indicate the end of a piece of music. (p5)

Doubled – duplicated pitches used in chords. (p184)

Double Flat – lowers the sound of a note a whole step or lowers the sound of a flatted note one chromatic half step. (p38)

Double Sharp – raises the sound of a note a whole step or raises the sound of a sharped note one chromatic half step. (p38)

Duration – one of the four characteristics of musical sounds; describes how long a sound lasts. (p5)

E

Enharmonic – two notes which have the same sound but have different spellings:–C♯ and D♭ for example. (p26)

Enharmonic Keys – major scales which have the same sound but use two different key signatures: C♯ and D♭ major for example. (p63)

© 2005. Eric Harris. All Rights Reserved.

F

Fifth – an interval spanning five letter names; the top note of a triad – named such because it is built a fifth above the root. (p99 & p168)

Figured Bass – Arabic numerals used to indicate the intervals required above a bass note to create a chord or its inversion; an old form of keyboard notation. (p187)

Final – the first note of a mode; functions much like the tonic note in more modern scales. (p86)

First Inversion – a triad written with the third as the lowest note. (p187)

Flag – curved line attached to the stem of a note. Can be replaced by a beam. (p18)

Flat – lowers the sound of a note a half step. (p25)

G,H

Grand Staff (or great staff) – a treble staff and a bass staff joined together with a left bar line and a brace. (p6)

Half Step – the distance from one key to the next closest key (with no key in between) on the piano keyboard. (p25)

Harmonic Interval – formed when two notes are played simultaneously (at the same time). (p99)

Harmonic Minor – one of the three forms of minor scales; created by raising the seventh scale degree of the pure minor scale one chromatic half step. (p140)

Hybrid Meter– a meter which contains both simple and compound elements (groups of two and groups of three); the top number of the time signature is usually five or seven (5/8, 7/8, 5/4, 7/4); also called asymmetrical meter or irregular meter. (p160)

I

Intensity – one of the four characteristics of musical sounds; describes how loud or soft a sound is perceived to be. (p5)

Interval – the distance between two notes (on the staff or on the keyboard). (p99)

Inverted – an interval in which the lower note has been made the higher or the higher note has been made the lower; a triad written with the third or fifth as the lowest note. (p124 & p184)

Ionian Mode – one of the seven church modes; follows the same step pattern as the major scale. (p86)

K,L

Key Signature – a list of the sharps or flats to be used in a major scale. (p61)

Ledger Lines – tiny lines used to extend the staff in either direction. (p6)

Locrian Mode – one of the seven church modes; follows the same step pattern as the major scale played from scale degree seven to scale degree seven. (p86)

Lydian Mode – one of the seven church modes; follows the same step pattern as the major scale played from scale degree four to scale degree four. (p86)

M

Major Interval – seconds, thirds, sixths, and sevenths found within a major scale. (p100)

Major Scale Pattern – W W H W W W H; pattern of whole and half steps required to create a major scale. (p60)

Major Triad – chord consisting of a major third plus a minor third. (p168)

Manuscript – handwritten music. (p7)

Measure – the distance or space between two bar lines. (p5)

Melodic Interval – formed when two notes are played successively (one after the other); can be ascending or descending. (p99)

Melodic Minor– one of the three forms of the minor scale; has an ascending and descending form; the ascending form is created by raising the sixth and seventh scale degrees of the pure minor scale one chromatic half step; the descending form is the same as the descending pure minor scale. (p140-141)

Meter Signature – see "time signature." (p44)

Middle C – the C found closest to the center of the piano keyboard – usually near the manufacturer's nameplate. (p6)

Minor – a quality created when a major interval is compressed a chromatic half step; a quality created when the third of a major triad is lowered a chromatic half step. (p107 & p168)

Minor Triad – chord consisting of a minor third plus a major third. (p168)

Mixolydian Mode – one of the seven church modes; follows the same step pattern as the major scale played from scale degree five to scale degree five. (p86)

Modes – ancient scale patterns used in the chant music of the Roman Catholic Church during the Middle Ages; there were seven: Ionian, Dorian, Phrygian, Lydian, Mixolydian, Aeolian, Locrian. (p86)

Musical Alphabet Pattern – the first seven letters of the alphabet (A, B, C, D, E, F, G) used to name notes on the staff. Once the pattern reaches G, it begins again on A. (p5)

N

Natural – used to cancel a sharp or flat. (p25)

Natural Minor – same as pure minor. (p140)

Non-Tonic Tones – notes which are not used as the tonic of a major scale; D♯, E♯, G♯, A♯, B♯, and F♭. (p120)

Note Head – part of a note that sits on the line or in the space of the staff. Stems are attached to the note head. (p18)

Notes – written symbols used to represent musical sounds. (p5)

O

Octave – The distance from one note to the next note (up or down) with the same letter name. (p5)

Order of Flats – B, E, A, D, G, C, F; the order in which flats are placed in the key signature. (p61)

Order of Sharps – F, C, G, D, A, E, B; the order in which sharps are placed in the key signature. (p61)

© 2005. Eric Harris. All Rights Reserved.

P

Parallel – major and minor scales which share the same tonic (C major and C minor, for example). (p155)

Perfect Fifth Rule – states that most perfect fifths are natural to natural (C to G), sharp to sharp (C♯ to G♯), or flat to flat (C♭ to G♭) with the exception of perfect fifths between B and F (B♭ to F and B to F♯) which do not follow this rule. (p105)

Perfect Fourth Rule – states that most perfect fourths are natural to natural (C to F), sharp to sharp (C♯ to F♯), or flat to flat (C♭ to F♭) with the exception of perfect fourths between F and B (F to B♭ and F♯ to B) which do not follow this rule. (p104)

Perfect Interval – unisons, fourths, fifths, and octaves found within a major scale. (p100)

Phrygian Mode – one of the seven church modes; uses the same step pattern as the major scale played from scale degree three to scale degree three. (p86)

Pick-Up Notes – see "anacrusis."(p49)

Pitch – one of the four characteristics of musical sounds; describes how high or low a sound is perceived to be. (p5)

Pitch Name – letter name assigned to one of the eight notes of the major scale. (p80)

Prime – a unison. (p99)

Proper Degree Name – names assigned to one of the eight notes of the major scale: tonic, supertonic, mediant, subdominant, dominant, submediant, leading tone, tonic. (p80)

Pure Minor– one of the three forms of the minor scale; begins on the sixth note of the relative major scale, follows the musical alphabet pattern for one octave, and uses the same key signature; also called natural minor. (p140)

Q,R

Quality – term used to indicate the specific type of interval or triad: major, minor, augmented, or diminished. (p100 & p168)

Raised Submediant – the sixth scale degree in the harmonic minor scale. (p155)

Relative – a form of the minor scale based on the sixth scale degree of a major scale; form of a major scale which lies three half steps (a minor third) above the tonic of a minor scale. (p132)

Rests– written symbols used to represent silence in music. (p18)

Roman Numeral Analysis – the process of assigning Roman numerals to the diatonic triads built above the scale degrees of major and minor scales. (p179)

Root – the fundamental pitch on which a triad is built; it gives the chord its name. (p168)

Root Position – a triad written with the root as the lowest note. (p184)

Rule of Accidentals – states that any accidental (which is not in the key signature) lasts for one measure and is then cancelled at the bar line – unless it is tied into the next measure at which time the accidental dies at the end of the tie. (p27)

Rule of Nine– states that intervals and their inversions will always equal nine. (p124)

S

Second Inversion – a triad written with the fifth as the lowest note. (p187)

Sharp – raises the sound of a note a half step. (p25)

Simple Duple Meter – 2/2, 2/4, or 2/8 time. (p44)

Simple Quadruple Meter – 4/2, 4/4, or 4/8 time. (p44)

Simple Time – time signatures with a top number of two, three, or four. (p43)

Simple Triple Meter – 3/2, 3/4, or 3/8 time. (p44)

Solfège – syllable assigned to one of the eight notes of the major scale (do, re, mi, fa, sol, la, ti, do). (p80)

Staff – a set of five lines and four spaces on which music is written. (p5)

Stem – a vertical line attached to a note head. (p18)

Stem Rule – states that notes written below the third line will have stems that go up (attached to the right side of the note head) and notes written above the third line will have stems that go down (attached to the left side of the note head); notes written on the third line may have stems that go up or down and generally go in the direction of stems on surrounding notes. (p19)

Subtonic – the seventh scale degree in the pure minor scale. (p155)

Syncopation – effect produced when the second eighth note in a pair is tied to the first eighth note in the next pair creating a quarter note value that begins on the "and" of the beat. (p47)

T

Tenor Clef – the moveable C clef centered on the fourth line of the staff. (p192)

Tertian – made of thirds; used to refer to the Western system of harmony which uses chords made of thirds. (p168)

Thin Double Bar Line – used to indicate the end of a section or movement within a larger piece. (p5)

Third – an interval spanning three letter names; the middle pitch in a triad – named such because it is built a third above the root. (p99 & p168)

Third Order – triad tones placed in root position so that the notes are stacked a third apart: C-E-G, D-F-A, etc. (p 184)

Tie – a curved line used to connect two notes of the same pitch and add their values. (p19)

Timbre – one of the four characteristics of musical sounds; the identifying quality of a sound. (p5)

Time Signature – large fractions placed at the beginning of a piece of music. (p43)

Treble Clef – also called the G clef; identifies line number two of the staff and calls it "G." (p5)

Triad – a three note chord. (p168)

Triplet – three notes of the same value placed in the same time/space normally occupied by two. (p47)

W

Wedges – symbol used to indicate sustained beats that exist within longer note values. (p46)

Whole Step – two half steps combined. (p26)

© 2005. Eric Harris. All Rights Reserved.

North🌲Land

All books in the Fundamentals of Music Theory
for the Windband Student Series were
designed and typeset by Eric Harris.
The text was set in ITC Stone Sans 10-point.
Headers were set in Futura Condensed 18 and 24-point.
Music examples and exercises were created using Finale®.